Transcending Turmoil

Survivors of
Dysfunctional Families

24
3, 33, 60,

Transcending Turmoil

Survivors of
Dysfunctional Families

Donna F. LaMar, Ph.D.

INSIGHT BOOKS

Plenum Press • New York and London

Library of Congress Cataloging-in-Publication Data

LaMar, Donna F.
    Transcending turmoil : survivors of dysfunctional families / Donna
  F. LaMar.
        p.   cm.
    "Insight books."
    Includes bibliographical references and index.
    ISBN 0-306-44127-6
    1. Adult children of dysfunctional families. 2. Adjustment
  (Psychology) 3. Problem families.   I. Title.
    [DNLM: 1. Adaptation, Psychological. 2. Child of Impaired
  Parents--psychology. 3. Family--psychology.   BF 335 L215t]
  RC455.4.F3L35   1922
  158'.1--dc20
  DNLM/DLC
  for Library of Congress   92-3216
                                                                     CIP

ISBN 0-306-44127-6

© 1992 Plenum Press, New York
A Division of Plenum Publishing Corporation
233 Spring Street, New York, N.Y. 10013

An Insight Book

To all transcenders
for their courage to be

Foreword

From a Therapist:

During my many years as a therapist, I have been privileged to be trusted by my clients, who have shared their stories with me. Many of these people who have sought out therapy seem to be successful, highly functioning individuals leading "happy, fulfilling" lives. Inwardly, they are suffering, often silently, with feelings of anxiety, depression, and confusion. Additionally, they have thoughts of unworthiness, loneliness, and insecurity. And they don't understand why. They also do not take credit for all they have achieved. Instead, they attribute their accomplishments to circumstances, chance, or something else outside themselves — anything except their own will, persistence, and intuition. They discount themselves, minimizing their ability to survive in a world where it seems everything was against them. Nothing was easy about their lives while they were growing up.

Time and time again I have been impressed and awed by the strength and undying spirit of my clients. I have often wondered aloud, "How did you do it? How did you survive — not only survive, but thrive in spite of your history? What was the secret spark that stayed alive and caused you not to give up or give in, and allowed you to overcome poverty, abuse, neglect? How did you maintain your independence and honesty, your sensitivity, and your ability to give and receive love?"

The answers usually start with "I don't know." After we explore the course of their childhoods, experiences, and family histories, we are able to understand where they have come from. We invariably determine that they possess several important attributes or ingredients that have accounted for their survival and ultimate transcendence of their chaotic childhoods. There is a common thread that runs through their stories and weaves a remarkable pattern. Their journey of self-discovery in therapy leads them to self-love and creates a greater understanding of their strength and innate wisdom. This reduces their inner struggle, and then the "inside matches the outside."

Many enlightening books have been written recently that explore codependency and dysfunctional families. They help us understand why we suffer, how we were affected by our families, and how we sabotage our own lives. My friend and colleague Donna LaMar has taken up the challenge to explore in depth the phenomenon of *transcendence*, an adaptation that goes beyond survival. Dr. LaMar seeks to understand the individual who soars beyond the limits of the dysfunctional family and breaks through the barriers into the realm of the exceptional. She has made it her quest to explore the secret place inside these exceptional people where the true self is kept safely tucked away, nurtured and protected from the destructive forces of emotional, physical, or sexual abuse, poverty, and neglect. *Transcending Turmoil* is an important book that examines how and why transcenders manage to stay healthy in an unhealthy environment. It is a book about life — about love. It is a book that celebrates and affirms the human spirit. Read it and be aware of the survivor — no, the transcender — in each of us. Thank you, Donna, for helping to answer my question, "How did you do it?"

DIANN BRAUN, M.A.

Psychologist and Administrator
Center for Realistic Living
Troy, Michigan

From a Transcender:

Dr. LaMar offers understanding, insight, and hope to those of us who have grown up in dysfunctional families. In reading this book I found a road map that explained where I have been as well as the direction necessary for me to arrive at my destination — that of a healthy human being in touch with all my feelings. This book is the first opportunity I have had to look objectively into the lives of other transcenders and realize that I am not alone. Those of us who bear the scars of abuse speak a common language, Shame. After finishing this book, however, I felt a sense of pride about what we have accomplished, often against great odds.

The author's commitment and dedication to those of us on the journey of recovery come through with great sensitivity and sincerity. She tells it like it is. My tears flowed freely as she took me back into the pain and loneliness. And yet, there is an awareness in Dr. LaMar's words of the determination and the strength that each of us showed as we found direction for our own lives.

For anyone who has grown up in a dysfunctional family or is close to someone who has, Dr. LaMar opens the doors to an understanding of the hard work involved in the recovery process. She challenges and encourages each of us to become all that we are capable of being — to take in the warmth and love from the light at the end of the tunnel that we so richly deserve.

MARIE

Acknowledgments

With Gratitude

It is with deep gratitude and love that I thank the many individuals who contributed and labored with me in the creation of this book. These individuals gave to me with caring, support, encouragement, energy, time, and prayers over the many years of preparation. The journey has been full of challenges, inspiration, and love. This book is the essence of our journey together.

First, I thank all the transcenders who have shared their journeys with me. They offered their stories, their struggles, their pain and joy, as well as their being. I was touched deeply by these many people, and they often enhanced my personal healing and growth process.

To my family goes some of my deepest appreciation. Darrel, Laura, and Don offered constant support, love, encouragement, and prayers. Without their understanding about not having a "regular" mother and wife, this book might never have been. Also, I thank my parents, Don and Athena Nelson, for their continued love during the process. A special thanks goes to my father for his continued faith and unbelievable patience in teaching me that my teachers had been wrong when they taught me that I couldn't write.

There are many who lovingly contributed by editing, typing, listening, sharing ideas, and even running my children to activities so I could write. They include Betsy Laney, Barbara David, and Diann Braun. Members of my doctoral committee who helped clarify the research and its essence are Drs. Clark Moustakas, Cereta Perry, Patricia Rourke, Steve Nett, Colleen McNally, Frank Campbell, and Larry Schmidt. I thank all of them for providing a special lifeline.

A different kind of lifeline was provided by my "barn people," with whom I ride. They helped reduce my stress by providing support, caring, fun, and a place to re-create my energies. A few of them are Deborah Butler, Bob and Carol Kerr, Chuck and Jackie Wilson, and Heddy Waggoner.

I express deep thanks to my two powerful prayer partners, Sue Miller and Dorothey Pangracz. In the darkest hours, these individuals brought light.

Finally, I thank the staff at the Center for Realistic Living for their constant support and encouragement. I always found love and unfailing belief in what I could accomplish.

DONNA LaMar

Contents

Introduction

Richard, my former fiancé, was kind, generous, loving, responsible, and emotionally stable. I was young and naive. When Richard invited me to meet his family, I was excited and a bit afraid. I was sure he had a wonderful family who loved and adored him. I believed they would be kind, generous, responsible, and stable — just like Richard. I had no expectations that they could be anything but the warm and loving family I had envisioned who supported and treated one another with dignity and respect.

Richard tried hard to tell me about his family before the visit. I was so convinced about his family that I couldn't hear what he was saying. It wasn't until after the visit that I recalled his saying such things as: "Donna, my family is different"; "My dad gets real angry"; "My mother is not a good housekeeper"; "My sister is not well and hasn't been for a long time." I decided that Richard was just nervous about my meeting his family. I wish I had listened.

The day of our visit arrived. I was anxious, nervous, and excited. I wanted to make a good impression. What if his family didn't like me? What if I made a social goof and insulted someone? I desperately needed and wanted to get along with them; after all, they were Richard's family!

Then we drove up to the house. I was surprised to find that the outside was untended and dirty. Inside, it was worse. The house was unkempt, filthy, and foul smelling. But this was only the beginning.

Once we were inside, Richard's mother invited me to sit down in the living room. As I started to sit on a three-person couch, four other people tried to sit there with me at the same time, including Richard's mother. She actually sat *on* me! It was comical in a way, but it was my next insight into his family. I soon learned that there was literally little space for any individual in this family.

I had eagerly looked forward to sharing with Richard's family. I had fantasized hearing stories about his growing up. However, I learned very rapidly that people in his family did not share. Instead, they talked exclusively about themselves in loud voices and tried to dominate all conversations. Communication was done by putdowns and/or excessive demands. Their voice tones were harsh, imposing, and cold. Individuals were told, "Move, I want to sit there!"; "Get me that!"; "Can't you even do that right?" When I asked one person a question, *everyone* tried to answer. When I was asked a question, no one bothered to listen for an answer, not even the person who had asked the question. There was a sense of desperation and few smiles.

I was shocked and confused. I had only one thought: "Get out now!" Yet I wanted so much to get along with my future in-laws. I was torn. For Richard's sake, I forced myself to smile, talk, and listen. As I did, I was bombarded by individuals demanding that I listen, accept, and give — give anything and keep giving.

I was totally dismayed when I heard how different family members lived. Their energy seemed to be used only to exist, to get through the day. Richard's family appeared to take little responsibility for their lives and had few life goals. One family member wanted to retire at age seventeen; another had been in and out of the state hospital; two others were on public assistance; and still another was abusing drugs. All of this was in direct contrast to Richard's goal-directed approach to life, his drive to succeed and grow.

I felt repulsed and empty. I had never witnessed such chaos, neglect, and emotional deprivation. I had expected to find a warm, loving, caring family. Instead, I found an emotionally destructive family who shattered my false belief that all caring, loving, responsible individuals come from caring, loving, responsible families. Nothing was further from the truth. Nothing.

Although I still wanted to get along with Richard's family, I suddenly found my behavior toward them changing. I began avoiding eye contact, hoping that there would be fewer demands. I stopped asking questions, and I answered in one-word sentences, hoping they would leave me alone. Nothing worked, and the demands actually increased. It didn't seem to matter to them how I felt. It just mattered what I could give. The more I withdrew, the more they seemed to force themselves on me. I felt drained, numbed, disappointed, and confused. It seemed nothing I could do was enough; perhaps nothing I could ever do would be enough. I became very tense and upset. My stomach was in a knot. I was losing me in the destruction and chaos. I had to leave soon in order to find me again.

Finally, after four seemingly endless hours, we left. As we drove home, I began to recover from the emotional shock and find myself again, but I was confused. Very confused. I began to compare Richard with his family. My questioning began: How could Richard have come from *this* family? How had he grown up to be the person he was now? Those questions were the beginning of over twenty years of formal and informal research.

What I had painfully discovered that day of the visit was the amazing phenomenon known as *transcenders*: individuals who grow up in difficult, painful, destructive families and emerge with a meaningful, productive way of life. These individuals, as children, somehow maintain a sense of self strong enough to withstand the onslaught of abuse and neglect from their families.

We realize the truly amazing accomplishment of the transcenders when we look at the families they transcend. These children are frequently victims of physical, emotional, verbal, and sexual abuse, as well as neglect from within their own families. Such painful, destructive families cause intense pain and loneliness. Families like this are called dysfunctional and do not supply the protection and nurturance necessary for a child's developing personality or sense of self.

Transcenders are neither magical nor invulnerable. They are children who work hard to raise themselves. From a core deep inside, *transcenders make important decisions that protect, nurture, and guide them through the difficult, painful family years.* These decisions, or turning points, are valuable commitments used for the individual's survival and future, and they appear to last a lifetime.

Through the strength of these commitments made in childhood, transcenders pull away from their families and preserve a precious part of their inner selves. This part is not touched by the abuse and neglect of their dysfunctional families but is held in reserve and used to nurture, protect, and guide the transcenders through the years ahead. Often these decisions are made at a young age. Transcenders develop and use remarkable techniques to sustain the inner self until they can leave their families and create their own world.

Once free of the family, transcenders work hard to rid themselves of the no-longer-needed emotional and behavioral patterns they used to survive their families. They also work to develop themselves in a positive, authentic direction. They seek to heal by grieving and by reclaiming their original personality, with all the talents and abilities that may have been blocked by their destructive families. They are not content simply to exist. They risk, work hard, and strive for changes for their development and personal growth. They overcome great obstacles and typically meet with success in spite of their backgrounds.

This description by a transcender relates the process well:

> Transcending a destructive family is like living within prison walls while expending constant energy trying to recapture and maintain that sense of self, that natural state of freedom and purity, that one has when one is born. Although there is a feeling of being trapped by the extreme limitations and boundaries established — whether these be poverty, negative family values, harsh criticism and or punishment, miserable, and gloomy and

unstimulating environments — somehow, there is an inner knowing or sense that I will be OK, that I can overcome these barriers.
I will push ahead and survive.

For over twenty years, I have observed and admired transcenders.
Through these years, my passion to know and understand has led me
to explore their processes in university research and everyday life.
During my many years of research, I asked many questions of
ministers, teachers, mental health professionals, and transcenders
themselves. Formally, in 1984, I finished a comprehensive phenomenological research project at the doctoral level on what I then called
"the survivor." I asked questions such as, "How did you survive? What
did others do for you? What helped? What did you do in the abusive
times? The lonely times?" My many years as a therapist working with
children, families, and many transcenders have added to my depth of
understanding of the process.

Throughout the years, transcenders have touched me deeply. I
am appreciative of them everywhere. Their courage to be is truly
heroic. I am grateful to the transcenders who shared their stories for
this book. Their names and some of the details have been changed
to protect their identities.

Even though the book had its origin in a disillusioning visit, from
that visit came wonderful knowledge. Too often in the mental health
field we have focused on what is wrong with people and how they
become ill. The focus of this book is on how individuals stay well in
spite of destructive families.

We have many organizations that help individuals recover and
heal from abuse: Adult Children of Alcoholics, Codependents Anonymous, Alcoholics Anonymous, Gamblers Anonymous, and Overeaters
Anonymous among them. These groups have seen themselves as
separate, believing that one type of abuse is different from another.
There may be different focuses, but the healing and growing process
is the same. Abuse is abuse and adult children are adult children, no
matter what the abuse and dysfunction. It's all damaging.

The information presented here is intended to enhance our

understanding of our ability to grow despite tremendous odds. Please take and use what fits for you. Add to it. If you wish, write to me about your learning and growth. This will help unite our knowledge to help others.

It is my ultimate hope and prayer that the information in this book will help individuals to heal and grow from past traumas, to feel less separate, and to learn that we can all help one another. This, in turn, will help us remember that we are human, with human needs to share, support, and give to our world. We are in this life together.

Chapter 1

Transcenders and the Dysfunctional Family

To love and be loved is our directive as human beings. We come into this world with many talents, facets, and abilities ready to be developed. With these abilities we can offer love; in return, we can be loved through others' abilities. We also come with specific handicaps, such as a learning disability, a physical handicap, or a personality trait. These handicaps usually make it difficult for us to get along with our world and to fulfill our love command. For example, a child may be supersensitive or strong-willed and may keep people away. Whatever we come into the world with, abilities and dis-abilities, composes our *original package*, the one we use to relate to others and make our way in the world. Even as early as the moment of birth, we are ready to grow, move, develop, learn, and relate by using this package. We work to develop and love ourselves as well as others.

Our love directive may become confused, sidetracked, complicated, infringed upon, and destroyed — or enhanced and developed — depending on our life experiences and how we personally view these experiences. *Life experiences* are made up of the relationships and situations in which we are involved as children and adults, that is, what happens to us in life. These experiences include family, work, leisure, religion, health, and the like. Children are especially vulnerable to early life experiences because of their great need for protection and nurturing. How children develop their abilities, their personalities, and their view of themselves depends a great deal on how they are treated and what happens to them in the growing years.

This book is about transcenders: individuals whose early life experiences were characterized by difficult, painful family environments from which they were able to emerge and pursue meaningful, productive lives. These individuals, as children, somehow, maintained a sense of self strong enough to withstand an onslaught of abuse and neglect from their families.

We see that transcenders' accomplishments are truly amazing when we look at the families they have survived. Individuals in these families may be physically, emotionally, verbally, ritualistically, or sexually abusive, as well as negligent. Such abusive families inflict intense pain and loneliness on those whom they victimize.

The majority of life experiences for transcenders in childhood are experiences that are damaging to the growth and development of children. Their families do not provide the nurturing, stability, or protection needed to sustain physical and emotional health, let alone the development of abilities and potentialities. Often, these families interfere with and damage the inner guiding forces the child uses for growth and development. This type of family is termed, in the field of psychology, a *dysfunctional family*. In a dysfunctional family, the system of relating and communicating is painful, abusive, damaging, and difficult. A *family system* is the way individuals relate to each other and to the outside world, as well as how the family members interrelate. Every functional family has a unique system that works to help family members relate within the family as well as outside it.

In a family system, all individuals are connected. If one individual changes, the rest of the family is affected. An example of how a system works is seen in a mobile. What happens when you pull or touch one part of a mobile? What happens in a family when Mom gets sick? When Dad leaves? When Sister goes to college? In each case, the entire system moves and shifts. One person's moving or changing causes another person to shift, and not always in a healthy, productive manner. In a dysfunctional family, if an individual grows and becomes healthier, other family members not only may try to block the growth but may actually sabotage it. That is why it is so very difficult for a person to change while still living in the family.

In a dysfunctional family, there is often abuse — physical, verbal, emotional, ritual, sexual, and/or neglect. The abuse may range from severe to subtle in intensity, constant to rare in occurrence, and minutes to weeks in duration. It may last for years. Abuse may be so severe that the individual is in danger of dying or losing his or her inner being and becoming mentally ill, or the abuse may be so subtle that it is extremely difficult to identify what has happened to the individual.

There may also be many different types and variations of abuse in the same family, from mild ridiculing to severe acting out. Abuse may be directed at all children, or at just one individual child. In the subtle forms, the abuse and the interference with the child's growth are hard to recognize because the family looks and functions as if it were relatively "normal." The more severe forms may be so devastating that I have often wondered how the individual can still physically be alive. Whether mild or severe, abusive behavior interferes with and damages the child's ability to develop and grow normally.

An example of mild abuse is a family that insists that the children be perfect and pretends that feelings do not exist (i.e., denies them). Children from this type of family may grow up not knowing who they are because a "perfect" person is not their real self. Their real or authentic self (the original package) is actually hidden and has never been developed. This kind of abuse translates to a young mind as: "Do not be yourself; you are not OK. Be what your parents want you to be — perfect." The individual then goes through life attempting to be perfect, or inauthentic. Often, persons with this background do not know what is wrong with them but are tense, depressed, and angry and have little sense of their own worth. They have no idea that their family damaged them and may even believe that they have a "perfect, wonderful" family. Their goal is to be the perfect person who they believe will please their parents and who will win them love and acceptance. As long as they work to maintain this "perfect" and false identity, they have little chance to develop their authentic abilities, talents, and personalities. This type of life is painful and damaging to the original package.

A severe example of abuse is physical violence toward children. Children who are physically abused work especially hard not to disturb the individual who does the abusing. Often, they don't know what they have done to deserve being punished. They may believe that they have legitimately brought on the abuse because the abusing parents tell them that it is all their fault: "If you had done the dishes right, I wouldn't have to hit you!" What the children don't know (and can't know because they are children) is that Mommy's and Daddy's anger is out of control and they are looking for any reason to strike out. The anger is not rational. Rational families do not beat up children for wiping a dish wrong. Rational parents teach children how to perform a task and allow for the imperfection of growing children. In abusive families, children learn to be very careful about what they say and do, learn that they do not count, and learn that surviving has priority. Again the result of severe abuse, like that of subtle abuse, is the hiding of the authentic self and a damaging of precious undeveloped abilities.

Every transcender has a unique story, which includes a painful and difficult childhood. Transcenders are different from children who become abusive or mentally ill like their parents. They may end up having some personality traits similar to those of their family, *but* they are different and work hard to be different. Transcenders do not go under. Somehow, they manage to maintain some contact with their original package. They are able to envision a more authentic world with love or, as one transcender puts it, "The way it should be." They work not only to maintain themselves in a difficult, painful environment, but they are also able to develop some of their authenticity in the face of life experiences that are violent and crazy.

This does not mean that transcenders, as children, avoided the pain and craziness of the family. Instead, transcenders survived the experiences with scars and grew in spite of them or, as we shall see in Chapter 2, because of them. This book is about this incredible phenomenon. Who are these transcenders? Are they perfect beings? Invincible? Invulnerable? Superhealthy geniuses? Actually, transcenders are varied and can be found in every walk of life: wealthy/poor; traditional/modern; liberal/conservative; professional/blue-collar; religious/nonreligious; permissive/rigid. The list goes on. Transcenders are different from each other in appearance, behavior, and personality. They may be athletic, studious, withdrawn, or outgoing. *But* they share one uniqueness: a dynamic ability to raise themselves in a dysfunctional family and to grow into adults who create meaningful and productive lives.

Transcending a dysfunctional family is a *process*, a process of surviving and then healing and growing. A process is everything I can't put in a wheelbarrow. A product is something I *can* put in a wheelbarrow, things like a hammer, a doll, an art creation, or even a building—if I have a big enough wheelbarrow. Processes are things like surviving, learning, healing, growing, and loving. A process unfolds from within us, takes its own time and direction, and has a life of its own. It usually has vague beginning and ending points. Occasionally, at the end of a process, there is a product. For example, at the end of my doctoral-level education, I had a research paper, a product called a *dissertation*, but the education was a process.

A transcender's process is a struggle to survive conflicts and feelings of loneliness and pain emotionally as well as to survive abuse and neglect physically. Transcenders have two ultimate goals: to get out of the family with all of its abuse, neglect, chaos, and pain and to create a more nurturing, loving, safe world. In spite of tremendous odds, they accomplish this goal. They create safety, structure, goals, authenticity, fun, and love. Transcenders create this world by working hard to overcome struggles, conflicts, problems, obstacles, and scars left over from childhood. They heal and go forward.

I have watched in amazement the transcenders' process, a process that takes years of concerted effort and courage. To understand the process, we need to take an in-depth look at what transcenders have overcome: their own personal dysfunctional family existence. In the first part of this chapter, I will share five stories about transcenders and their dysfunctional families to give you an understanding of the variety of their backgrounds. These stories are not exclusive or inclusive — every transcender has a unique family story, and each individual member of that family has a unique perception of his or her experiences in the family. This unique perception of the family is very important, as we will see in Chapters 3 and 5. Each family has its own secrets, its own particular type of pain, its own history. Each history is important to the person who is struggling to understand and recover from the family. In Chapter 3, I will describe general characteristics of dysfunctional families.

The stories of Marie, Chris, Steve, Paul, and Tiffany follow. I ask you to put yourself in their place. Feel their pain and imagine what their childhood was like. Some of you will have little problem doing this because you are, or have been, in their place.

―――――――――――――――― *Marie* ――――――――――――――――

Marie is the only child of a schizophrenic mother and an alcoholic/schizophrenic father, who were both ritualistically abusive. Schizophrenia is a severe mental disorder that sometimes causes the person to live a dark, delusional existence. It is characterized by disorganized speech and behavior, delusions, and hallucinations. The person with schizophrenia often has very little, if any, contact with reality, and the personality can continue to break down over time. Medication is usually used to maintain even a limited contact with the environment. Marie's parents' condition was severe and untreated and was allowed to run rampant. Normal functioning for them was limited or nonexistent. Abusive functioning was the norm.

Marie's descriptions of her childhood are beyond belief. During intensive therapy, Marie has remembered tortures by her parents from day one:

My mother would give me ice water enemas that caused horrible stomach cramps. She forced me to satisfy her sexually (she was bisexual) and then would punish me for being a "bad girl." At times, she would tie me to a tree for several days and nights or lock me inside a coffinlike box with only small holes for air to get in. Frequently, these "punishments" were for things she had done herself (wetting the bed while sexually excited, vomiting on the floor, etc.). After being locked in the box for long periods of time and not being able to hold my urine any longer, I would have an "accident" and urinate in the box. I then dreaded being let out of the box because I knew that punishment would follow. She would become furious at seeing my wet clothes, and her eyes would glow like pieces of coal as she would defecate and then smear my face with her feces.

Once she tried to sew up my vagina because she was mad at a man and wouldn't allow him to have sex with me. (I was about ten at the time.) I often passed out from the pain (physical and emotional), which would only make her angrier and more violent with her tortures. My mother and father both demanded that I satisfy them sexually (either individually or both at the same time) as well as anyone else they decided could "use me." Beds are still terrifying to me.

My father was just as cruel as my mother. He used me sexually at his convenience and tried to kill me many times. He made me help bury the remains of babies from abortions he would do on women, sometimes with a razor at my throat or a gun at my head. He would bring home little kittens and puppies for me and would tell me that, if I was good enough, the animals would be allowed to live and I could keep them for my own pets, but if I was bad, the animals would have to die. I was never "good enough," and to this day I can see and hear those pitiful little animals as he killed them while I was forced to watch, all the time being told that they had to die because I was a bad girl. No matter how hard I tried, I was never a "good girl" by my parents' sick standards.

My parents were also both into satanic worship. They sacrificed animals as well as babies, and I had to help bury the bodies. I know it sounds so unreal, so awful, and it was. It was so horrible and terrifying that I had a hard time believing it myself when the memories first began to return.

At times, as I got older, when I tried to tell other relatives or teachers what was happening, my parents had already set the scene. They had convinced everyone that I was a liar and had severe emotional problems. When dealing with other people, my parents presented the facade of the perfect, warm, caring, loving couple. How often I was told how lucky I was to have parents like this. It is no wonder that, when I did try to confide in people, they did not believe me and would tell my parents what I had said, and once again, I would be severely punished. It did not take long for me to learn that no one could be trusted.

I felt total relief when both of my parents died, even though I was accused by relatives of killing my mother in a car accident. I wasn't even driving the car!

One of the ways Marie survived was to block out the memories until years after her parents died. Then, after years of intensive psychotherapy, she was able to allow herself to remember her past. Marie's experience is the most severe and abusive I have encountered as a therapist. Often, as I worked with Marie, I would wonder how she physically stayed alive, let alone sane, in her obviously severely dysfunctional family. The above experiences are only part of the horrors she lived through. In spite of the tortures from infancy into adolescence, she earned a B.S. degree, is a respected member of the community, has raised three children, and plans to return to school to develop her abilities further.

Chris

Chris has been a scapegoat in his family. That is, anything and everything that goes wrong is blamed on him—accidents, behavior, feelings, thoughts, family history. Here is his story:

I was born a scapegoat. I was the middle of ten children of, obviously, a Catholic family. I was blamed for everything. I think I was blamed even before I was born. I felt as if I could do nothing right and they all hated me. They hated me if I tried; they hated me if I didn't try; they hated me no matter what. I have an image of myself at about age three that describes my childhood: I am looking toward my mother and sister, and I'm deciding if I'll try to get some attention. I reach out my arms, and they walk away. I then turn away from them and find a place to cry.

I never understood it. Never! Why me? Was I odd-looking? Did I hate them? I guess, at a very deep level, I suspected it wasn't really me. That's what helped keep me going. After being in therapy for a while, I came to know that it was really them. My mother used to go into these rages. I tried real hard, as a kid, to avoid her when she was in those moods, but she could shift so fast from "OK" to "monster," and I'd get caught. When she would catch me, I'd have to get my dad's belt, go into the bathroom with her, strip to nothing, and be beaten until I had welts. This occurred until I was in my late teens. Here I was, either a little kid who had to bring her a belt bigger than I was, or old enough to beat her. It was all real crazy.

I remember one time the family planned to go to see *Around the World in Eighty Days*. I was so excited. But my mother got in one of her moods and found something I had done wrong. She locked me in my room while the rest of the family went to the movies. I can remember looking out the window and watching them go . . . it was so painful. Other times, she would make me kneel down on the old-fashioned heating grates on the floor for hours, or she would lock me in my room and not feed me for a day. Dad just let all of this happen. He never stopped her. Never. He just watched as if it was OK to do this to me.

My brothers and sisters would also join in and ridicule me when they were in a bad mood or something had gone wrong in their lives. I was never included in play and never included in family affairs. Even now, the family exchanges Christmas presents with everyone but me. In the past, I sent presents to them, which they either never acknowledged or criticized. It's crazy, really crazy. Recently, when my father died, my other brothers and sisters cleaned out his stuff. I was not told and was not offered any of his possessions. Everyone else got something.

It never stops. Now, even my nieces and nephews are part of it.

They believe I'm to blame for their problems even though I never even see them and am no part of their lives.

One time when I was seventeen and still in high school, my mother threw all my stuff out on the driveway—she did this regularly—and told me to leave. It was February, and I had to sleep in my car, go to school, and then go to work. I was so cold and hungry. Finally, I asked to come back home, and she let me come back. Again, my dad did nothing. I don't know which was worse, her direct abuse or his total neglect and nonaction. I know all I ever wanted from my family was to be loved and for them to accept my love. I was always rejected, and so was my love. In later years I wrote this:

Cradle Pains
Cherry red splashes on velvet baby skin—
The fury of your Hell had landed

Tiny soft arms ending in virgin baby hands—
They open, they close,
They hold tight the dead weight of empty air.

A lullaby tune of whimper and moans
Sung not too loud
By a broken heart that's two days old.

Steve

Steve is the oldest of ten children. He lived in total poverty with his parents. He describes his story this way:

All I can remember is how poor we were. There was never enough to eat and only a few clothes and never any shoes. When I was about four years old, I was taken to live with my grandparents. I was lucky to live with them for a couple of years because they could provide better than my parents could. At least with them I had food, shelter, and clothing. When I lived with my mother, we barely existed.

It was awful when I had to go back and live with my parents

again. I was about nine, and once again, found myself scraping for enough food to live on. I can remember being so hungry that I was weak and couldn't go to school. On rare occasions, when I had enough energy to go to school, I didn't have clothes or shoes to wear. Most of the time, however, I was too weak from hunger to go, let alone concentrate. Once I got there, I can remember so much pain from the hunger and the cold and no one to help us. My parents did almost nothing. My father eventually abandoned us. I can remember everything about growing up with my parents. I never want to forget what it was like.

The worst part was the neglect. There was no love, no sharing, no caring, no nothing, just neglect. My parents were just sort of there in a world of their own. They would have all sorts of men and women over and never knew we were around. It was awful.

Being the oldest, I was totally responsible for my brothers and sisters. I was responsible for trying to get food as well as firewood for the family. For firewood, I'd have to walk into the woods a long way. If I got lucky and found some wood, we would quickly build a fire and kneel so close to the heat our legs would burn and turn black because we were so cold. Sometimes, for food, we'd go to a neighbor's house, and they would give me the scraps from the table to take home for us to eat. I'm not talking about good scraps. I'm talking about just the stuff left on the dishes after you eat. It was bad, so bad.

I knew it wasn't right, but I didn't know why. I tried to take care of my brothers and sisters, but at times they would turn on me and ridicule me for trying to help or for not helping enough. I think I was the target because I was the substitute mother. I hated it. We were just all hurting so badly.

At the end, I watched my mother die of cancer. I was sixteen then. All of us were farmed out to relatives or orphanages. I was one of the lucky ones and went to live with my grandparents. I had it a little better there. At least I had something to eat and clothes to wear and could go to school.

My grandmother, however, was an alcoholic and often drank up most of my grandfather's wages. Money was again nonexistent, but at least I ate, had clothes, and went to school. I still had a load to carry because my grandmother was so out of it. I had to run the house and do all the errands. I don't remember any love or caring there, but I at least did not have the heavy responsibility of my brothers and sisters that I had when I lived with my parents. I knew early that learning was important, and I never wanted to go back to what it was like with my parents.

Steve graduated from high school and went on to earn a B.S. in health care. He is married, has two children, and works for the government's health department.

Paul

Other types of dysfunctional families create emotional chaos, as in Paul's case. Here is his story:

There was little money in our house, and there was always tension and stress. Dad was an attorney and struggled in our early years to establish his practice. Mom worked for him at home while trying to run the house and raise five children. I was the middle child and was lost in the chaos. Mom gave everything I wanted to the other kids. For example, I wanted to take dancing lessons; my sister got them. I wanted to be in sports; my brother did it. Everything, just everything I wanted was given to others. I was never driven anywhere for any activities or helped in any way. It's as if I didn't exist.

What I remember most was the chaos: stress, neglect, severe ridicule, and, at times, verbal and physical abuse. My mother was gutless and abusive; my father was absent and critical. I was forced to go to a church school, which I hated, and I begged to be allowed to go to public school. My younger brother and sister got to go to public school while I was forced to stay in church school. I could never figure out the reason and tried to be perfect. It just felt real crazy.

There was always fighting and screaming at our house. Either the kitchen wasn't clean enough or a bed was not made right or something was not perfect. If it wasn't, I would then be spanked and beaten, but

I never really knew what I had done or not done. I would be beaten again if Mom felt I needed it or if Mom wasn't done getting her anger out.

The worst part for me was never having a niche of my own at home. I never fit. I was always wrong, bad, and ignored. I really was lost in my family. One time, when I was about twelve or thirteen, we were going up north for a fishing vacation in Canada. The family got everything ready by the front door. I got up early and packed everything in the car before anybody got ready. We went out and got in the car and started to leave the driveway. My father stopped the car and said he had to check the trunk. He got out and opened the trunk, looked inside, and said, "How could you possibly pack it that way?" He began to take every article out of the trunk and repack it. I remember how that made me feel: like a piece of shit. I sat in the car and cried and cried. I felt so bad about myself.

Paul is now in a career transition that he finds very difficult. This transition has thrown him back into some old patterns. However, he put himself back into therapy and is working through these difficulties. He is confident that he will work through the transition and the feelings that the transition has triggered. Paul is single and was successful in his previous career.

---------------------------- *Tiffany* ----------------------------

The last transcender's story is Tiffany's. Tiffany's story is a little different because the dysfunction is so subtle. The damage is just as hurtful, and therefore can still cause chaos because she feels abused but can't pinpoint why. A person from this type of background may feel "crazy" but does not know why. The "whys" usually come after a long, hard, sorting-out process in therapy. Here is Tiffany's story:

My family was traditional and strict. My father was a professional, and my mother stayed home and took care of everything and everyone. Dad was rarely home because he worked so much. I was the only girl among four brothers. In my family, *traditional* meant that men were the superior breed. They were to be taken care of, waited on, and watched over. My father and my brothers ruled the roost. Whatever they wanted, they got. In so many ways, I was discounted because I was a girl, and this constantly chipped away at my self-esteem. Girls had to do woman's work — dust, cook, wash dishes — even though I really enjoyed working on gardening and other projects. The chaos for me, which I came to understand after working hard in therapy, was being the only girl, who was loved and wanted for being a girl and not for who I was as a person. I tried very hard to please my parents and be the "good girl" who would someday become the "good little house-wife" and continue taking care of the men in her life. The tragedy was that this wasn't really me, and I felt discounted and not wanted.

In addition to all this, I was expected to be perfect, to act perfect, to buy perfect products, to speak perfectly, to accomplish the perfect goals, not to feel, and above all, to be an intellect and to be totally successful. To make a mistake was to be ridiculed and severely criticized about it by my brothers forever. Even the friends I picked had to look and act perfect or I'd be criticized after they went home. In time, I learned not to bring anyone home.

I never felt accepted or loved because my parents loved an image of a "good girl." My brothers made sure that I was kept in my place with ridicule, criticism, and threats of physical violence. I was never OK, but they never really got to know me. Eventually, I went into a deep depression as a teen and went underground. That is, I func-tioned at one level, trying to be the good girl, and at the same time, I held my real self underneath and hidden from others. I became totally isolated and alone. I was told not to share any family situations with anyone because of the rule "Don't hang your dirty laundry out for the neighbors to see."

At at early age, I was expected to be independent and not to rely on anyone for anything. At the same time, we were strictly controlled and not allowed to do much of anything other than be home with the family. I never could gain support or another perspective to help me with the pain I experienced in the family. I had to be mature beyond my years so I could figure out how to raise myself. On top of all this, I was also my mother's mother and felt I had to take care of her.

The real crazies were that my family looked and acted typical; wonderful and loving with perfect, wonderful children. God, no wonder I felt crazy! I lived in the world of "I have a perfect family, yet I am abused and neglected."

Tiffany is a successful professional and mother. She struggles at times when life experiences trigger past memories and feelings, but as she says, "I am different from my parents and I intend to stay that way."

* * *

Basically, children in dysfunctional families do not get the nurturing or the protection they need to grow and develop into healthy, productive adults. At times, the family like Steve's is at a physical survival level. At other times, there is a lack of affirmation and validation (a confirming and sorting out of feelings, thoughts, and the growth process) as seen in Tiffany's family. A wide range of abuse and neglect is seen in all the families. Often the children do not count and are only seen as being there to service others. Usually, no adult takes any length of quality time to be with the children and teach them how to get along in the world. This teaching is crucial to healthy emotional development and includes helping children to set limits, to follow an established value system, to feel loved, and to develop their original package.

If the most basic of needs are not met, such as food, shelter, clothing, and emotional nurturing, children grow up extremely needy and dependent on others for life resources. Too often, children in these families may become aggressive, withdrawn, emotionally ill, or dysfunctional in other ways, like their parents. They may become so afraid that existing in the world is too difficult that they withdraw or commit suicide. Too often, these children develop characterological disorders, that is, lack conscience, morals, and values, with little or no original package left. Our jails are full of them. None of these patterns are healthy or desirable. The cost of the damage is great, and the children who survive accomplish a great feat.

Chapter 2

Dysfunctional Family Characteristics

What do transcenders overcome? Particular interactional and family systems are characteristic of dysfunctional families and provide a basic understanding of the manner in which dysfunctional families communicate, function, deal with pain, and relate to the world. Each family is unique and may have one or many of these characteristics, which range from mild to severe. These characteristics are learned and passed down from one generation to another. As you read, please keep in mind that the children who survive overcome a number of these obstacles and manage to create a world that leads to healthier functioning.

INTERACTIONAL CHARACTERISTICS

The term *interactional characteristics* refers to how individuals in a family relate to and communicate with each other. Different families may have all, some, or none of these characteristics, depending on the amount of dysfunction in the family.

1. *Nonexistent, or poor, interaction.* Some families don't interact. That is, they do not communicate on any level. The parents may ignore or neglect the children, and the children may become more like objects than human beings. Some families are actually silent most of the time. Others may yell and scream about everything and at everyone, their accusations having little basis in reality. If there is no healthy interaction, there is no shared interest and no chance for the children to gain emotional support. If there is a lot of yelling, there is also tension, stress, and conflict. None of these patterns, or combinations of these patterns, brings about any meaningful communication.

2. *Nonexistent, or little, sharing and/or feedback.* This means that children receive little or no confirmation (affirmation or validation) of who they are as persons. They do not gain the information essential for development. Receiving feedback through sharing is the process through which children normally develop their identities and personalities, as well as their limits, values, morals, and abilities. If feedback is not available, children seek out information from television, the street, or other poorer sources. For example, the child needs to answer questions such as: What am I capable of? What are my special talents? What things can't I do in my world? What things will get me into trouble? How do I handle being angry?

Without a significant caring adult sharing and giving feedback, children may become other-oriented (taking care of others and trusting others to lead them in their lives) to the point of losing themselves, becoming delinquent, or underachieving. At times, they may become so attached to anyone who will give them direction that they will put up with abuse for the attention. They often become very good at reading others' facial expressions and intonations of voices to pick up cues about how to act.

3. *Isolation of the individual.* Many children who grow up in a dysfunctional family experience isolation and intense loneliness. The isolation may be created in many ways: the family's saying they don't trust anyone; the children's being kept from playing with other children; the children's choosing isolation as a form of protection from embarrassment and an onslaught of the abuse; or perhaps, the children's being seen as objects and little attention's being paid to them. In any case, there is usually no attempt to help the children out of loneliness or to relate to them in any meaningful way.

4. *Denial of problems, feelings, and thoughts.* Some families pretend that everything is great and there are no problems. They may even believe their children are the most wonderful, well-adjusted children in the world. Yet, underneath this facade are problems that may include perfectionism, ridicule, denial of feelings, and abuse. An example is a family with an alcoholic parent in which everyone pretends everything is wonderful in spite of Mom's or Dad's drinking up the weekly grocery money or abusing family members. It is pretending there is no "elephant in the living room" when there really is one. Everyone pretends, adjusts, and goes around the elephant.

5. *Distorted or "unreal" feelings.* Individuals in dysfunctional families often warp or distort their feelings. Feelings can become a major problem when they are not valued because feelings are very important for growth. Individuals may act out feelings in distorted ways because of emotional illness, inability to deal with the world, or generational learning (patterns of handling feelings that are passed on from one generation to the next). For example, I may feel afraid to cross the street, but instead of dealing with the fear and then taking precautions for safety, I totally lose control, scream, or abuse another person because I fear that if I cross the street I will die. Anger is another example of a feeling that is greatly distorted. Anger is a normal feeling and needs to be felt; however, my being angry does not mean that I will beat or kill another person.

6. *Not meeting individual needs*. One of the basic tasks of a family is to support each other and to provide a way for each member to have his or her needs met. As human beings, we all need food, shelter, and clothing for physical survival. We also need emotional support and nurturing to develop our original package. In dysfunctional families, parents or other adults are unable to meet these needs in themselves, let alone in others. Because the children are unable to have their needs met, they become the next generation of dysfunctional people who are needy, dependent, isolated, and hurting. This cycle continues through the generations.

FAMILY SYSTEMS CHARACTERISTICS

How the family as a whole functions is known as a *family system*. Specific systems have specific characteristics, which are the rules governing each person in relation to the others.

1. *No clear boundaries*. In healthy families, there are distinct, clear boundaries between individuals. A boundary is an unseen line where "you" begin and "I" end. There is not only physical space, such as one's bedroom or clothing, but also psychological space, which is one's feelings, thoughts, and responsibilities.

In a dysfunctional family, these boundaries or limits may be weak or nonexistent. For example, one parent may make one of the children responsible for the parent's anger; the child may be blamed for making the parent angry, or the child may be required to act out the parent's anger. In either case, the boundaries are enmeshed and entangled, and the children get lost in the entanglement.

The accompanying diagram may help the reader to understand boundaries.

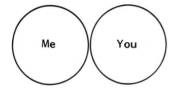 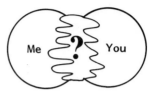

If boundaries are poor, individuals may not know who they are and whose feelings belong to whom. This is a natural state for the infant, but this symbiotic state must develop into a more independent and separate state. The two-year-old stage of temper tantrums is all about separating and setting up boundaries. Poor boundaries encourage poor self-concepts.

Without a personal boundary, saying no is not only difficult, but painful, because it is like saying no to oneself. Individuals cannot distinguish between their needs and feelings and those of others.

2. *No clear values.* How we function in our world depends on the values or beliefs that we've decided are important. Values are traditionally passed down through families and transmitted to the children through examples in daily living. If values are not clear or are nonexistent, children suffer from the lack of direction and guidance needed for their growth and development. Without values, the sense of right and wrong may be lost. For example, if parents use lying as a way to get along in the world and never punish their children for lying, the children also learn and use this pattern of getting along in the world.

3. *Expecting children to be adults before their time.* I have often heard, "I raised myself" or "I had to be mature beyond my years." These individuals are saying that they had to supply the support and guidance needed for their own growth and development, which should have come from their parents. These children learn early,

sometimes as early as infancy, that they have to rely on themselves for the knowledge and wisdom needed to make it in their world. This process requires constantly thinking ahead and figuring out how to handle something because no one will be there to teach or help. Basically, it requires "knowing before you know" living. Children are not ready to do this developmentally and often succumb to the dysfunction in the family.

Perhaps a child is required to run the household and to watch over the younger children while the parents neglect the needs of the children or act like children themselves. Steve's situation is an extreme example. In his family, he was required to supply food and fuel for the family because of his parents' lack of responsibility. This can also happen when the parents are alcoholic or codependent. No matter how it happens, the child is robbed of the needed support for growth, development, and, in fact, a whole childhood.

4. *Problems of the couple acted out through the children.* In some dysfunctional families, the parents take little or no responsibility for their feelings or the problems in their relationship and dump them on their children. The children are expected to feel, act out, and handle these feelings and problems for their parents. After all, it is more acceptable to have an acting-out child than an acting-out adult. Sometimes, the parents may look wonderful but have one or more children who are delinquent, underachieving, sexually promiscuous, lying, or abusive of drugs. These children are responding to their parents' feelings, problems, and expectations. Although this undercurrent or feeling tone of the family may not be shared with the outside world, the real atmosphere is one of conflict and tension.

The job of the children in this type of family is to act out and divert attention away from the parents' feelings and problems and to refocus the attention on themselves. This distracting system relieves pressures, tensions, and conflicts not only between the parents but also between other family members. It works to keep the entire family in a balanced state. This balanced state enables the family to continue to function in the world.

5. *Nonexistent, or poor, support for individuals.* Dysfunctional family systems don't usually support or help individuals to develop and grow. The individuals may not even feel that they're noticed. I have often heard, "I was only a number"; "No one knew I was alive"; "They really didn't care about me"; "All I was good for was to be their slave." If an individual child works to develop his or her unique talents and abilities, there is usually little support or acknowledgment. Some family members may sabotage or even scapegoat that individual. For example, the parents may not ever attend any of the child's events or activities or acknowledge academic achievement. Some children continue to strive under these circumstances, while others may give up and become lost in the system.

6. *Rigid family structures that do not change with the individual's needs.* The structure of a dysfunctional family may be so set and rigid that no one can move. That is, rigid limits, rules, and/or roles in the family keep the individuals trapped. For instance, the parents may make one child a substitute mother for the family so that there is no escape from that role, no matter what the individual needs. The individual then feels trapped, controlled, and isolated. Growth is stifled. Limits in a healthy family move and grow as individuals', and especially children's, needs move and change. If you think about the things you needed as an infant and those you needed as a teenager, you will get some idea of how limits and structures must be flexible and change to support growth. Rigidity works to keep everyone controlled, limited, and deindividualized.

7. *Family secrets that are kept and played out in feelings and behavior.* I once worked with a child who, when emotionally hurt, would cover up the hurt and make it a secret hidden deep inside her. The secret and its pain, however, caused the child's behavior to change because it took energy to keep the pain hidden and because feelings intensify when not expressed. The hurt had no release, and it festered, grew, and intensified, creating tension that had to be released, as it was in her behavior. She would go from a sweet child to an aggressive, out-of-

control child in a matter of minutes. Secrets in families function in the same way, causing tension, festering, and shame. Secrets affect all members of the family through feelings, thoughts, behavior, and stress. The more secrets, or the larger and more serious the secrets, the more acting out is done in the family. This acting out may take the form of aggression or withdrawal, depending on the individuals and on the family system that has been developed from one generation to another. Secrets are often handed down from one generation to another.

8. *Secrets that create shame.* Part of having family secrets is the underlying feeling of shame. There is a deep fear that people will find out about the secrets and that the individual will be considered the guilty party, as if she or he had actually done the awful deed. The individual then takes on the responsibility of the shame and feels as if she or he should be punished for being the cause of the family's ruin in society. The damage to self-esteem of such shame is intense and deep.

Even the deep feeling of shame becomes a secret to keep hidden. There may be an intense fear that once the secret is found out, everyone will know that the individual (not just the family) is not OK, and this becomes another secret to keep hidden. This shame may be acted out through aggression, withdrawal, or denial. One person put it this way: "I just knew my family was not OK, but I had to keep the secret hidden. If I didn't, well, the thought was so awful I believed I would die and my family would be destroyed."

9. *Myths that surround the family to "protect" secrets from the world.* This characteristic goes hand in hand with the previous two, secrets and shame. To protect and keep the secrets hidden from the world, myths or lies are created about the secret. These myths may be passed down from one generation to the next for decades, or they may be created in the immediate family, depending on the need. For example, if my mom is a heavy drinker, irresponsible, and an embarrassment to the family, I may tell others that Mom is sick and can't do much. My siblings and I take over the household responsibilities and raise ourselves. As a family, we try to project an image that says we are

OK or, better yet, that we are wonderful and everything is terrific. The outside world doesn't suspect the truth, and no individual within the family is free to tell the truth. The fear and shame keep the secrets and myths in place. For children, this process causes poor self-esteem, poor or no boundaries, and confusion between fantasy and reality. If Dad is great and everything is wonderful, why does Dad beat up Mom, and why does she pretend that she's happy?

10. *The use of blame, guilt, and shame to handle family problems.* Dysfunctional families use blame, guilt, and shame to shift responsibility from the person to whom it belongs to someone else. For example, if I can blame my spouse for all (or most) of my failures, feelings, and problems, then I don't have to struggle, suffer, feel pain, or be responsible for my feelings or actions. My spouse then feels guilty, and the shame continues underneath the relationship to keep everything in control. Basically, if I can blame you and make you feel guilty and ashamed, I'm OK.

The scapegoat in a family is the most extreme example. Everything that goes wrong in the family is blamed on one person, so that the rest of the family is "OK." All the yelling, abuse, and punishments are aimed at this one person, and, in turn, the family's tension is relieved. The family, as well as the scapegoat, may truly believe that the scapegoat is responsible for all the bad that occurs. This is one of the most difficult roles from which to recover.

11. *Different types of abuse and neglect.* Physical, emotional, verbal, ritual, sexual, and drug and alcohol abuse, as well as neglect, occur commonly in dysfunctional families. Abuse and neglect occur in different forms, depending on the individuals in the family. Typically, neglect and abuse come from out-of-control, inappropriately expressed feelings such as anger, jealousy, and sadness. Abuse and neglect also work to relieve tensions, deal with problems, and punish, all in inappropriate ways.

12. *Imbalance of power.* Often in dysfunctional families, certain individuals control the power, individuals' power as well as the family's

power. This is imbalance. In a balanced family, each individual has his or her own personal power, and the family works together in a cooperative, noncontrolling way. In an imbalanced family, the father, for instance, runs the house and whatever he says goes. It doesn't matter if Mom or the children have needs. All that matters is what Dad thinks or wants. The entire family system is then developed to take care of Dad and to give Dad what he wants, or Dad may act out by punishing or abusing. Another example of an out-of-balance family is one in which there is a pecking order. Dad picks on and demands from Mom, Mom demands from the son, the son demands from his sister, and so on. In these families, individuals learn very early that they are not important. No one feels good, and everyone loses.

13. *Profound disorder in family responsibilities.* Dysfunctional families deal with responsibilities very poorly, including physical work around the house, caring for the children, and being responsible for one's own feelings and behavior. Such families range from promoting total permissiveness to being so rigid in demands that no one can begin to meet them. At both extremes, the children become lost. In an extreme example, one person is assigned the role of caretaker in the family. As one person put it, "I worked hard to clean the entire house all the time. My family yelled at me constantly, saying I didn't do enough and I was lazy. I actually believed them until a friend told me I did more than anyone else in the family and that that was the reason I was always tired. I was so caught up in it, I really thought I was lazy."

The above characteristics are important to keep in mind as we further explore the world of the transcender. They provide the background for understanding just what transcenders have lived with in their daily lives and what they have overcome. They have worked to find ways to grow, to develop, and to protect and nurture themselves in spite of the dysfunctions. Out of the pain and the dysfunctions, transcenders create a turning-point decision — a decision *not* to be like their families. This turning-point decision is the pivotal point of survival.

Decisions: The Turning Point

How does one grow up in a dysfunctional family? Cope with intense stress throughout one's childhood? Raise oneself because no parent is really available? How does one do all this and not become severely emotionally impaired? When asked these questions, transcenders respond matter-of-factly with, "I did what I had to do"; "Doesn't everyone do what I did?"; "I'm no different from anyone else." Transcenders, though, are different. They are different from the child who grows up in the same or similar circumstances and becomes severely emotionally ill, extremely dependent, or delinquent. They're also different from the emotionally healthy child who grows up in a loving, nurturing family.

What transcenders accomplish in the face of great obstacles is nothing short of miraculous. Their incredible process begins with feelings of intense pain and loneliness that lead to a monumental turning-point decision: to divorce themselves emotionally from their family of origin, to take responsibility for their lives, and to raise themselves to be different from their family.

PAIN AND LONELINESS

Transcenders suffer emotionally, as well as physically, from the many kinds of abuse that occur in a dysfunctional family: physical, verbal, emotional, ritual, and sexual abuse, as well as neglect. These abuses include assaults on the self as well as on the body, and they cause great pain. Experiences of pain and loneliness are described again and again by transcenders.

The pain, whether physical or emotional, is a chronic condition of growing up. Transcenders describe the sharp, temporary pain of physical beatings. Never-ending pain comes from unmet emotional needs, lack of support, struggles for identity, embarrassment, deception, not belonging anywhere or to anyone, and fear of the uncertainty in their world. The worst pain is a gnawing, aching, ever-present emptiness. The pain is heavy, depressing, and chronic.

Loneliness is another part of transcenders' experience of suffering. They describe the loneliness of being-in-the-world with no one to turn to for help or support. (Being-in-the-world is the individual's unique way of relating to his or her world.) They feel that no one cares, no one regards them as special, and no one accepts or loves them. Transcenders also express feelings of alienation from themselves and others and a strong sense that they can rely only on themselves. Their loneliness is like a constant ache, a deep inner emptiness.

For transcenders, the suffering is chronic, intense, deep, and painful. Incredibly, it is this suffering that is the positive, motivating force and the grounding that causes transcenders to move out of their families into more growth-directed channels. Their intense suffering forces a realization that they do not want to live as their families do. It focuses them on a world without the pain. Psychologically, the transcenders' suffering is the trigger that shifts their internal frame of reference. (The internal frame of reference is the view that an individual has of his or her world. This includes thoughts, beliefs, and feelings. This view helps determine how we function in the world and what decisions we make. For example, if I believe that the world is wonderful and exciting, I will choose different activities than if I believe that the world is a terrible, fearful place to live.)

In the following descriptions, Marie, Chris, Steve, Paul, and Tiffany share some of their experiences of pain and loneliness.

―――――――――――――――― *Marie* ――――――――――――――――

I grew up in a family where there was no way to win. I was never "good enough" to win my parents' approval. When I was a child, my only goal was to be good enough to be loved by my parents. With each baby animal my father would bring home, I prayed I would be "good enough" so it wouldn't have to be killed because I was a bad girl. Each time, with childlike faith, I believed him. Each time, with satanic madness, he tortured them and killed them while making me watch. The pain was horrible, and I felt so alone and so guilty because I couldn't save any of them. They all died.

I was kept isolated from other children all through my childhood, and I was allowed to be with other adults only when my parents wanted to use me sexually or for the satanic rituals. They tortured me with hopes of having friends. For example, my parents would tell me I was going to have a birthday party. I would anxiously wait for the big day to arrive, standing at the door, full of excitement, waiting and waiting for the first guest to arrive. But no one ever came! I thought no one had come to my party because I was a bad girl. No one came to my party because no one was ever invited. For years, I thought it was because I was a bad girl and not good enough to celebrate my birthday. I can never remember being wished a happy birthday by my parents. That was a day neither of them wanted to remember. I felt responsible for making them unhappy by being born.

The times I was being tortured by my parents I felt loneliness beyond any description. I learned to retreat into myself in order to escape the pain. At times, I would be tied up in a chair and would watch the hands on the clock move ever so slowly, hour after hour. I would be punished if I wet myself because I couldn't hold the urine any longer and no one would untie me. The fact that I had wet my pants was "proof" of what a bad girl I was. How I hated that clock. I always hung onto the belief that, if I could just last a little longer, someone would come and untie me. (Crying out for help brought more punishment.) No one ever came, unless it was with a belt or a whip.

Verbal communications in our house were almost nonexistent. My mother would go for weeks without speaking a word to me, and I would have to anticipate what she wanted of me, or from me. If I didn't anticipate correctly, I would again be severely punished. I longed to talk — to anyone, about anything. This was never possible in our house because I would be punished for "using up my words."

When I went to school, I had never played with other children, and I was terrified. My mother added to the terror by telling me each morning as I left for school that she might have got "sick and tired" of taking care of me and that she would probably leave town while I was at school and I would never see her again. I was terrified she might "go away" while I was at school and I would be all alone.

An "A" was the only acceptable grade on a test, paper, or report card. When I did make an "A", however, I was punished for "calling attention to myself." Once a teacher wrote my parents a note telling them how well behaved I was in class and how he wished he had more students like me. (Unfortunately, this teacher didn't realize that I was "too good," that something was wrong.) I'll never forget the explosion when my parents read the teacher's note. I was supposed to be a "good girl" and never have to be corrected by my teachers. Here was a letter confirming that I was being a "good girl," but were my parents pleased? I was severely beaten for again "calling attention to myself." The funny thing is, I knew what my parents' reaction would be when the teacher wrote the note. In fact, I begged him not to, but he said that good behavior deserved to be rewarded. Little did he know what kind of reward I would receive. Truly, I grew up in a home where there was no way to win.

──────────────────────── *Chris* ────────────────────────

The scapegoat of a family experiences pain and loneliness not only from growing up in a dysfunctional family, but also from being blamed for all the problems in the family. Chris describes his pain and loneliness this way:

They hated me. I kept trying and trying to get along, to do something right, something that would make me OK and accepted. Nothing worked. Nothing ever worked. I was always on the outside looking in, hoping. The pain, God, the pain! I was so anxious. I thought at times I was going to just die because the feelings were so intense.

The pain and tension would overwhelm me. There were times when I couldn't function, and I would just go to my room or a place in the park and sit there. I wouldn't think, feel, or anything. I would sit in a stupor just trying to stop the pain. Other times, I just kept going because it hurt too much not to.

The pain of the beatings was awful, but not half as bad as the loneliness and the emotional pain of being isolated in the family. That pain lasted forever. It was like an empty, black void where my pain accumulated. My family just kept pouring more and more pain and suffering into it. One of the ways they did this was to play emotional games. They would pretend that I could be part of the family. I would get so excited about finally being a part, belonging, but at the last minute, they would change their minds and reject me. They would invite me to a movie or to go and visit relatives with them, but I always had done something bad and had to be punished by not going. It really hurt. I was tricked so many times. I felt like an unacceptable, awful kid who could not be given to because everyone knew I was awful, bad, and not worth anything. I was so alone, so incredibly alone. There was no one there to fill the void, to tell me that I was OK or that the problem was not me but the craziness of the family. There was no one. I remember always being cold, hungry, and left out. I was never OK in my family.

—————————————— *Steve* ——————————————

Steve, who lived in poverty and took care of his brothers and sisters, experienced a combination of physical and emotional pain. The feelings included isolation and being overburdened with responsibility. He describes it this way:

It was just terrible. The pain and loneliness were awful, just awful. I can still feel the pain in my legs from trying to get close enough to the fire to get a little warmth and how horribly cold the rest of me was. I will never forget that no one helped us except for table scraps from the neighbors. We were always so hungry. No one should have to live like that, so hungry and so weak, too weak to go to school.

Later, when I was able to go to school, I never looked OK. The other kids, including my brothers and sisters, would make fun of me. I was always made fun of. I was awkward, weak, dirty, and hungry. They'd call me retarded and dumb, and I believed it.

I would study for hours and hours and get so frustrated I'd beat my head on the table saying, "Why can't I do this! I must be dumb the way they say!" But there was so much physical and emotional pain that I didn't have room for academics. It was all taken up with pain and just trying to survive.

I always felt so very, very alone. My parents were never there for anyone. They were only there physically. I realized there was nobody I could get close to. So, I was lonely in the worst sense of the word. I think I felt so unbelievably alone for a lot of years. One of the worst things about being that alone for so long is you believe this is the way it is suppose to be or someone would have helped out and changed it for you. You begin to believe all life is like this, with all the pain and loneliness. At times, you just lose hope.

Paul

Paul experienced a variety of abuses. What he remembers the most is the chaos and stress. Here are his words:

Most of all, I remember the stress, the unending stress. There was always yelling and screaming. I was always being beaten by my mother. I can remember not being able to sit down for three days after one of Mother's beatings. I was black and blue. It was the stress and the chaos that were the worst, though. The physical beatings, yeah, they hurt, but it was the constant turmoil and confusion that created the terrible, never-ending pain.

I never felt loved or accepted. Everyone else got to do what I wanted to do: public school, art lessons, dance class. I never knew what was wrong with me because me wasn't OK, and I really did not know how to be anyone else. I couldn't be perfect because I couldn't get the rules right because the rules were always changing. I was lost in the chaos, which was like not having any ground to stand on. I didn't know who I was, didn't know how to figure me out even though I tried, really tried. I didn't have anyone to adhere to, to begin to figure it all out.

My loneliness was like a deep, gnawing monster inside me that kept eating up anything and everything that did get to that spot deep inside me. That empty spot never got filled when I was a child, and it took me years to begin to fill it as an adult. No one should ever feel that empty.

Tiffany

Traditional roles often create isolation and loneliness. Perfectionism also creates a different pain: isolation from within oneself. Tiffany, being the only girl, was commanded to play a traditional role, combined with sibling abuse. She felt alone and trapped. Her pain was deep and full of fear. Here are her words:

Fear. All the fear. I was so afraid. The fear in my family was everywhere. I had a fear of not being safe, of not having enough to eat, of not getting enough love, of not being perfect, or being handicapped, of being criticized. I can't pinpoint the exact age when I started being afraid, but it seems to have always been there, always. I desperately needed someone to guide me and teach me how to live, but no one was ever there for me. But I was expected to be perfect or I would be severely criticized, even though there was no one to help me figure out and understand what perfect was. At times, I would hear deep inside of me: "Please, I'm scared. Please help me. Tell me things, teach me things I should know. Hold me. Tell me it will be all right." I didn't know how to grow up. I needed someone so desperately. I would tell myself to be a big girl, a good girl, and then Mommy and Daddy would love me. Part of the crazies for me was that you could never show you were afraid because that meant you were not perfect, and here I was, not just afraid, but terrified!

So I tried to be perfect and hide my fears so that my parents and brothers would love me. I felt so afraid, so alone. I believed no one loved me — at least, not the real me. One of the worst parts of growing up was knowing my parents really did want a girl, but a girl in the traditional role who was prim and proper, who acted, felt, and thought like a good girl. They wanted a girl, but they didn't want me. I just didn't fit. Lord knows I tried, but I just couldn't do it. I felt so unwanted. They never saw or accepted me for the person I was, and I couldn't fit the mold they wanted as their "traditional good girl." I just knew I had to find a way to ease the pain and go on.

It was such a terrible waste, so sad. I just remember having no one there for me. No one I could talk to or be the real me with. It seemed as if every time I talked or tried to share something, I was criticized and made to feel wrong. I don't remember anyone ever trying to listen to me.

I was so lonely and the pain was so intense at times that it seemed intolerable. I was so depressed at one point; I read every one of John Steinbeck's books, which are horribly tragic. When I got to the last one, *The Red Pony*, I couldn't finish it when I realized the pony was going to die. That was the beginning of my turning point!

THE TURNING POINT

Suffering is the core of the turning-point decision. Transcenders experience intense depression, anger, pain, and loneliness throughout childhood. At times, the suffering is so overwhelming that they honestly believe they won't survive. Amazingly, it is out of coping with this intense suffering that the turning point emerges. It is as if the individual feels the pain so deeply and so intensely that she or he comes to a point of knowing life is not supposed to be this way and begins to seek out a new direction. To the transcender, the turning point sounds like this: "This is not my family. I am not like them and I don't belong here. Someday I will get out of here and create a world that is less abusive, less neglectful, and in other ways less hurtful to me. Someday I will be me and have a life I want. I will be different from my family for the rest of my life."

Transcenders' awareness of their turning point includes (1) not being able to go through the suffering again; (2) feeling challenged by and attracted to alternate lifestyles; (3) wanting to maintain the "good" within themselves; and (4) realizing that they are in their world by themselves and it is up to them to make the best of it.

The turning point is an emotional divorce from the family of origin and that family's way of living. It involves a crucial shift from pain and loneliness to goal-directed, productive living that radically alters the transcender's internal frame of reference. This alteration includes a feeling of liking and loving oneself as well as feeling good about oneself. It is as if a miracle happens that begins to change the person's view of herself or himself.

What transcenders decide in this divorce is to make it in spite of family problems, obstacles, and handicaps. The decision is so powerful that it becomes the pivotal point, the motivating force, for survival. Transcenders use it as a support and grounding to sustain them throughout childhood and often as a guiding force for the rest of their lives. The turning point is a powerful leap into the future. It is the essence of survival; without it, the transcenders would not have made it.

Sometimes one crisis brings the turning-point decision into focus; sometimes it is a series of crises over a period of years. However it occurs, transcenders often feel forced to accept the painful reality of their families, to reflect on themselves and realize their families will never be capable of giving them the love and acceptance they so desperately need.

The cost is great. It often means emotionally divorcing themselves from the little, if any, closeness they may have had in the family and maintaining a state of independence long before they, as children, are developmentally ready to do so. It also means taking care of their own physical and emotional needs and being wise and mature far beyond their chronological years.

Transcenders are not superhuman or immune to pain. The major difference between the transcender and the child who succumbs to the family's dysfunction is the turning-point decision. Instead of becoming dysfunctional and/or emotionally impaired like their families, transcenders choose to find ways through the struggle. They work to be different from their families and to divorce themselves emotionally while still physically living within the family. They seek out what they need elsewhere. This means reaching out to others for support, guidance, and information on how to live in the world differently from their own family. At the same time, they are coping with tremendous stress at home by using survival skills. Through survival skills, transcenders work to create meaningfulness out of chaos, nurturing out of barrenness, and protection in the face of violence.

The turning-point decision occurs at different ages for different individuals. For some, it seems to occur as early as infancy, whereas for others, it occurs in the late teens. The average age, from my research and experience, is ten to thirteen years of age. The study did not include transcenders who made their turning-point decisions as adults. The time of the decision is not really important. What is important is the decision itself.

What follows are examples of turning points that give a flavor of these decisions.

Marie

I am not able to identify the particular time of my turning-point decision, when I decided to be different. I know it was at a very early age, before I could identify my emotions. Actually, there were probably several turning points, each one stronger, more determined than the one before. I suppose the real turning point was when I internally rebelled against my world and said, "No, I will not be like these people. I will be different. I will make other choices for myself." It was a definite, conscious awareness. I decided that I might be "*from* the mud, but never *of* the mud." Deep inside myself I knew I would rise above this insanity. I knew there was a better way, a different way, and I just had to make different choices from those my parents had made in their lives.

To make these different choices, I had to weigh and measure actions, behaviors, and values in order to determine what was real and worth keeping. At the same time, I had to decide what to discard, reject, or remove myself from. Basically, I had to be my own parent, a terrifying way of life for a small child, and for a teenager. I just remember so many things in my life that did not feel right.

I don't remember the first time I was sexually abused or subjected to sexual encounters no child should have knowledge of. I do remember it did not feel right and I did not want to be there. I grew up "knowing" that I could never let anyone know what my family was really like. My mother always told me that, if anyone found out how bad I really was, I would be put up for adoption. As crazy and abusive as she was, I was terrified of her leaving me.

During therapy, I remembered being with my parents in a department store. They would walk just behind me, and then all of a sudden, they would be gone, hiding from me. I remember so well the terror of looking for feet that I recognized so I could find my parents again. I didn't dare act lost or cry. After all, I had been a bad girl. At the time, I really thought I was such a bad person that I deserved this kind of treatment and abuse. And yet, at other times of sexual abuse, I would cover my eyes or try to put my fingers in my ears in an attempt to block the sights and sounds from a world in which I did not belong and knew I did not belong in. No, I can't say there was any one real turning point, but rather an accumulation of turning-point decisions, not to ever be like my mother and never to have to do those horrible things again. That has truly sustained me and been my focus for life.

Chris

I became determined again and again and again, like a mind set, to take care of me in spite of my family. I simply did what I had to do until I could get out of there. For example, I can remember this mind set being part of me when I was very young. I came home from school when I was four, and I said to my mother that I didn't need to walk to school with anybody. I mean, even at four years old and school a mile away, I've got this goal. So I don't know. I even think that it can be prenatal; I sensed that I would have to tune out the world until I got out of the family in order not to be like them.

Sometimes I'd get angry and say over and over to myself, "I'll show you. I'm not going to be like you guys, because I'm not. Life doesn't have to be this way."

Steve

I remember deciding that I would never live in poverty again with the neglect, hunger, cold, and no parent. I never wanted to go back. That's what kept me going. It was my drive, my energy for working, getting ahead, and moving forward. Nothing could ever be as bad as that. Nothing. I won't let it.

It was fear, but also a commitment to myself to keep moving forward and not to stay in a spot where I just kept rehashing my life over and over again and became like my parents. I never wanted to do that. I knew I couldn't be that poor again. Ohhh, it was so awful. I wanted to keep moving forward and never, never to repeat how I grew up. I wanted to be different, very different. I wanted to be different from my environment, different from my abandoning parents, different from all of it. I wanted to be me, and whatever risks it would take, I'd take them. I never again wanted to put myself in a position of being cold, hungry, or neglected.

Paul

I was always scared shitless that I would be a fool like my father. I considered my father a fool, and he really was. That's harsh language, but his behavior was so strange that it was kind of like a buffoon's. I do imitations of people who are out of control. For example, people you meet in bars, people who are just squirrelly, and how their mind gets going and they talk about things that really don't make any sense at all, and yet, they don't know that. My father was always that way, so I grew up thinking that if you are yourself you will be a fool. So I monitored everything that went on in my mind before I said a word because I was scared to death that I would say things like my father and I would come out sounding like a fool and not know it. I worked really hard not be like my father.

Tiffany

It was from the pain, so much pain. I can still feel it. I was so alone and so afraid and yet I had to act so independent. I can still bring back the terror of it and my body shudders with it. I had become unbelievably, painfully shy but out of this pain came my decision. I can remember the day of my decision. It was sunny and beautiful out but all I could see was darkness, pain, and emptiness. I was reading Steinbeck's *The Red Pony* and had come to the place where the pony was going to die. I closed the book, and I said, "I'll never do this to me again, never. I'll never be this depressed and in this pain again." I never have finished that book.

I decided that someday, somehow, I'd be me with a world where I could be me and not have to hide. I'd be me no matter what it took. That's what it felt like; the real me was hidden because the real me wasn't OK. To exist, I functioned on two levels: one, the girl my family wanted that cooked, cleaned, helped my mother, got good grades, did what she was told, and took whatever my brothers dished out, and the other me, the creative, vital, authentic me, who withdrew, fantasized, and was nurtured underground.

It was this decision, to be me in my own world, that has continued to be my focus for life. It is a special, powerful promise I made to myself and one that I have rarely veered from. This promise meant that I emotionally divorced my family and looked in other directions for my life.

I still use it when I become lost in the world of others. It helps, even now, when I have a hard decision to make. I ask myself, "Is this how I want my world?" If the answer is yes, I go ahead, because not to do it would mean going back to that suffering and losing me, and I couldn't ever do that again. Ever!!! Just the thought of it shoots a feeling of fear and pain through me with a scream, "No!" This promise is absolutely one of my most precious possessions.

Somehow, deep inside me, I was in touch with a kernel of truth — that part of me that was good, precious, and worth everything. It's this kernel that I protected and nurtured as much as possible. I cared for it and affirmed it. I believed in my abilities until the day I would have my world. It was as if I kept the real me protected from the hurts of the family. It was tucked away, safe, waiting for its time to surface. It helped ease the pain.

Here are more descriptions of transcenders' turning points to help illustrate how varied they are and yet how similar:

---------------------------------- *Tim* ----------------------------------

Tim transcended a family in which the parents were totally enmeshed and that left little room for a growing child.

My turning point was around my mother's hospitalization for a hysterectomy; she had ovarian cancer. It was shortly after we moved to a new town, and I was just very, very, lonely. I had a real hard time making friends, and I felt very out of it. I tried to be the teacher's pet and be smart. I found no support whatsoever at home. I was put out into the world of school and new friends and a strange town with no support from home.

My father was zoned out. I can't remember him during that time, even though it was just the two of us for two weeks while she was in the hospital. I do remember him taking me to the hospital to visit her and then telling me I couldn't come in because I had to be fourteen to visit — I was only ten or eleven. I was really angry and hurt. What I did was I would take a step ladder (my mother was on the first floor of the hospital), set it up, and wave to her from outside her window. One time, I made a little snowman for her.

I think the symbolism of being outside the window in the cold, looking in and seeing my parents in the warmth together, hit me very hard. I wasn't really conscious of it, but I think after that time I checked out of my family. I had tried to be part of the family. I tried to make them into my parents and kept banging on their doors. After a while, I didn't bang on the doors anymore.

I made the decision to divorce myself from the family; I really had left them. The situation was an exaggeration or magnification of what was really going on all that time in everyday life. It was a symbolic thing because my mother was always acting like a little girl. She was so dependent, almost like an invalid. Basically, she was flat on her back in the hospital, and my father was ministering to her emotionally — and me, standing outside on the ladder in the snow.

I felt a lot of sadness, hurt, and anger all mixed up. I wondered what it was about me that was so unlovable. They were always in the warm, well-lighted room, and I was always out in the snow. I would wonder what it was about me and turned it on myself: Maybe it isn't them; maybe it is me. And then again, I felt really helpless to do anything about it. God knows I was trying. I felt like a victim and was really helpless. There was nothing else I could do because I had tried everything there was to try. At that time in my life, there was nobody, nobody I could adhere to, and so I began to seek what I needed elsewhere and divorced my family.

Bill

Bill grew up in an ethnic ghetto with an alcoholic father and a deep, symbiotic relationship with his mother. In this type of relationship, the connection is so close that there is little separation between mother and child. Here is his turning-point process:

Part of my moving away from the family occurred when I went to high school out of my old neighborhood. It was a parochial school. It wasn't an ethnic parochial school; people actually spoke English. They did not speak Polish or Italian, but everyday common English in a school run by Irish nuns. There was a mixture of kids, and I was forced to adapt. I blossomed, and I became aware of other lifestyles, values, and attitudes that were different from mine. I met people who were sons of doctors, successful insurance men, and attorneys who did not drive ten-year-old clunkers, but who bought this year's car this year. They were successful that way but were also successful emotionally. I saw real closeness between parents and son. It was as if I was in a different atmosphere in a different way.

I started shifting away; my father and mother were no longer going to be the yardstick of how I measured life; my father was not capable of giving me guidance or direction, and he was always going to drink and be crazy. I also came to realize that I couldn't rely on my mother. I started pulling away from that kind of emotional relationship. I began to invest in other relationships and to create my world.

Tom

Tom's turning-point decision was a shift to more positive messages rather than a major decision.

No, I didn't make a conscious decision. I don't think I did. But I did make a kind of shift where I was looking for positive messages. I remember especially in terms of girls. I felt very ugly and got real crazy about it. I was just acting out the message I got at home: a lot of criticism, a lot of nonverbal messages that I'm not much of a human being, not very desirable as a human being. So, I just gave up girls altogether. And then I remembered hearing in my senior year a rumor that some girl wanted to date me. It just blew me away. I was so surprised. So, I did it. I dated some girl, someone I never would have thought would have been the least bit interested in me, and that was a real help. From there, I continued to look for more positive messages.

* * *

Transcenders create turning-point decisions as a result of an inward shift triggered by intense suffering. There are three important parts to the decision: (1) a separation from the family emotionally and physically; (2) a refusal to be like the family; and (3) a commitment to personal growth.

In the first part of the decision, transcenders realize there is a different, healthier way to live without so much pain, loneliness, and anger. Separating, or "divorcing," the family often includes leaving emotionally, socially, and/or physically until the transcenders are able to move out permanently. Transcenders come to a strong realization of the need to separate and detach in order to survive. They describe this part of the turning point as a strong will to live, an intense inner drive to go beyond or transcend the family, as well as determined internal independence.

The second part of the decision is a refusal to be like the family. There is a realization that the family is wrong, horrible, violent, and ignorant, as well as an awareness that the transcenders do not have to be like the family. This part helps maintain the separation by reminding the transcenders of the intense fear they have of being like their families. They describe the refusal as an inner drive to be *much more* than the family. This area requires an active, determined commitment to be different, which in turn maintains and encourages growth in other ways. For example, they feel forced to seek role models in other areas of their lives.

The third and last part of the turning point is a strong, long-lasting commitment to personal growth. This part of the turning-point decision seems to begin at the time of the decision. It includes (1) a fear of ending up stuck like their families; (2) an awareness of their potentialities and talents; (3) the search for a way to make up for time and opportunities lost because of the family; and (4) the search for growth at all cost. To create growth, transcenders use their will (that part of us that focuses all available resources for our use) and seek other areas for developing competencies, overcoming anxieties, and finding needed and available resources. Their commitment to personal growth is a continuing, lifelong process. One transcender describes it this way:

> I feel very proud of what I am because I worked hard to be able to be here. It's a lot of hard work, hard work. I see people today who want to make changes overnight, and it doesn't work that way. It takes a long, concerted effort. You have to work, work, work, and when you can't stand it, you work some more. Sometimes, you just have to go to sleep. Many nights, I just sat up reading books, trying to find something to hang on to. Somebody gave me a copy of *The World's Greatest Salesman*, and, boy, there were nights I sat in the bedroom and just read the same chapter over and over again, just trying to hang on. I'd wake up the next morning and read it over and over again, just trying to make it through the day. Sometimes, I'd just go to bed at night and say, "Go to sleep and you won't feel it." And it helps, it's

helped to deal with those things, to reach part of the potential that I have. I've still got a long way to go, but I'm excited about the growth I've gained.

PROCESS OF THE CHANGE

Transcenders create a remarkable internal shift. They change how they view their world, their families, and themselves. To do this, transcenders make a concerted effort that they maintain over a long period of time — even years. Some transcenders remember a very conscious decision, and others remember beginning to look for more positive messages in their world. No matter how the shift occurs, it is amazing that it can be maintained over years of dysfunctional family life.

Transcenders describe two processes in changing their internal frame of reference. The first is the creation of a more positive self-image and a better lifestyle. To accomplish these goals, transcenders struggle to overcome feelings of self-doubt, self-degradation, and a fear of life. They work to be accepted and accept themselves as persons (not as objects or numbers in the family), to be independent, and to move away from the family. They find ways to help themselves through traumas, to be first-class citizens, to seek positive messages rather than cynicism, to continue working to change their old internal frames of reference, and to create a new way of being. They protect themselves from the negative influences and work to gain the nurturing they desperately need. Transcenders are persistent and stay focused on their goals. They refuse to give up.

The second process that transcenders use in the struggle to change their internal frame of reference is a shift to more positiveness in their lives. Transcenders describe a dawning awareness of the world's beauty and goodness that kindles a sense of warmth. This connection inspires them to take control of their lives, to have the courage to move away from their dysfunctional families, and to gain the strength needed to continue working to "make it." They begin to believe in, rely on, and be responsible for themselves.

Once they decide to be different from their families, their belief in themselves helps them to know that there is something better and that they are capable of creating it. This belief connects them to their potentialities, talents, goals, and hope. Often, it provides an internal affirmation of themselves. In this process, their being-in-the-world is in transition, and they apply the needed work, persistence, active willing, and a belief in themselves that sustains the effort through many years.

In summary, the process of creating the turning-point decision involves individuals' examining their lives and making a commitment to themselves for the future. It is in this way that they become free from their family's control and free to seek what they need in other areas. Additionally, inward shifts become pivotal points in their lives. Transcenders work to create a more positive internal frame of reference, relying on their belief in themselves.

Chapter 4

Techniques of Survival

How do transcenders get through the day while coping with the extreme stress in their family life? How do they create a new and different life for themselves? Where do they get needed information, protection, and nurturance to survive? This chapter details the every-day skills or techniques of surviving that work to create a different lifestyle while managing and coping with extreme stress and trauma.

Survival depends on *actively* developing techniques that gain two very important supports: protection and nurturance for the body and the precious core, the authentic self. Often, one technique offers both protection and nurturance.

Protection is an absolute necessity because transcenders have to become less vulnerable to the dangers in their world. They need to escape, seek refuge, and defend themselves whenever possible. Protection techniques shield, curb, hinder, and, at times, stop the onslaught of injury and destruction.

Even in the most abusive situations, transcenders also have to develop techniques that gain nurturance. They seek out people, places, organizations, and situations that offer assistance, support, and learning. These, in turn, help the transcender maintain and develop the original package.

From these techniques, transcenders gain feelings of being gratified, bolstered, rescued, relieved, encouraged, and reinforced in their battle to survive. The nurturance and protection that transcenders obtain may not fill the emptiness or take the pain away, but they are enough to maintain the self and give hope for the future.

Eleven survival technique categories used by transcenders have been identified: (1) using inner personal resources; (2) using fantasy; (3) using the available environmental resources; (4) transcending the family; (5) getting out and staying away; (6) developing a style of relating to others; (7) developing roles in the family; (8) seeking relationships with significant others; (9) developing competencies; (10) playing; and (11) developing spirituality. In the following descriptions, each category is illustrated by many different transcenders, including ones we've already met in previous chapters. These categories demonstrate how transcenders use the techniques to provide protection and nurturance, as well as what creativity they use to do so. Techniques can also overlap; that is, they can belong in more than one category. While reading, please remember that some techniques protect, some nurture, and some do both. Take the time to feel what it must have been like to develop and use these techniques. Many of you, I am sure, can easily add to the list.

USING INNER PERSONAL RESOURCES

Inner resources include those abilities, talents, or skills that originate from within the person. Transcenders reach deep within and use what is available. Intuition, manipulation, withdrawal, reverse psychology, and solitude are a few examples of the inner resources used by transcenders to deal with their assaultive world. Other examples are distancing from others, drawing close to others, feeling one's feelings fully, and choosing when to use a certain technique.

When transcenders must be at home, their inner resources function to preserve the self when the world is working to destroy it. Their deep commitment to the turning point, along with their strong will, helps transcenders in this process. The following illustrations are examples of how transcenders use inner personal resources for protection, nurturance, or both. Inner resources are listed under seven different aspects of the category. They are (1) affirming oneself; (2) reality-basing the abuse; (3) using intuition; (4) being alone or withdrawing; (5) yelling; (6) observing; and (7) others.

Affirming Oneself

Transcenders often have to affirm and support themselves. The following quotations describe some of the ways they do this:

> First, I had to immerse myself and work on getting my self-image together. At times, I wondered if I was ever going to, but it was really necessary for me to invest in me, because there wasn't anyone else who was going to. It was an absolute necessity for survival.

> I really felt my mom gave my sister a lot more credit than she gave me. I've always felt she believed my sister was more intelligent and more attractive. In my own mind, I felt I was every bit as intelligent and as attractive as my sister. It was a knowing that supported me all through growing up.

Reality-Basing the Abuse

In dealing with the abuse, transcenders realize they are not to blame and often express this to themselves. The following are some of their words:

> During the physical abuse, I remember many times crying, "Why am I being hit? What am I being beat up for?" I hadn't

done anything, and it really bothered me. I'd get slapped in the face or get a lot of verbal abuse, which I hated. I was awfully mad about it. I would think, well, I wasn't wrong, they were wrong.

I didn't have any cognitive awareness because it wasn't safe. I did think, "Well, I didn't do anything that bad." But I'd pay the consequences and shut my mouth because something worse could happen. For example, my parents would say, "Go clean that room again with a toothbrush because you didn't dust it well enough." That's insane! I'd say to myself, "What did I do wrong?" It's like looking for some sort of reasoning, except it wasn't there. There's a part of me that knew it didn't make sense, a positive core of me helping to sort out their crazy reality from mine, and that helped.

Using Intuition

Another part of inner resources is intuition, the area of knowing something, but not really knowing how we know. Transcenders not only rely on this area but develop it fully:

I was given myriads and myriads of opportunities to develop my intuition and my handling of emotionally difficult situations. For example, I can remember thinking, "If I say such and such, OK. However, if I say this, boy, they're going to get mad." I would work and figure this all out. I also had to learn to manipulate my brother because he was stronger and he'd tear up all my comic books. I tried psychology on him, some reverse psychology, and I found out it worked—it really worked! My brother didn't tear up my comic books.

When my dad was drunk, he would have DTs (deep tremors that cause hallucinations), and I was smart enough to handle them. For example, I'd be in the bedroom, and he'd say, "Get the snake that's on the wall." He was hallucinating. I'd think, "Dad, I can't. Where in the hell is the snake?" I knew there was no snake there. I was trying to sort out what was real and what was not. There was a real battle going on in me. But I was smart enough to say, "Yeah, Dad, I got it. It's not there anymore." I had to go with the system to survive.

Another time, Dad put his head in the stove and I was scared. I think I said something like, "Daddy, you don't want to be with the devil." That snapped him out of it and helped him not to die. It's like I could go into his craziness. I could understand what he was doing, and if he was dead, he was going to be with the devil.

Being Alone or Withdrawing

Transcenders found being alone and withdrawing into themselves very comforting and nurturing. During these times, they did not have to be on guard and could relax:

> I think being alone, being in a world of my own that was not connected to the bunch of crazy acting-out people in my world, helped the most. It was not too real, as far as a "normal" reality because I had to create my own, but it was safer and saner than what was in the family.

> There was a difference between my outer and inner world that goes back to daydreaming and my withdrawal into reading. Yeah, because in the reading and the daydreaming, I could be in a world that was my own creation and not somebody else's. These were the seeds of my survivorship. I used to say to myself, "I'll be what you want me to be, but when I'm not around you, when I'm among my friends or by myself, when I choose to, there are some things you cannot take away from me. You can't take away my daydreaming, you can't take away my fantasies, and you can't take away what reading means to me as long as I am a very fantastic student academically." And they would actually defer to me that way. They'd say, "He's studying" or "He's forgetful because he's reading his book," and they'd leave me alone.

I would get so angry, and when my father would get mad at me, he would just criticize and be all over me. I felt so bad about myself. I would go off by myself and just close everything off. I would hear my mother say I was just going into my shell, and then I'd just go blank. I heard the words but didn't feel anything. The only way to protect myself from my father was to shut him off and shut the words out so I couldn't hear what he said. I couldn't fight him. I would then just go off somewhere.

I stopped sharing me because it hurt too much to put me out there with my family criticizing, smashing, and making me wrong all the time. So, I literally went underground. One part of me functioned on the surface, and the other, the real me, was underground, protected and away from the people that could hurt it. It was like escaping inside of myself.

Yelling

Yelling serves as a release and an outlet for built-up emotions. Here's how it works:

When things got real bad around the house and the pain had built up inside me to the point of being more than I could handle, I'd explode by yelling, screaming, and throwing things around. I'd have a major temper tantrum! It felt so good to release all that stuff. At times, I felt I could go on screaming forever. After the temper tantrum, I could go on again. It felt like a limit I was drawing inside myself that screamed, "That's enough, back off," and for a little while they did.

I used my anger to keep people away, especially my family. I would yell, scream, throw things, and really pitch a fit. I did anything I believed would keep them away from me.

Observing

At times, transcenders pull back and observe others intensely. From this, they learn many things, such as other ways to live and how to relate to their world:

> I watched and watched. In school, I may have been observing more than working and getting involved. That's how I learned what to do and how to fit in. I needed to observe in order to know what normal was because all I knew at home were crazies. Finally, I quit watching and began to act, to be a part of life. I got involved.

Others

Techniques are limited only by the creativity of the person involved. Many variations are possible:

> There was always a difference between my outer self and the inner real me. I would screen all incoming stuff and decide if I was going to let it go deeper, to the real me. If it wasn't OK—that is, not matching what I thought I needed or wanted—I rejected it. I had to be very strong-willed. If it was something I needed, I would allow it in, and I would use it to nurture myself. I wasn't always successful in keeping the pain away, but it helped.

> My brother and I always had a strong German pride that kept us together. When we first arrived at the farm and wanted to discuss something but didn't want our foster parents to know, we would speak in German. They were Italian and didn't understand what we were talking about. It gave us privacy and a sense of family.

USING FANTASY

Fantasy is a part of the inner resource techniques, but important enough to be put in its own category. Transcenders give themselves in fantasy what they do not, or cannot, have in reality. It's almost like having the real thing. Through fantasy, transcenders create another, different life. For example, in fantasy, they can be powerful enough to overcome abusive parents or have everyone love and take care of them. They can be in demand, liked, confident, pain-free, and even playful like a regular kid. Fantasy offers escape when escape is impossible, relief from the trauma when trauma is everywhere, and hope for the future when there is none. Fantasy can even help set goals for the future:

> I daydreamed a lot. Fantasizing really helped me survive because I could be in another world, a world of my very own, and have things the way I wanted them. I controlled this world, and I decided who and what happened in it. I felt relief and power over the insanity that was in my family. I can remember also setting goals back then that I am still working on today.

> Through pretending, I dealt with my world and experienced my feelings. For example, if I was really upset or scared about something that was going to happen, I'd pretend how I wanted to handle the situation. I'd act it out in my imagination and try many different solutions. At the same time, I would experience and release all my feelings about it that were not safe to release at the time. It was such a good release for my feelings and helped me get ready for what was going to happen. I also did this with things that had already happened that I was still upset about and wished I could change.

> I lived in a dream world. I even had a dream when I was five years old about having a better life. I wanted to be the king of England, and I fantasized it all the time. I read *The Prince and the Pauper*, in which the two kids change places. I said to my mother, "How come you did away with my twin?" She said, "What are talking about? You are my kid." I wanted to be knighted, to be

the English heir. Actually, my mother's heritage goes back to Scotland, to the Ross clan, and the earl of Ross became James the First, king of England. So, my fantasy and dream for a better life was based in some reality.

When I was in school I would pretend a lot. I would say, "Oh, there are my friends. This teacher is a lovely person." When I was in Boy Scouts, everyone was my friend or brother, and my Scoutmaster was my dad. I found people and made believe they were my family, my real family, not the one I was stuck in. It felt so good and gave me such support.

USING THE AVAILABLE
ENVIRONMENTAL RESOURCES

The third technique category acknowledged by transcenders is using the environmental resources discovered or offered in their world. Transcenders view these offerings as opportunities to learn, grow, and develop areas of security and competency. These resources include educational, recreational, organizational, and situational, along with other personal opportunities. Through these environmental opportunities, transcenders find support, caring, and encouragement. In addition, they become involved with the available protection and nurturing resources:

My growing-up world was made up of sights, sounds, and smells of a multiracial and multi-ethnic neighborhood. My senses were stimulated viscerally, visually, and tacitly, so that my preparation in the world was indelibly imprinted. To see, to hear, to touch, to taste, to smell, to sense the tacit filled me with such stimuli and imagery that I wanted to know more. I became an observer, a wanderer, and an explorer at an early age. I was an intensely curious child, and I got into difficulty at times for experimenting with household elements or wandering away from home without permission. The smells and tastes and sights and conversations of countless delicatessens, bakeries, and ethnic markets and music of dozens of languages will remain with me to the end of my days. I am still able to recognize the sounds of a dozen or more languages even though I am not conversant in all of them.

I had a wonderful seventeenth summer. I went to muscular dystrophy camp for the first time and really loved it. I felt really good about myself. I liked helping those kids because it made me feel really good inside. Also, five boys liked me.

For the first time, I was liked, and it was a very sharing, giving, good experience, and I loved it. I found out I could feel good by doing good. I got this wonderful reward that is very hard to get anyplace else.

In the seventh grade, I began to live in convents to escape my father's violence. When one no longer wanted me (which happened for a variety of reasons), I found another. The nuns accepted me because they had no background from the other convent. I was clever and would find another place.

I remember arriving at the farm for foster care as a big date in my life. It had a lot of exciting things for boys to do, such as trapping, hunting, chasing rats, playing with the dog, and playing with the cats. There was all of nature, with insects, wild animals, pheasants, and wild swamp birds of different kinds. The farming life had a powerful influence on me because it showed me that if I work hard, even though I'm not the smartest, I will succeed at something.

Probably one of the most exciting things to me happened when I was thirteen years old. My aunt and uncle took me with them on vacation. We went to New England. I remember they had a Mustang, a brand new Mustang that had just come out in the 1960s. I remember riding in this Mustang all the way out east and seeing things like the *Mayflower*, Plymouth Rock, battleships, and Niagara Falls. I really enjoyed it, and it gave me a vision for the future.

TRANSCENDING THE FAMILY

Transcendence is a technique that enables an individual to rise above and go beyond the immediate situation. In doing so, individuals consciously shift to and gain another perspective of themselves and their world. Their ability to transcend helps them to overcome difficult, and what seem at times to be insurmountable, obstacles.

Relationships, activities, and fantasies, as well as other techniques, help transcenders transcend the family situation. For example, they use fantasy as a way to give themselves what they do not, and cannot, have in reality. This is one type of transcendence. Using educational opportunities to see the world in a new way is another. Once a situation is transcended, transcenders gain a heightened awareness of their situation. They see more clearly how to create nurturance, protection, hope for the future, and goals for their lives. Above all, transcendence offers relief from the immediate situation:

> I struggled to invest in activities with new and different people. To compete, socialize, and date, and to have an awareness that people outside my family saw and experienced me differently from my family. Without this different perspective, I would not have sustained my will to survive.

> I used many things to transcend my family situation. I worked with clay, fantasized, read, prayed, and spent time alone. Basically, I did anything that shifted me out of my present world into a less tense, less vulnerable, more nurturing and warm place. At times, I'd "leave" my world completely and fantasize I was in another. Other times, I'd be half in and half out of my family's world. That is, half of me was in the family's activity and half was focused on the future. My fantasy world often contained my hopes and dreams for my future. I could actually feel what it would be like to accomplish those goals. Now, in real life, as I actually do those things, I feel them "for real."

> At times, I had to just leave the pain and get time to sort me from the family—sort of like rising above it so I wouldn't be affected by it. It's as if I went to another level inside of me,

where I was detached from the pain and I could think and feel clearer. I felt relief and a separation or distancing from my immediate situation. This was a major part of my survivorhood.

GETTING OUT AND STAYING AWAY

A *major* technique used by transcenders is getting out and staying away. Transcenders physically leave their families as often as they can, for as long as they can. They get out through activities and organizations or by adopting other families. They go to churches, schools, convents, neighbors' homes, and friends' homes. They go for bike rides and walks. They go out with friends and significant others. They go to sanctuaries. Getting out and staying away are purposeful actions; they do not just happen.

By getting out, transcenders escape their home situations, release feelings, relax, and gain nurturance. They also refocus, spend time being their authentic selves, and gain a sense of freedom as well as safety. At times, the family gives the transcender the freedom to get out by being negligent or having an inability to cope with the situation. Basically, for some parents, it is easier if the children are "out of their hair." At other times, transcenders have controlling parents and leave by rebelling. In any case, getting out and staying away involve using safer, available, and accessible people and places. The final getting out and staying away occurs with the move out of the house into the adult world through marriage, work, or college:

> One time, my father tore the basement to pieces coming after me and beating me. I didn't fight back. I just ran out of the house and headed for a field and lay there for a long, long time, just trying to figure out what I was going to do next with my life. Eventually, I started walking back home.

> I just adopted this other family as mine. I used to spend all my weekends there during most of high school, which enabled

me to leave home emotionally and definitely physically. I was about fifteen or sixteen. As I look back on it, it was a great adaptation because if I had gone any other route, I would have landed in juvenile court and probably in a home somewhere. This way, I was able to get away from my home, which was a dynamite keg ready to explode. It finally did explode a couple of times with my dad and me.

I spent lots and lots of time with a close friend who was also a survivor. We drove around town together and helped each other survive. Tom and I found each other basically to hang on to. We put thousands and thousands of miles on his car, driving around town, doing nothing but staying away from our respective families. Round and round and round—we were such experts on that town. We probably put 200,000 miles on his car, literally. That was part of surviving: getting out and staying out.

I left home quite often, especially when I was feeling anxious or lonely. I got out in the evening when I played for dances and got away in the summer in college by playing at resorts all summer. I was very involved in school activities— thank God, because I was able to stay away from home as long as possible and get connected to really nice people. That's how I maintained my sanity.

There is something about adventuring or exploring that I have always liked. I like to travel, and I like to venture out into the world and explore. I think, in a sense, that has been my theme from day one. The running away was venturing out into the world. It's sort of like there's nothing at home, so let's go see what's out there in the world.

I was just very distraught over all the stuff that was going on at home, and frankly, I avoided going home. It was lonely, but I preferred it over going home because it was just that old tension again. It was just the pits, and I avoided it as much as possible. There was nothing I could do about it, so why subject myself to that?

I was always on the go, always running. My sister stayed at home more, and she got worse. I kept at it. I went to places that were crazy but sane, that is, the same thing as my family because even the nuns couldn't talk and they'd walk around the halls with their heads down. At least, they weren't acting out violently. I knew that I would come and scrub the floor today or buff the chapel with the big buffer machine or wherever I'd be working. In the ninth grade, I lived there and joined the order. It was more or less like going away to school, wanting to become a nun someday. I left home in the ninth grade—actually, I left way before that.

If I hadn't got married, I would probably have run away from home. I couldn't stand living there, but I was afraid to leave because my parents would have come and dragged me back, no matter where I went. So I got engaged. I knew that the only way to get out of my parents' clutches was to get married. My husband was the first to ask, so he got me.

Sanctuaries

In the category of getting out and staying away we find the sanctuary. This is any special place that transcenders use to get away from the family. Sanctuaries offer protection from the family and nurturance for the self. Above all, these special places offer a chance just to be, where transcenders can escape their homes, release feelings, relax, gain nurturance, and, in general, regroup within themselves. The sanctuary is a safe, accessible, available place to go when the world closes in:

I loved the out-of-doors, with the sun and woods. That has always been my sanctuary, warm, sunny—on walks, bike rides. Relaxing with the warmth, comfort, and good smells. Most of all, it was relaxing and safe. I could pray, cry, and let it all out. It was my special place to be just me.

I had a special place in our basement. When I felt as if I had absolutely had it with the stuff going on in my family, I would crawl in the space and stay until I could face the world again. For some reason, my family never realized I was there or just didn't care. I would spend a long time there, thinking, feeling, being alone, and being lonely. It was my special sanctuary, a place to be just me. There was part of me, however, that wished someone would notice that I was gone and come and ask me what was wrong. I wish someone had tried to talk to me about it. No one ever came.

I used to get away as often as I could—go anywhere. I did have one special place, my sanctuary. It was near the lake, and I'd spend hours there. I would be alone, and it was peaceful, calm, and there would be no fighting or criticizing.

DEVELOPING A STYLE OF RELATING TO OTHERS

Many transcenders develop a style of relating to others that helps them gain protection and nurturance. A style of relating is a way of communicating with others, a way of being with the world outside the family. It's not the same as a role in the family, even though, at times, it may be. Among these styles are being rebellious, witty, or entertaining, or even playing dumb. Styles of relating can fend off negative influences, keep people at a distance, bring people close, and help reaffirm the sense of self. Often, transcenders hope that someone will take the time to discover the intense hurt that is causing their style of relating. The following illustrates how styles help children survive:

I was totally out of it. I mean, I played dumb to the point of being labeled retarded in the second grade. I was smart to do it because it wiped out all that was going on in my family. (Taken from a doctoral candidate.)

My school friends lived nearby. I visited them, and their parents liked me. I received affection from my friends as well as their parents by being a witty, entertaining child. In return, my friends offered applause and encouragement.

My ability to tune out was amazing. I realize that I didn't relate in my family. Instead, I shut down, avoided, and stayed aloof when I was at home and related when I was among my friends. When I had to be home, I would study, eat dinner, watch TV, listen to the radio, and, at times, even read the newspaper, all at the same time. I don't know how I did it, but it sure kept my family away because I was not available to anyone for anything. I didn't even hear my name if someone called me. I only tuned in the things that were important to me, which were usually outside my family.

At times, I kept myself together by making promises to myself, for example, "You've had your day; I will get you. You will pay. It's not going to be very subtle or very tricky." I remember one of my aunts, she was disciplining me and she said, "As long as you're in this house you're going to obey this rule. You're going to do this and do this," and I'm saying, "No, I'm not. No, I'm not. Who do you think you are? You can't make me do that." She'd say to me, "Look, you are an eight-year-old, and you will not be that bold with me. You're so bold." I'd sit there and I'd say, "Sure, here I am this little brat." It gave me a security inside of myself to fend off the oppression.

I was a real character. I was labeled the class cynic under my high school picture. As a matter of fact, I organized a group that seceded from their own class. They had their own float in the homecoming parade. That was my style. I wasn't willing to conform to anything without a fight.

I think all the crazy things I was doing—getting erratic grades, skipping school—were kind of intellectual rebellion. For example, a friend and I were going to do a survey of sexual activities at school for psychology class. The board of education went crazy, and I was suspended for a day. But things like that would just get under my skin. In my gym class, there were teachers who were more authoritarian and ran the thing like the military. I gave them holy hell in various ways. I was very bright, so I figured out real creative ways to screw them and enjoyed it immensely. I would get in trouble and sometimes get caught. But that was the fun part, getting caught and sticking my tongue out at them. But what I really was hoping was that someone would take a step back and say, "This kid is hurting." Instead, they got embroiled in a battle. I felt that if they stopped me, that would show some kind of caring about me. But I wanted more than that. I wanted more than being stopped. I wanted them to see why I had been doing that. I wanted them to ask, to take a moment to stop the battle, stop the game on their end, and spend more time with me. Maybe, too, I was hoping that the school people would discover my crazy home life and do something about it.

DEVELOPING ROLES IN THE FAMILY

A role is a way of relating, but it is usually assigned by the family and is rigid and nonchangeable. Roles include good child, rebellious child, scapegoat, mediator, family hero, and others. Roles can also be a wonderful adaptation for survival and offer protection from abuse and trauma as well as some nurturance. For example, the good child, if "good enough," may receive special privileges. A mediator may receive strokes for stopping a fight, even if the reward is only to have the screaming stop for a while. Roles give a niche, a place to belong, and a way of dealing with the crazies in the family. On the other hand, some roles are devastating and isolating, such as that of the scapegoat, who gains little, if anything, for being blamed for all the family's problems:

> I had to be there for others or I was worthless, totally worthless, with no value to anyone. This is what I learned in my role growing up. My only value was as a helper—to pack for a trip, to clean, to cook, to support Mom, and be a good girl. The real me was underground and well protected. I knew I had to

protect my real self, and my role did help keep it away from the family's ridiculing and criticizing. They needed me, so they weren't going to hurt me.

There was no place for me, nowhere, except I had this role that allowed me to fit in and be OK, at least on the surface. I also received much-needed praise in this one area of my life, even if it was just for cleaning or helping. It was at least some support, acknowledgment, and attention, which I desperately needed.

I wasn't against whatever my father had to do at that time, even when he was having DTs (hallucinations) with his alcoholism, but I think my role was to let him know that I was scared and shaky. I had to deescalate him. My parents would be yelling, and I'd start with "Stop it, Daddy. Stop it." My mother would say, "Don't you hear the kids?" because all three of us would be yelling, "Stop it," so that would deescalate him because he was really violent.

I'd been conditioned by adults to deal with matters such as legal documents and adult-type discussions. For example, they'd tell me, "Here, read this. Do this. Talk to this person. Tell them to set it up." I could mouth all that was needed but really did not have the comprehension either socially or emotionally to know what I was doing. I was the prince of the realm and the rest of the people were like a court in very subordinate roles. I felt powerful and in control and had support in the world.

I got all kinds of privileges from being the "brain." I remember that I was paid by an aunt fifty cents on Saturdays to take my cousin to the movies because my family needed the money. I wasn't really good working with my hands, doing chores, or being mechanical. I wasn't even very quick on my feet. Also, I was the kingpin. So I was paid to be this little escort for my cousin for two years. It was terrific. I would take her to shows, and I would see Hopalong Cassidy, Tarzan serials, and Superman serials.

My mother described my relationship with my sibling to me one time. It became clear to me that I had escaped the pain through becoming a surrogate mother in my family. My mother helped me feel as responsible for the baby's care as she was. When company would arrive, she stated that I would insist they come and see the baby's crib in my bedroom.

My parental role of caretaking and responsibility continued to grow as the family did. The effect it had on me was that I felt robbed of my childhood. I grew up too quickly. I can remember refusing to play with dolls by age eight. Any dependency needs I had were overlooked because I was taught to focus on the needs of the younger children. I can remember being blamed and punished when the other children got into trouble. This reconfirmed my feeling of responsibility for their actions. As a result, I internalized feelings of guilt when things didn't run smoothly in the family. However, I never gave this up because there was a lot of power in the role and self-esteem in knowing I was needed and depended on. Teaching and leading the way for my siblings helped strengthen my feelings of adequacy as a person.

I worked to have people like me. It was a way of nurturing me and getting what I needed. If I could nurture others, then I could get some of it for me. Also, it was a way of relating, a way of being needed and being with others. It was a basic way to connect. It gave me a role, a relationship, a connection. Besides, if I weren't a caretaker, then what? How would I relate to people? What I did was a form of therapy with people. I would listen to their problems and help them with their feelings. So, I would pick out people I could be in that role with so I could get what I needed.

I was the family hero. I was the one who announced to the world that our family was not only OK, but terrific. It went like this: If I was such an accomplished person, then my parents had to be wonderful because they raised me. I got almost straight "A's" and was involved in all sorts of school activities. Teachers liked me, kids liked me, and I got a lot of praise and support and a feeling of being special. It also gave me a separate identity from my family, thank goodness!

SEEKING RELATIONSHIPS
WITH SIGNIFICANT OTHERS

Significant others are the *most important* factors in surviving. Most transcenders actively seek relationships that involve them with a more nurturing, protective world. These important relationships offer love, acceptance, support, kindness, and a feeling of being special. Significant others also provide role models, examples of alternate lifestyles, and hope for the future by demonstrating another way to live. The nurturing and protection that come from relationships are remembered vividly for years. Even what seem to be the smallest of gifts from others are priceless gifts to the transcender. These offerings are desperately needed to maintain the self and provide substance for growth.

This area is so important that its effects extend into the adult healing and growth process. Individuals find survival as well as healing less difficult and painful when there is even minimal nurturing from at least one human being over the years. Here are a few of the offerings from significant others that transcenders remember:

Significant Others outside the Family

I always had to have one really good friend. My friends have always been very important to me since I was little. They offered nurturing, support, love, acceptance, and being special to someone. They liked me, and I liked the mutual respect. We liked being together, and I liked that feeling because I, obviously, wasn't liked at home. I was much more comfortable, accepted, and at peace with my friends, having a good time or even talking about something serious, than being home waiting for the world to explode.

I was a Girl Scout. It was a wonderful experience and helped me a lot. The troop we were in was very friendly and sociable. I started out as a Brownie in second grade and went until the eighth grade. I had the two greatest leaders, who were very kind and loving. One of the leaders was the mother of one of my best girlfriends, and I loved going over to her house. The activities were fun, but it was the relationship with the leaders that really counted. They were kind and nurturing, and they treated me so well. They were really special ladies.

I used to idealize other kids' parents. I had a pal with an alcoholic father, and I thought his parents were just the greatest thing in the world. Basically, their main attribute was that they weren't mine. Also, they were very bright and artistically oriented, and I thought they were really neat, creative people. I adopted them as my family, and I used to spend all my weekends there during most of high school. In essence, I left home emotionally and physically. I worked to create my own family and find supportive people because my family wasn't going to be around for that.

I had a high school teacher who stopped me in the hall one day when I was in about ninth grade and said to me, "Do you know you're going to be a great politician someday?" I looked at him because I was probably some type of officer in every class, and he said, "You're really a politician." I was sort of hurt by that, and I guess it showed on my face because I thought of a politician as being someone nasty, and he said, "No, no, I swear. You go for it." He just said, "You can do anything." That was just something he stopped me in the hall one day to say. In my senior year, I was very popular, and I was this and that and really ran the whole high school if you want to get down to the brass tacks of it. He stopped me again and said, "See, I told you years ago you can do anything if you want to. You're a politician." He kept using that term, but I knew what he meant. I came to believe I really could do anything.

I found families in church who really liked me and were so sincerely thankful for all the work I did for the church. I felt gratified that someone appreciated me, because my parents never did. Never, ever. There were some families in the church who were very important to me because they made me feel so much a part of the church and their lives.

It was interventions by people, feeling people, that really helped. Sometimes, just the little things would help keep me going, not as if they were on-going, full-time confidants, but somebody who would notice that something was wrong and give that little extra bit to say, "You're OK. You're special to me. You're important as a human being. You deserve to live and be OK on this earth. You have something special to offer in some kind of way." That made such a difference to me.

Our foster mother showed us caring and love through what she did for us. She would take us to town, let us buy our own clothing, make sure we got to church, help us get work we got paid for so we could have some spending money, and make sure we were clean and dressed properly. It doesn't seem like much, but it was more than we had had, and it felt like caring.

I blew up during a softball game and got really angry at this teacher. He got angry back at me and I screamed at him. He took a step back. He was getting all hooked up and getting all involved with this sixth-grader. I think he realized what he was doing, and he stopped and said, "Hey, come here" and walked in with me. He spent just ten minutes talking to me and said, "You really seem upset about this game, but it seems as if something else is going on besides just being upset on account of this game." I'll never forget him. He wasn't even my teacher in school, and he cared so much more. He was able to give, just a little bit; you don't have to bend over backward. I think that was what was missing—the bending over backward or my parents' ability to do that.

I was looking for a different way to live, like shopping new avenues. I had a feeling that there had to be a better way. Something about my family just didn't hit me right, so I was always looking and watching how other families lived. I watched how other mothers related to their daughters, and I'd think, "Oh, aren't they lucky." Friends in high school were important to me because they opened my eyes to other values and lifestyles outside my family and neighborhood.

I would go to the neighbors' and sit in the backyard. I remember being a friendly kid, and sometimes, I would start to shoot the breeze. They'd ask me if I wanted a glass of pop, and that was such a big deal for me. I'd want to go back to that house again but I was so afraid to let the good stuff in (to be nurtured). At the same time, I ate it up and needed it desperately. I also had to keep this stuff secret all the time because of what my family might do if they found out.

I remember how delighted I was when a kid in the seventh grade invited me over to his house. I still remember his name. I felt so damned good. I had a bacon, lettuce, and tomato sandwich, and after twenty-five or thirty years, I still remember this kid inviting me over and even what I had to eat. I can still remember sitting in the kitchen and his mother saying, "Well, what do you young fellows want to have for lunch?" It was Christmas, and I remember "Winter Wonderland" playing on the radio. They had a little Hot Point refrigerator, and I thought, "Gee, they have a nice refrigerator. Gee, why don't we have a refrigerator like that? All we have is an old Kelvinator at our house, and here is this brand new Sears Hot Point." That lunch offered me acceptance and being seen as a person, as a little kid, and not as the illusion I was living at home.

In junior high and high school, my steady boyfriend kept me from being lonely. He took up a great deal of my time from the age of fifteen to age eighteen. He was always there.

I had this huge cat which weighed nineteen pounds, and this cat was a dear friend. I can remember many times going to my room, closing the door, and curling up with my cat, just sobbing and saying, "You are the only one I can talk to." Then I would blow it all out. This poor cat had to take all this in. As I look back on it, it was one of the ways I could release all this pain inside me.

I remember a French teacher in high school, and I was getting worse and worse grades. I would get an "A" one quarter and an "F" the next, just because I was angry at authority. Anything that symbolized authority I hated. I was also reading all this heavy existential literature and getting more and more depressed. So my French teacher said, "Why don't you lighten up?" She gave me a Book of the Month Club novel about a World War II adventure and spent a little time with me just to let me know that she knew I was hurting. She thought I was very special and bright and hoped I didn't blow it all by being Mr. Rebel. Boy! Did that make a difference! I felt support and knew someone had really noticed my situation.

Significant Others inside the Family

Not all significant others are outside of the family. Sometimes, a family member offers some of the needed protection and nurturing even though the relationship may also include pain:

It was pitch black out. It was nighttime, and my father always left us outside in the dark. I don't remember necessarily feeling afraid because I always had another kid there, my sister. We were company for each other and we helped each other keep the fears away.

My father had the personality of Dr. Jekyll and Mr. Hyde. He worked three jobs so we could live in the suburbs and avoid the ghetto. He was also a former professional basketball player and instilled feelings of competition in us. His method of relating to us was mostly through harsh judgments and criticism. He was narrow-minded and set in his opinions. On the other hand, he had a great sense of humor and was artistic. He also played the accordion and entertained us with his talent. He was ethnocentric and had a strong sense of family. My warmest family memories seem to be involved with my father and food. I felt a strong sense of family each Sunday, when all of us joined my father to spend the entire day making homemade noodles, ravioli, gnocchis, and pizzas. After working all day, we would share family dinner by eating enormous amounts of food. I always found eating and food to be comforting.

My mother would often starve me in order to punish me. Once in a while, my grandma would get me something to eat if Mom had locked me in my room and wouldn't let me eat. It's a kindness I'll always remember.

The attachment to my mother for so long was symbiotic and beyond the normal stages of symbiosis. What this relationship did for me was to somehow add to a deep level of awareness that I was special. This is one of the reasons why I am a survivor.

My mother believed I was more of an intellectual than my brother. She noticed my bookworm tendencies, which my brother lacked. I was also more artistic than he was, which is a similarity with my mother. We were both artistic and liked to paint. She and I both had a great sense of humor and a gift for telling stories. We both loved to dance and dress up swank and go out on the town. I think we shared the need to be "somebody," and my mother knew that that need in me would give me ambition and push me to make something of myself.

My grandmother just loved me dearly, kept me going, and gave me a feeling of being special in my life. I guess she lived vicariously through me, and I took after her. She was quite an aggressive lady in her day, and I think she saw her youth in me. She was my father's mother, and basically, he treated her the same way he treated me. He never bent over backward to really go see her or do anything with her. I cared very much for her, and she enjoyed seeing me with all my success and achievement. She thought the sun rose and set on me, which gave me a lot of special feelings. She was very complimentary on anything I did and made sure she was at every activity she could attend to see me. She was a focal point in my life. It was obvious that I was her favorite. Yeah, I've never been anybody's favorite, but I was her favorite. I felt very special. I still have that feeling of being special inside me, and it still helps me.

My father gave me a sense of good morality, and I knew he loved me. When I say morality, I mean a sense of right and wrong; a sense of caring about people and a sensitivity to their needs. He gave me a consistency in the sense that he really tried to provide someone who was caring and nurturing while we were shipped from one place to another. He even tried to give me the little extra things.

I was visiting my aunt and uncle on their farm, way out in the middle of nowhere. I was very close to them. My former step-father showed up out of nowhere, and I was devastated. It really upset me to see him again. All I can remember is my aunt coming into the living room after he left. I had tears rolling down my face. She came over to me and kissed me on the cheek and said, "I love you," and it was so comforting. It was years and years ago, but I will always remember it.

My two oldest sisters and especially my brother offered me someone to whom I could relate; I could get feedback and reality-test my anger, disappointments, and rage, and to get assistance from them. It was a true reciprocal friendship.

Before my father left our family when I was seven, he clearly favored my brother, and I had very little interaction with him. I handled this situation emotionally by transferring my father-figure needs to older males in the family. One older male relative I had gave me piggyback rides and took me fishing and camping, and some summers my whole school vacation was spent with him. My stepfathers provided some fathering, and I also had a step-brother ten years older who enjoyed having a little brother tagging along after him. He responded by playing the big-brother role. He was kind to me, and it helped fill the emptiness and pain left by my father.

DEVELOPING COMPETENCIES

In the process of developing competencies, transcenders gain confidence, friends, healthier role models, meaningfulness in life, enjoyment, proficiency, and a foundation for creating a different lifestyle. Competencies are vital to helping the transcender develop positive self-esteem, success, support, and hope for the future. The development of these competencies often involves activities such as academics, sports, work, and anything else that helps the individual feel important and accomplished. These activities provide a way for transcenders to get out of the house and connect to more nurturing people.

I didn't belong in my family in one way, but in another way, it's OK because I did get something from it growing up. I did get something that formed a foundation from my old neighborhood. What I gained was a gift of words — a gift of language in order to survive. I became very proficient in listening to Polish; I can't speak Polish, but I can recognize the language and pick out some words. Our neighbors next door were Greek. Down the street were Lithuanians; some were Polish and Slovaks; there were blacks in our neighborhood and Jewish people ran the deli. I learned to listen and developed a gift for listening. Now, being a therapist, this gift is a constant blessing.

I had music, and that's the thing that really kept me going through school. I was in band, and when I was in high school, I started playing in dance bands. Music was something I was really interested in and good at and enjoyed doing. I first started taking lessons when I was in junior high school, and when I went into senior high, it was a whole different thing because I was in a great band. It was just really a fantastic band. That was what gave my life meaning. It offered something to do, something I really enjoyed, and the friendships with the kids that were in it. It offered another life.

I just found out that I had leadership ability and could keep everybody happy. I just had a way of handling people and found

I could lead without one part of the group getting angry. I kept everybody pacified and had the ability to keep things together. I became popular naturally. It started in fifth grade, when I almost won a trip to Washington, DC, through the national and regional safety patrol. They selected the candidates on their attributes. Things snowballed from there.

I started working in eleventh grade for the cooperative program (part-time work counted for school credit) in school. This is the only time I ever got encouragement from my mother about school or help in picking classes. She told me, "Whatever you do, take shorthand and typing." So, I took shorthand and typing and immediately became a secretary and have been one since. In eleventh grade, I worked for the board of education as a clerk doing odd jobs and typing after school. It gave me a lot: spending money for school, competency, and a feeling of confidence.

I had earned respect at school in the student council, and I was president of the prep club. I earned a lot of respect and it was a really good feeling. People become really impressed by the fact that I was doing all these things. These feelings gave me the extra impetus to keep doing and achieving.

PLAYING

Through play, transcenders can be something that isn't part of a dysfunctional family: a regular kid. They can giggle, laugh, and just be. Play includes anything that the individual perceives as play: informal sports, organized sports, theater, reading, mental challenges, playing alone, playing in the neighborhood, playing with toys and games, or even work that is perceived as play. From play, transcenders gain escape from the dangers and traumas of the family, release from tensions and stress, and relief from the seriousness of life. The experience of playing offers good feelings about oneself, encouragement, nurturing, and acceptance. In addition, play helps transcenders create hope and important support for the vital and often fragile self. In essence, transcenders experience and nurture their authentic child:

> The reason I liked school so much was that I could get away from all the hard work I had to do. I'd go and play, especially at recess time. We'd go out at recess time, and all we'd do was run and play tag, baseball, kickball — play, play, play. That's probably one of the reasons I liked school — the play part. We played baseball, and I was on the varsity baseball team for four years in high school. We won the county championship the last year. I also used to go skiing and do some tobogganing. All of these things helped me forget some of the things that had happened earlier in my life. Playing helped a lot.

> We'd act and we'd laugh and we'd giggle. There wasn't much fun when we reached a certain age in our house, and I would just crave that fun. I used to like to play with dolls, ride a bide (I just loved to ride bikes), talk, giggle, and play lots of typical little girls' games. I could be a real normal everyday kid and go play.

> We would have a crop cutting, and everybody in the whole community would come out with their wagons, men, teams of horses, and their tractors. We would load up all the machinery and things and take them up on the farm. Sometimes, we used to see if we could be as big as a man, a big, grown man, and see how fast we could pitch the bundle of oats, wheat, or barley into this big threshing machine. All the straw would be blowing way up in the air out of the big chute or a big pipe, and we would pitch it fast enough to plug it up and make the machine stop. Then we used to get a big kick out of climbing up onto the engine — it was a steam engine — with the owner and blowing the whistle. That was fun.

> I played by myself and did a lot of fantasizing. I played with my dolls, created objects out of clay, and pretended they were real. I would imagine what my life could be and how I really

wanted it. It helped me escape the reality of my family. I could also release and deal with all sorts of feelings. For example, I even played out my death. I imagined what it would be like to die and how my family would miss me, cry endlessly, and feel bad that they had not taken better care of me. It was a way of having a family that did care and love me. This playing kept the inner me alive while I was growing up. This playing also eased my intense loneliness.

The pain, God, the pain! I was so anxious, and I just knew that to ease it all, I had to keep playing on sports teams. I played baseball, basketball, tennis — really, anything that was available. It also brought me friends, eased the loneliness, and released the anxiety.

DEVELOPING SPIRITUALITY

Many transcenders turn to their spiritual base as a source of guidance, strength, support, and help in dealing with their dysfunctional families. Most important, spirituality offers a belief in a power greater than themselves and their situation. Transcenders are in touch with their spirituality and find a force powerful enough to help sustain them through the onslaught of their world and through their pain.

Expressions of spirituality for transcenders may take a traditional Christian or Jewish form, or they may be unique to the individual. There are transcenders who attend regular religious services and find an entire support system by doing so. Other transcenders find it difficult to attend religious services on a regular basis because of a lack of family cooperation, and they create their own rituals at home. Many view God as their real father and look to him for all their needs and as a replacement for their family:

God was involved in my life from the time I was a toddler and is part of my earliest recollections. My firm belief in God has been a large part of my ability to survive. There have been many times when I needed to believe that not only was there a God, but also an afterlife, a promise of something more than the misery or the dilemma that I was in.

When the oppression, stress, fear, and frustration became overwhelming and came to the point of explosion, I'd sometimes explode by yelling, screaming, and airing all that was within me. Other times, and more often, I'd pray—pray so deeply and internally that my being, or root, bared itself in seeking help from God. After the intense praying, I'd feel better. Nothing had really changed, but I'd feel better, and my explosive frustration would subside. In its place would be a sadness, but also a peace. This sadness would be a deep and alone sadness; yet there was also my commitment, which grew stronger and said that someday I'd be me. Someday, I'd pick a different way of being, someday! God supported me and helped sustain that commitment to myself.

The church helped me a lot as a kid. I don't think I would have survived if I hadn't had it. I'd go to church everyday, and I'd pray. God was real to me. He was going to help me. I was able to focus on God through his pictures or religious objects, and it helped me to sort myself out from the crazies.

Church was wonderful for me. I gained in personal growth, in my own feelings, and the feelings I'd get from attending and being part of a worship service or environment. I also had a lot of really good friends there. The minister was a friend of mine, and I had a lot of other good friends from the church. And musically—I'm very moved spiritually through music—it really nurtured me; the church was so full of wonderful music.

I used to get to the point of cracking and have no strength left to battle my family. My connection to God gave me comfort and strength. Once I was comforted, I could again enjoy the good that was in my life. It was a type of surrendering. I knew he was taking care of me.

God was and is my core. If I went beyond my energy, beyond my ability to cope, and beyond feeling sane, I could always go to

God and find energy, support, love, and deep caring. I would find relief and rest, as well as understanding and acceptance from him. Thank God! The way my family was structured, with such control, it was the only thing that I found that deeply helped. I was strengthened and renewed through my relationship with God, and I just knew he wouldn't let me crack up. It was a strength and comfortableness. I could talk to God about anything.

SUMMARY

All transcenders develop and use techniques to protect themselves from the traumas and terrors they experience as they grow up in the dysfunctional family, and to nurture themselves. The more assaultive the world, the more effort is needed.

In the beginning, their skills may not be adequate, but through determination and perseverance, they develop to a level strong enough to maintain the self, gain hope for the future, and, when possible, promote growth.

Survival techniques are like a haven in the midst of a stormy sea, helping to maintain a sense of self and a belief in the self by creating barriers, escapes, resistances, and defenses that hinder, limit, and, at times, stop the violence. In essence, by the use of these techniques, transcenders gain enough protection and nurturance to survive.

--------- Chapter 5 ---------

The Self: The Heart of
the Transcender

Transcenders are in a struggle for life: a struggle to not only exist, but to be authentically themselves. Five philosophical and psychological concepts are at the foundation of survival and are important in understanding the survival process. They are the self, the will, the internal frame of reference, Being-in-the-world, and transcendence. Each of these concepts is presented in more depth in this chapter.

THE SELF

Everything an individual is and experiences is processed through the self: thoughts, feelings, situations, talents, beliefs, values, view of life, behaviors, spirituality — basically, the entire original package and the available environment. It is through the self we learn and grow; we decide what kind of person we are going to be, and how that person is going to behave. The self is the core, the essence of life, the who of what we are, the foundation for all growth. Heidegger (1952), an existential philosopher, calls it our *being*. The self is the sum total of the "me."

From this core (the self), the individual's will develops, decisions are made, the internal frame of reference is processed, and a way of being-in-the-world is developed. It is from this core that transcendence and the turning-point decision are created and survival occurs.

Transcenders make and maintain the turning-point decision by processing all available information impacting on the self. From this processing, transcenders decide — powerfully decide — to make it and to be different from their families.

To make it, or to be different in a dysfunctional family, the self has to be protected from the onslaught of neglect, abuse, criticism, and all other forms of aggression. In addition to protection, nurturance is essential for growth and development. Transcenders, as children, learn to nurture and protect themselves on very little. They take in, absorb, and savor tidbits of offerings. These offerings are used for growth over many years and, as was seen in Chapter 4, may come from anyone and anything.

Transcenders, in spite of the onslaught of their world, maintain their precious self on some level. It is through the self that they work to maintain the spark of authentic life. Often, while they are growing up, part of the self is compromised in order for them to survive. However, there is always a part of the self that no one can touch. This part is protected, nurtured, and tucked away until a future time when it is safe to come out. Later, this very important protection of the self during childhood causes intense pain when it is time to develop a growing, close, trusting adult relationship.

THE WILL

The second concept to be explored is the will. The will is a basic ability of the self. It has a central position in the self and functions to regulate, balance, direct, and use forces from within the person. These forces include emotions, impulses, desires, thoughts, information, values, intuition, imagination, and potentialities (Assagioli, 1973). The will works to organize all available information and resources with the purpose of making decisions and creating behavior. Without the person's ability to will, there is no turning-point decision, no survival.

The will varies in strength, ability, and flexibility. It is a guiding force within the developing, growing self (Assagioli, 1973). The will acts in accordance with an individual's needs and is the pivotal point around which meaningful behavior occurs. May (1969) defines the will as "the capacity to organize oneself so that movement in a certain direction or toward a certain goal may take place" (p. 215). James (1899) believed that the will's primary functions are to focus and guide behavior, to attend, to enable action to occur, and to overcome obstacles to action.

The process of willing is intentional (that is, it is focused with intent) and begins with the individual's having a thought or an idea. As we contemplate an idea, our will works to organize and make available all information and resources. The idea becomes action or behavior when contemplation is finished, a decision is reached, and meaningful action is created.

The process of willing, according to Assagioli's phenomenological description, has six stages: (1) purpose, aim, or goal, based on evaluation, motivation, and intention; (2) deliberation; (3) choice and decision; (4) affirmation of the command of the will; (5) the planning and working out of a program; and (6) direction of the execution.

The turning-point decision is an excellent example of the process of willing. Transcenders first deliberate over all available information with the purpose of evaluating their experiences inside as well as outside the family. Next, their will works to organize the information, to focus it according to their needs, and to create the turning-point decision. Finally, they create a plan using survival techniques and execute it over many years.

To maintain the turning-point decision, transcenders learn to use different qualities of the will as described by Assagioli (1973): (1) energy, dynamic power, and intensity; (2) mastery, control, and discipline; (3) concentration, one-pointedness, attention, and focus; (4) determination, decisiveness, resolution, and promptness; (5) persistence, endurance, and patience; (6) initiative, courage, and daring; and (7) organization, integration and synthesis. These qualities also help in the creation of survival techniques and in the setting of goals for the future.

The transcenders with whom I have worked usually have a well-developed ability to will. Their will has strength, patience, persistence, and the ability to use and integrate the available material. Their will helps guide them, direct them, satisfy their needs, accomplish their goals, and find direction for growth. In essence, it acts like a beacon of strength to keep them focused on getting the needed nurturance and protection to maintain the self and the turning-point decision.

Assagioli also describes three types of willing: good will (will used for the good of self and others); transpersonal will (every need creates a will and the drive to gain its satisfaction); and universal will (the supreme reality, i.e., God). Transcenders use all these different types in dealing with everyday crises and in gaining needed growth.

Rank (1950), James, and Assagioli believe that our ability to will can be improved in all areas of functioning through training. Transcenders need an efficient, flexible, and strong will that adapts to the situation at hand. The more they use and train their ability to will, the more it develops and is able to function in all crises. Over the years, it becomes finely tuned, extremely adaptable, and wonderfully efficient. For example, a child may not be able always to avoid difficult family situations that lead to abuse. But after years of practice, avoidance may become almost routine.

Healthy willing is important in dealing with conflicts and in coming to decisions, according to Rank and Maslow (1971). Obviously, transcenders face many difficult decisions while growing up. They learn to use their ability to will to make enough adequate decisions to help them develop their potentialities. They use the available resources and their needs, desires, wishes, and goals as guiding forces.

In addition, Rank stated that our ability to will enables us to affirm, negate, forget, or become free of the past (this becomes crucial in the healing process). Transcenders use this area of the will to handle the difficult, painful, and abusive experiences. For example, the will can block memories from awareness. These blocks protect one from being overwhelmed by the pain. At a later time, that is safer, saner, and freer, these memories are released and put into awareness.

Frankl (1963) describes another type of willing important to transcenders, the will to meaning. The will to meaning is the will that guides us to our personal search for meaning in life, our sense of purpose in life. It is a primary force that is unique and specific to the individual. This search for meaning is directed by our ability to will and our personal values. To Frankl, who lived through the concentration camps of World War II, the will to meaning means survival. Frankl also believes that we must have a meaningful and authentic life. If this is overlooked or blocked, the person may cease to grow or even to survive. In the concentration camps, it meant, "I'm going to survive these tortures and the starvation." For transcenders, it means; "I'm going to live. I'm going to make it and be different in spite of my family."

The beginning of will training may occur as early as infancy. It is not unusual for transcenders to process back to childhood memories (to heal where the hurt begins) and find that they made a major decision to survive in infancy. Contrary to what many people believe, we can remember infant experiences: thoughts and especially feelings and awarenesses. Somehow, some transcenders gain in infancy the perspective that their family is not going to be there for them and that they are going to have to take care of themselves. This decision is amazing. It's as if the infant decides whether to be a "failure-to-thrive" baby or a growing, dynamic self. The following is a poem written by a transcender who reexperienced her infant decision:

> Deep, deep,
> Into the depths of my being, my soul
> lay the child, the infant.
> The small, quiet, strong infant
> She was afraid she'd die.
> She knew she'd die.
>   no breast, no food
>   no food, no life.
> The choice was to live or die
> The infant made it.
> She decided to live, somehow live.
> She set her mind to it—
> To live in spite of them.
> It was in this choice
> her will developed and became strong.
> She had to live—to choose to live
> Or   die.

Transcenders, incredibly, choose to live and create meaning from chaos and conflict. They sustain continued growth and in some form maintain their authenticity. For transcenders, not to survive is a source of terror, a form of death.

THE INTERNAL FRAME OF REFERENCE

The internal frame of reference is part of the functioning self and is of the utmost importance to transcenders. The internal frame of reference is the perspective or view of our world from the inside out. Contained in it are values, beliefs, attitudes, feelings, purposes, goals, desires, needs, self-concept, trust of self, and view of self.

The internal frame of reference is active, growing, and constantly changing. It works to integrate persons, places, situations, and experiences into meanings and purposes. The reverse is also true: Meanings and purposes are automatically assigned by us to persons, places, and situations. Each person's internal frame of reference is unique. None of us has the same view or can totally understand another's frame of reference. We also may make changes in our reference points, depending on incoming information and the current situation. For example, at one point I may view my mother's mood with fear and avoid her. Later that same day, her mood changes, and from my past experience, I know it is OK to get close to her. As my internal perspective of my mother changes, so does my behavior.

Behavior originates from the internal frame of reference. We behave according to our personal belief system. Husserl (1962) believes that the perception of the individual is the basis of behavior and human functioning. Cantril (1959) states that the purpose of perception is to create behavior that is effective and need-satisfying. Behavior and perception are directly related. For instance, if I believe that the world is a safe, nurturing place, I will be open to exploring and experiencing it. However, if I view the world as dangerous and difficult, I will relate to it in a fearful, shy, or defensive manner, and I will not be free to explore the opportunities in my environment.

For transcenders, the internal frame of reference is vital. If transcenders view the world outside the family as a place to be nurtured and protected, they can explore it. If they see the possibility of getting out of the family, they can create another lifestyle, that is, another world. Basically, behavior follows perspective.

To make perceiving easier, we group and organize information into constancies. Constancies are units of learned information about the world. We create and use constancies when confronted with similar situations (Kuenzli, 1959). Constancies are part of our internal frame of reference and are unique and directly affected by our perspective. Here's how constancies work. First, we take in information from the world, usually randomly. We then assign the information to a group of information (constancies) according to our beliefs, values, knowledge, feelings, needs, and previous perceptions. This information is then stored in the constancy until we need it. Constancies protect us, conserve energy, and increase the flow of relating. They also minimize guessing in all situations, prohibit having to develop new choices each time a similar situation arises, and enable information to be used easily and quickly as situations arise. When a situation does arise, we can quickly sort through our available constancies and pick the one(s) that is personally meaningful.

An excellent example of a constancy is the turning-point decision. Transcenders' turning-point internal frame of reference is "I'm going to be different from my family." Contained in this constancy is all the information they used to create the turning-point decision: the experiences of abuse, hurt, and rejection, as well as information about other ways to live. If transcenders had to sort through each piece of the information each time they need to reinforce the turning point, they would lose vital time, energy, and strength. Also, they might not be able to get out of a situation fast enough to avoid injury. Transcenders do occasionally sort through all the information in the turning-point constancy to reaffirm and strengthen the decision.

Having a constancy system is like having many huge filing cabinets. Each cabinet contains information on a certain area of our life, such as infancy, relationships, school, friends, love, work, Mom, Dad, and the turning point. Files stay in storage until a life situation requires the information. Most of the time, we are aware of the file, but we may need only a part of it, such as a perspective or decision it contains. Sometimes, we sort through the entire file and examine each piece of information to reevaluate our perspectives and decisions. This reevaluation is often the core process of psychotherapy.

What is unusual about the turning-point constancy is that it remains constant and stable for years, even after many reevaluations. Actually, it becomes stronger. Transcenders' worlds teach them over and over again that the turning-point decision is not only right but has to be kept strong and has to remain the primary focus. This constancy helps to guide them to safety, growth, development, and achievement.

Let's go a step deeper into philosophy as it relates to surviving. According to Heidegger, the internal frame of reference is part of, or is grounded in, caring. We, as human beings, are concerned about and care about our world. Because of this caring, we relate to and are involved with people and activities, that is, life and the world. This is called being "grounded in care." We are curious and want to know about our world. Unless prohibited or inhibited, we are automatically motivated to explore, discover, and experience our world through our perceptions and awareness. Awareness is the knowledge, realizations, and perceptions that come from our senses, feelings, and thoughts. Basically, it means that we are alert to our world and can draw inferences from it.

According to Combs (1962), to be aware and open to experiences in our world is essential for growth, let alone survival. The transcenders' world, however, also demands protection. What transcenders do is two-fold: (1) they close themselves off from the family's violence and craziness, and (2) they open themselves to experiences in the world outside the family. This is a difficult process for a mature adult, let alone for a child who must maintain herself or himself in this way for years.

The danger in this process is closing off the self to all aspects of the world. This closing off can cause a distortion of the perceptions coming into awareness. This distortion occurs because we need contact with others to test, adjust, and find the truth of our reality. It is absolutely necessary to completely close off at times of severe abuse or when we are totally overwhelmed. However, if this closing off continues, our reality grounding may be altered. To survive, it is vital that transcenders be open to some experiences in their world to gain a healthy grounding; at the same time they must screen out violence.

The available perceptual field is another important part of the internal frame of reference process (Combs, 1962). The available perceptual field is defined as "all that is going on within the envelope of the organism (individual) at any given moment" (Fadiman and Fragen, 1976, p. 530). It is in the available perceptual field, or world, that needs are satisfied and behavior originates. Because behavior is "the goal-directed attempt of the organism to satisfy its needs as experienced in the field as perceived" (Rogers, 1968, p. 531), it is important that the individual seek out the best available perceptual field. Sensing, feeling, and thinking create our perceptual ability, which takes in and discovers the available field (Rogers, 1968). The perceptual field is always unique and specific to ourselves and our world.

Transcenders see a choice of perceptual fields in their world and use the best available field. This field is different from their family and also offers substance for growth. This field may include church, significant others, schools, organizations, and, often, just a thought, comment, feeling, or behavior. The internal frame of reference is a dynamic, learned in process/internal perception. We have the ability to learn, unlearn, and change. We can alter our internal frame of reference as we need to or as the situation demands. Kelly (1980) believes this ability to change is so important that his definition of education is based on it:

> The capacity for the individual to become educated depends . . . on the capacity of the individual to relinquish what he had held and learn new habit patterns in keeping with new environmental demands. (p. 52)

Transcenders use this ability to learn, unlearn, and change to survive. They remain flexible and alert to modifications in their perceptions of the world and at the same time stay true to their turning-point decision. This flexibility helps them to maintain the turning point and to develop survival techniques.

The ability to learn and change the internal frame of reference may be used to educate individuals who have not identified their family as dysfunctional — when it is. The change process begins with a gathering of many details about the family until it is clear that the label *dysfunctional* fits. Previous constancies are then reevaluated and changed. This reevaluation creates a freedom that allows the creation of a different way of living. In addition, techniques can be taught to help individuals in survival situations. These are the steps that one needs in order to survive: (1) learn to detect subtle details that signal danger in the family; (2) learn to put all these details into a constancy; and (3) learn to use techniques that protect and nurture the self. In essence, we can teach the survival of dysfunctional families.

BEING-IN-THE-WORLD

Being is the essence of our person, of life itself. Being expresses itself in a world that is perceived by us, that is, Being-in-the-world. The world is the basic, essential state of all Beings. We are always in a perceived world. There cannot be a person without a world. For example, even if I am locked in a closet for my entire life, my world is that closet and all it contains and is. The world consists of people, places, and situations; that is, the entire environment that we experience and perceive; it is seen as a unified, integrated whole.

The world, in essence, is a "medium" in which Beings exist. It helps to determine our expressed Being or that part that relates to the world through thoughts, behavior, and feelings, but it is *not* the essence of Being. However, to understand our essence, it is very important to know our relationship to our world.

As we experience the world, we develop a special bridge between ourselves and our world. This personal discovery of the world is meaningful and unique to us. It is here, in our experience, that the self is maintained and supported while growing and changing. Because we are grounded in care and care about our world, we can cope, manipulate, encounter, and produce in the world. We can also work to satisfy our needs and to develop our potentialities.

As stated in the section on the internal frame of reference, Being has a basic curiosity about the world as well as about itself. This curiosity encourages us to know and understand our Being and the world. Through curiosity and caring, transcenders explore, seek out, and find a world beyond their family that offers what they need to survive. They sustain themselves by relating to and creating a world beyond the immediate family—a world that is more in tune with and that nurtures their authentic self. There are three important facts to remember about Being and the world as we explore further: (1) Being and the world are interrelated and form a unity; (2) they are inseparable and dependent on each other—there is no such thing as a "worldless" person; and (3) Being and the world are in constant interaction with each other. The world is the part of which we have direct personal experience. It is explored, searched for possibilities, and used according to our needs and desires.

If our world is rich in experiences and full of meaning, our potentialities can be discovered and developed. Our *potentiality* is the entire original package, which can be developed and actualized. As explored in the section on the internal frame of reference, our world is restricted or enriched according to our unique internal frame of reference. Our world can also restrict or enhance our Being.

Being and possibilities (one's utmost powers, capacities, or abilities) meet through relationships in our everyday situation in the world. Our Being is self-sustaining and continuous with our world. We experience the world and from this experience are given a chance to develop possibilities and potentialities. In turn, we gain support, guidance, confidence and, encouragement toward more experiences. Transcenders use this cycle, and it moves them to a world more in tune with the authentic self. Thus, the more positive experiences they have in the world, the more transcenders gain the support, growth, and development that enables them to survive.

We can experience or encounter our world by moving closer to or further from persons, places, and situations. In other words, we have the power to encounter our world at various psychological or physical distances, depending on our needs or situation. We can make a face-to-face contact feel extremely close or put the distance of a continent between ourselves and the contact. Our abilities to hear, smell, see, touch, think, and taste enable us to experience our world at the distance we choose.

We, as Beings, determine the distance of the encounter or relationship, as well as its meanings and relationships to our life. Distance becomes an important factor in helping us experience the world we choose. For example, transcenders bring needed healthy role models close so they can experience and select appropriate values, feelings, thoughts, and behavior. These personal encounters may include teachers, coaches, employers, heroes, neighbors, a friend's parents, and so on. Through these experiences, transcenders' internal frame of reference is enriched, expanded, and shifted, as well as supported. On the other hand, an abusive parent can be distanced emotionally and/or physically for protection. Transcenders actively seek out and respond to healthy experiences and choose to gain all they can from them while distancing traumatic, damaging encounters.

Some transcenders also have an awareness that they have freedom of choice in the world to support and protect their authentic self. This awareness of freedom is always internal. Basically, this means that transcenders see a choice of how to live. Whenever possible, they choose experiences that offer support, guidance, and encouragement to lead them to their possibilities and potentialities. These experiences, in turn, help them to gain achievement, success, confidence, growth, and the energy to continue.

Another important part of Being-in-the-world is assertion, the ability to master Being's mood. Mood is a state of mind, a sensing that occurs within a person that can change and vary from moment to moment. We're always in a mood in the world, and to master our mood is to be in charge of our moods and to be able to change one mood to another. To do this, we use assertiveness, knowledge, understanding, and countermoods (those that are different from and, perhaps, in opposition to the present mood). For example, a transcender who is at home when a fight occurs and who becomes angry about the family situation can change his or her mood and choose to distance himself or herself emotionally and/or physically. The mood shifts from one of anger to a freedom to choose. This does not mean that pain is not experienced. It does mean reframing the mood, tuning back into the turning-point decision, and transcending the situation.

A core part of Being-in-the-world is understanding. If something is understood, it's available and can be experienced in the world. Conversely, if it's not understood, confusion remains. Once something is experienced and understood, we gain knowledge of and insights into previous concepts so as to form new ones. This is the continuing challenge of living an authentic life: taking previous knowledge and understanding, adding new information to it, and creating new growth and insights. Understanding works to expand and reframe our internal frame of reference and also creates new or deeper levels of personal meanings that support us in our world. A basic knowledge and understanding of their world gives transcenders the ability to cope, manage, and be competent. At a deeper level, understanding enables them to deal with their existence, possibilities, and potentialities. Transcenders do develop an understanding of self, family, and world that creates an ability to cope as well as to hope.

We can become more of the world and others than of ourselves and lose our authenticity. This important aspect of Being-in-the-world is called *being thrown* from our original package or being unauthentic. Being thrown happens whenever we decide to give up part of ourselves for someone else. This does not mean loving acts. It means changing ourselves unauthentically in order to meet our needs or to survive. Even though transcenders work to maintain their selves, part of them *has* to deal with the crazies of the family for survival. Dealing with the family's crazies often throws them away from their authentic selves. For example, caretaking of others offers protection and nurturance but focuses transcenders on others and puts them in danger of losing part of their authenticity. Transcenders do what they need to do to survive and then heal and reclaim the self later in adulthood. Healing and reclaiming constitute the process of getting emotionally straight and changing old patterns. These old patterns that are needed in childhood often block healing, growth, and healthy relationships in adulthood.

TRANSCENDENCE

The final philosophical and psychological concept, as well as survival technique, to be explored in relationship to the transcender is transcendence. Transcendence is a process of "stepping over, going beyond, surpassing, being above and beyond" (Hora, 1961, p. 501). It is a state of "enlightened consciousness" (p. 501) that expands the state of consciousness and that enables us to go beyond the everyday and create new worlds and possibilities (Privette, 1968). In a state of transcendence we seek to discover the specific meaning for us that enables us to be open to our world, its meanings, and its responsibilities (Sutich and Vich, 1969). Privette (1968) states that transcendent functioning is preferred to normal behavior and defines it as:

> behavior that goes beyond, or transcends average behavior. It is more creative, more efficient, more productive — in some ways better — than habitual behavior. [It] is a level of behavior rather than a type of behavior. (p. 122)

Frankl (1966), a psychiatrist transcender who studied the behavior of himself and others in the World War II death camps, believes that the ability to transcend or "self-detach" is a "constitutive characteristic of being human [and] it always points, and is directed, to something other than itself" (p. 98). Transcendence, according to Frankl, is the ability to rise above oneself, to go beyond the personal who and what. We can transcend feelings, thoughts, behavior, situations, experiences, and families. At times, transcendence can be a strong idea that drives us forward, or values and morals to live up to, to strive for. Frankl relates this strong idea to the values we hold in life that go beyond the everyday, the immediate, the concrete, and the material, to ideology and spiritualism. The turning point and the survival that follows are good examples of transcendence.

Through this technique, we can discover other worlds, possibilities, and potentialities that help us to develop as unique individuals. Our ability to transcend reaches beyond the everyday into deeper levels of our being. It's somewhat like shifting gears within oneself to another level that puts distance between the everyday self and the everyday world brings our possibilities and potentialities in closer. Thus a person can gain encouragement, protection, inspiration, and refreshment by embracing a higher level of beliefs, values, and ideals. The core focus of transcendence is the authentic, ultimate, best self.

There are many different ways to transcend. Jourard (1968) includes perceiving, remembering, learning, achieving, surviving, and personality organizing. Transcending can be done through time, space, self-awareness, death, pain, sickness, one's past, needs, opinions, culture, environment, God, spirituality, values, feelings, another person, and love.

Privette (1968) indicated three conditions that enable transcendence to occur: (1) a concentrated focus on an object, task, problem, personal need, or other person which gives the person a chance to respond to the possible or impossible; (2) needs that demand attention and focus; and (3) a concrete and/or psychological obstacle to overcome, or an obstacle or entity with intrinsic value to the point that other obstacles are diminished.

Transcenders find many obstacles to overcome, needs to satisfy, and problems to face. They use transcendence to shift from the family situation to a level of living that offers hope, inspiration, protection, and support. It is through the transcending process that transcenders become aware of their potentialities and possibilities and thus become encouraged. Through transcendence, transcenders seek their personal meaning and authenticity from the situation or experience. An understanding of themselves, their life, the situation, and a way of handling their family is developed through the transcending process. Transcenders described using transcendence this way:

> I sensed a basic striving from within at an early age. I told myself that to be happy, I must strive to be the best I could. I knew that I wanted, deserved, and expected more from life. There must be more than what I had at home. I didn't know why I knew; I just knew and went after it.

> Transcending a destructive family is like living within prison walls while expending constant energy trying to recapture and maintain that sense of self, that natural state of freedom and purity that one has when one is born. Although, there is a feeling of being trapped by the extreme limitation and boundaries established, whether these be extreme poverty, negative family values, harsh criticism, punishment, or miserable, gloomy, and unstimulating environments, somehow there is an inner knowing or sense that I will be OK, that I can overcome these barriers. I will push ahead and survive.

The transcending process seeks the truth of a situation, the truth for each of us, whether it is an illness, survival, or creativity; it seeks to discover our specific unique meaning (Privette, 1968). It is our ability to will that enables transcendence to occur. The transcendent process uses the available resources to go beyond the present to a higher or different plane of existence (Heidegger, 1952). In addition, it uses fantasies to relieve tension and invoke hope (Assagioli, 1973).

How does an individual transcend? Jourard (1968) lists the following steps: (1) a letting be of what is and the creation of a clearing of the experience and letting it alone; (2) an openness to sharing experiences with oneself and with others fully and freely, with little defensiveness — there is a sense of safety in interpersonal relationships and an ability to cope with one's own world (this is not always true of transcenders); (3) a focus and involvement to the point where nothing else exists, such as in the turning-point decision; (4) a commitment to the self in which values develop into goals, achievements, or tasks — the individual may also be inspired from transcending experiences to develop more values and commitments; (5) a sense of self-confidence or trust in oneself to cope, the confidence to succeed, and the determination (will) to follow through; (6) symbols, which are metaphors for ideals, values and beliefs, that are involved in releasing transcending behavior and can be experienced as "insistable [constant] images of possibility" (p. 223); and (7) challenges that unite with the above factors in a way that requires the person to respond to the situation. The situation

> entices, or demands, a full focusing of attention and resources to the matter at hand . . . It acts [to] bring forth from [the individual] achievements and feats of endurance which might be impossible for persons less challenged. (p. 223)

One or any combination of the above is powerful enough to create transcendence. Here are some examples from transcenders:

> In the tenth grade, I had a history teacher who was young, attractive, and enthusiastic. I used to watch her, examine her

closely; I liked her and thought maybe that what I could be was a history teacher just like her.

"You can't go to college and waste all that money. You'll just get married anyway. You have to work too hard for your grades," Mom said. I received a scholarship and I went anyway — something told me she was wrong.

I remember saying that when I got older, I would have a housekeeper. Others laughed at me. They didn't believe me. I felt angry that others denied what I said I wanted. It challenged me to continue achieving.

Jourard (1968) summarized transcendence this way:

Perhaps the element of mystery, surprise or unpredictability that seems associated with most of the examples of transcending implies that man, to function most fully, must transcend the programming and shaping of his behavior and become less predictable and controlled. (p. 224)

SUMMARY

Through willing, transcenders guide their energies, use their resources, and make decisions that are sustaining and growthful. Transcenders' internal frame of reference connects to their Being-in-the-world because it is in the world that transcenders find the resources and the energy to continue. Transcendence is the process of gaining energies, touching potentialities, and invoking hope for the future.

---- Chapter 6 ----

Adulthood: The Process

All human beings are given natural life processes as part of the original package that help us to experience the world. We are programmed from conception to develop physically, mentally, emotionally, and spiritually into our fullest potential by using these processes. These processes help us to learn from our experiences, to grow in our potentialities, and to heal from traumas. They are *powerful* interconnected life forces helping to lead and guide us ever forward in our growth. At times, these processes flow easily and effortlessly from within us. Other times, we are in an intense struggle, where everything is an effort.

When trauma occurs, there is a disruption in our life, and our entire being works to heal and reestablish a normal flow. If, for whatever reason, healing can't occur, our natural flow is altered. Dysfunctional behavior then develops to cope with unhealed traumas. In dysfunction, we learn to live with the unhealed trauma as if it were natural and normal. It is neither. What we are actually doing is working around the unhealed trauma by avoiding, masking, transforming, and/or storing it in our body. This is not natural to us, and our authentic flow is stopped or altered. The essence of the healing and growth process is to heal from traumas and to reestablish the natural flow of our being.

Healing and growth occur as a well-choreographed unit; movement in one area triggers movement in another. They combine to make a wonderful process that is an authentic, dynamic, everyday function. *Ideally*, the healing and growth process results in the development of an authentic self. The essence of the process looks like this: We experience a traumatic situation. This experience may be a past, unhealed trauma or a present experience. The experience affects us in many different ways: physically, emotionally, mentally, and spiritually. It triggers discomfort or pain on many levels. We struggle with and feel our pain. Our struggle may be very intense or an easy flow. After feeling, we go over the information and work to gain all the meanings it has for us and our world. We take responsibility for this learning and apply it to our lives. This is growth. Growth, in turn, creates patience; patience creates strength; strength creates wisdom; and all of it creates the character of our authentic self.

This is authentic living. We don't have failure; we just have learning and growth from experiences. No matter what I do, no matter what I experience, I gain. I grow. I learn. I develop. I personally view life as a huge experiential school. With this view, I never lose. No matter what happens to me, I am never the victim, never the failure. I'm the learner. Every time I heal and grow, I take one more step forward into the development and strengthening of my authentic self.

In the healing and growth process, transcenders go beyond surviving their families and work to develop their authentic selves. They truly transcend. As adults they work hard to create the life they dreamed about as children and surpass the dysfunction of the family. They work to heal and grow as authentic human beings. In this chapter, the basics of the transcenders' process of healing and growing are presented.

DEFINITION OF TERMS

The following are definitions that will help you to understand the healing and growth process that is presented in the next three chapters:

Directives in life. To love and be loved physically, mentally, emotionally, and spiritually. Love supports, encourages, and helps growth to occur. We must live fully in love to be truly authentic.

Feeling feelings fully. To feel our feelings to their fullest extent in the present moment. Feelings are always felt in the present because we are in the present when we feel them. They are never in the past. When feelings are fully felt and experienced, they are then complete and settled in the past. This is the magic of feeling feelings. Feelings must be felt in order for us to release the pain they cause. The more we ignore, avoid, and push our feelings away, the stronger and more painful they become. Feelings are stored in our bodies until we feel them. And until we feel them, we don't heal or grow fully. As we feel, pain is released and important life-changing insights into the past and their effect on our present living occur.

Growth. The movement of the individual toward becoming *all* our Creator originally intended. Growth involves feelings, thoughts, learning, potentialities, talents, spirituality, and love.

Healing. The process of releasing pain and changing old patterns to develop and enhance our original creation with the addition of growth. Healing allows the darkness of the trauma to give way to the light of being. Our Creator never intends for us to stay in our pain and darkness. The original package intention is always for us to work through the pain in order to learn and grow.

Learning. What we know and understand *and* are in the process of knowing and understanding about ourselves, our world, and others in

our world. Learning supports and enhances growth. We learn by
staying in our struggles and gleaning all we can. We then move on to
our next experience and all that it contains.

Love. A commitment to fulfill our directive with ourselves,
others, and our world.

Revisiting. Revisiting is the reexperiencing, remembering, and
refeeling of the past to gain an adult perspective and understanding of
what happened to us as children. Revisiting is handling all the
feelings as well as the problems and conflicts (issues) left from the
experiences of childhood. The feelings include anger, sorrow, pain,
resentment, loneliness, shame, hurt, and rejection, as well as guilt.
The issues include relating to family members and resolving unresolved problems from childhood.

Struggle. The internal wrestling with behavior, emotions, thoughts,
and spirituality that works to create growth in the individual. Old
patterns of being are challenged by life experiences so that we create a
new, third way of being that fits. Struggle occurs when the old is
challenged or no longer works and the new has not yet been learned.
Sometimes, the struggle occurs with little effort, and at other times,
incredible effort is needed to move forward. The struggle continues
until a new way is created.

There is always some sort of discomfort or pain that throws the
individual into the struggle that shifts the old and creates the new.
Otherwise, there is no reason to change, no reason to grow. Without
the challenge, the old way is not seen as obsolete and no longer useful.

Struggle may feel like suffering at times, but there is a difference. In struggle, I am moving forward; in suffering, I just stay in
pain. The following is an excerpt from Tiffany's journal that focuses
on her struggle with being "good" and "bad." In it, you can get a
flavor of struggle and its back-and-forth energy:

Tiffany

I don't want to be a bad girl; I want to be a good girl. I'll try harder; then Mommy will love me. I'll be the good girl she always wanted me to be. I'll work hard, Mommy. I promise. Just please love me — please, please love me. Please don't be mad at me. I need you. I love you. I know you never liked me; you wanted me to be someone else, not me. You wanted me to be that perfect girl. Help! If I do that, I'll lose me again, and I don't want to do that, not again. It's too hard to come back. Why can't I just be me? Isn't me OK? Why not? I seem lovable. I seem OK to me. Why aren't I OK to you?

Please love me just for me. I can be different. I'll try. I'll change me. I'll be good. Please help me to grow up. Why didn't you? What was so awful about the real me? But I've been judged by you. It's not fair! I'm not bad. I am OK. I am good. God created me good, so I'm good, but you think I'm bad — so I'm bad. BAD! Mommy says I'm bad, so I'll have to cover it all up. Cover up all the bad so no one can see it and so people know that Mommy is OK. I must hide. I'm embarrassed of all of me. But I'm not bad; I'm good and OK. I don't know who's right — me or Mommy?

*   *   *

Trauma. A physical, emotional, mental, or spiritual assault. Traumas usually include intense feelings of fear, terror, anger, and hurt. Often, there is disbelief that the event is actually happening. For example, a child who is assaulted by his or her parents is in a state of shock: "It can't be happening! How could my parent, who is suppose to love me, do this?" Then, reality sets in: "God they're going to kill me!" Usually, all these feelings have to go underground and are stored in the body until later in adulthood, when it becomes safe to feel.

The terror involved in a trauma can be so powerful that the blood in the body leaves the head, hands, and feet and goes to the vital organs of survival, such as the heart, and lungs. The hands and feet may feel cold, and the head may feel light, as if one has a head cold. If this state lasts very long, there is energy only for basic survival and nothing for academics or other pursuits.

Traumas, if worked with in the healing mode, can be healed. The healing of one trauma may trigger the healing of other, deeper and older traumas. For example, if I feel the fear of one trauma, I can release other stored fear from other traumas. Healing may also trigger a trauma that has been blocked from my memory.

THE HEALING AND GROWTH PROCESS

Healing is often called recovery in the mental health field. I believe that true healing is more than recovery. Healing is a deep and life-changing process that is interconnected with the growth process. Together, healing and growth work through the pain and darkness of trauma to create life in freedom and light. They are a wonderful integration of releasing the pain, gleaning learning, and applying the learning to our lives so we live more authentically in our natural flow. The two processes work together so that we find our true selves from the inside out.

By growth, I mean learning from all my experiences and taking risks in my unknown areas. It means expanding my limits and not accepting my self-imposed prison bars as permanent. It also means exploring these self-imposed limits to see how far I can develop.

An example of pushing these self-imposed limits is a decision I made when I was a teenager. When I was fifteen, I was *painfully* shy and couldn't talk to teachers. I turned beet red and speechless if they tried to talk to me. I made a decision when I was seventeen that I would no longer be shy and that, no matter how painful it was, I would step out and be assertive. I had no idea how I would develop with this decision. I just knew I had to be out of that awful pain. Now, decades later, when an assertiveness program was announced in my church, my daughter begged me not to take it because I am already "too assertive." If I hadn't taken those first steps, I would never have known how I could develop, and inside, I'd still be that shy, speechless teenager.

The greatest gain in my "shy" process is that I learned many things about me, the real me. One of the things I learned is that I am not a shy person. I enjoy people and also love my quiet, alone times. The essence of the healing and growth process is eliminating what is not authentic and enhancing all that is authentic. I compare it to Michelangelo and how he created his wonderful sculptures. He first imagined his creation in the stone and then removed all that was not the image while enhancing all that was. We have within us all we need to develop our original package. We, like Michelangelo, need to remove the damage caused by traumas while embracing and developing our authenticity. It is in this way that we find our strength, growth, original package, and relationship to God.

Healing takes on many different forms. It is basically anything that helps heal the effects of trauma, in safety, for that individual. It may, but not necessarily, be formal therapy. The healing process is unique to each person. I've seen healing with just a phone call to set up an appointment, with a client receiving a special card in the mail, or with a hug or a smile. Basically, as a dear friend of mine says, and I believe, the essence of healing is love — the giving of love in any form possible. We need to give it to ourselves and receive it from others.

Our dynamic healing and growing process works to keep us emotionally, mentally, physically, and spiritually healthy. It uses all our resources to guide us in healing from traumas, in learning from experiences, in continuing to grow, and in keeping us straight in all areas of our lives. By being *straight*, I mean developing and being our authentic selves. We are honest in our communications, thoughts, and feelings, and we back them up with authentic behavior. What we are inside matches what we are outside. When we are straight, there is little or no game playing or dysfunction in our relationships with ourselves or others. In essence, we are real.

Authentic living involves a constant healing and growing process. This process helps guide us in handling *all* our traumas and experiences. It works to integrate our perception and knowledge of each experience to create growth, learning, and development. If we resist our process, as we all do at times, we experience frustration, depression, anger, and lack of learning. While processing an experience, we may have pain, sorrow, and other intense difficult feelings, *but* we always gain learning, growth, peace, joy, and love.

Healing occurs on many levels at the same time. For example, I may be feeling sadness when a friend dies and, at the same time, feeling the sadness of the loss of never having had a healthy family. Or I may be angry about something at work, but when I express the anger, its intensity tells me that old anger is also being released. I may not always know what healing is occurring, but I can become aware that it is.

After any kind of physical, emotional, mental, and spiritual trauma, there is an incredible surge of focus and energy to release the pain, reestablish the natural flow, and grow. Our internal processes work to establish a normal life again. These processes of healing and growing may become blocked when we are either unwilling (because it is intense and painful) or unable (because it is not safe) to work through an experience or trauma. Working through a trauma involves feeling it and learning from it. When we are not able to do this, the trauma and the damage it causes become trapped or frozen in our bodies and interfere with the flow of energy, feelings, and learning, and we cannot function efficiently. We become stuck. When we try to adapt and handle the trauma by denying it, masking it, running from it, covering it with an addiction, or not trusting ourselves and depending totally on other people for our needs, we create dysfunction. Being our authentic selves by staying in our process can be exciting, joyful, sad, intense, difficult, and, at times, very painful. But it is the only way to really live. It is only by knowing ourselves that we can heal, grow, learn, and be real. This does not mean that we won't have rough, difficult times that will challenge us down to our core. It does mean that, as we heal and grow, living will become easier because we have *all* of us available to handle our world and its obstacles.

When we are authentic, we trust ourselves, our feelings, our intuition, and our process, and we learn from our experiences. We know our authentic selves and processes are not only OK, but fantastically wonderful and perfect for us. The tragedy in our society today, let alone in a dysfunctional family, is not knowing this. We, as individuals and a collective society, have forgotten how to support ourselves and others in the healing and growth process. Sadly, society believes that the only way to feel good about oneself is through financial and/or status success. The only way to *really* feel good and be successful is to be our authentic growing, dynamic, process selves.

With each experience we face in life, we have the choice of growth or nongrowth. In this choice, we face going forward and developing new parts of us or dying on some level. Each of us is personally responsible for our choice. Even in the midst of healing and growing from a dysfunctional family, the decision can be made to stop. We may stop for many reasons: it may be too painful, too life-changing, too terrifying, too threatening (like having to leave a relationship), or just too time-consuming. But by not growing, we are saying, "I don't want the rest of me, and I am choosing to stay stuck!" Nongrowth sounds like "That's enough!"; "I've had it"; "I don't want to grow"; "I don't want to change"; "It's too scary"; "I'll stay where I am." If we continue to say no, we are at risk of becoming nonrecognizable because our real selves are no longer truly alive. We are then in danger of becoming nonproductive *and* definitely narrow-minded and set in our ways.

Nongrowth creates a slow, painful, and tragic death of the authentic self. If I choose not to grow, I have not only denied my internal spiritual vision of all that I can be, but also denied and squelched my original package program to grow and develop. This choice takes an enormous amount of energy and a concerted effort. Nongrowth means using energy in a way that does not embrace the natural flow of the authentic self.

Growth, thank goodness, is so powerful and its benefits feel so good that we usually want to continue growing once we have experienced growth. I may struggle and suffer in growth, but I gain the authentic life that goes with it. In nongrowth, I have a form of death. In growth, I have life of the self.

Everyone is unique in this area. Some individuals seem to have little determination, strength, or courage to face the healing and growth process. Others are so determined that they leap into any experience that supports and encourages growth. Transcenders are among the latter and have the ability to use even a little encouragement to go forward.

Sometimes, we give the responsibility of our process to another person. By doing so, we give away our personal power and become inappropriately dependent. If this happens, the message is "You take over. You know more than I do. I'm too scared and don't know how to handle my own life." Usually, this occurs because we have been taught by rigid and abusive families never to be responsible for our lives. This is actually an illusion because only we can be responsible.

When we choose to support and encourage our process, we develop our wonderful original package and our potentialities are virtually limitless. In addition, we gain personal power and freedom, which create healthy *interdependent* relationships. Interdependency is being dependent and independent at different times in the same relationship. There is a flow between the two extremes. My needs in the relationship, as well as my significant other's needs, determine whether I will be more independent or dependent. Sometimes, depending on my mood and situation, I'll need to be very dependent, for example, during heavy grieving times or after surgery. At other times, my significant other will need to be dependent on me. At still other times, I will need or want to function in the world very independently of anyone.

Once we learn to live in our natural process, we usually can't, and don't want to, return to our old, inauthentic way of living. We are on a continuous self-discovery journey. We become excited about what we just learned and look forward to what we will discover next about ourselves and our world. We also learn to trust ourselves at a deeper level. We find within us a comfortableness and have a deep knowing that says "I have what I need to live." We also find a strength, a deep internal strength of being.

Every person's process of healing and growing is unique, special, and perfect for that person. My process is not like yours nor yours like mine. You can't live authentically in my life nor I yours, but we are perfect in our own process. The following is description of Steve's experience of his process:

Steve

I was swimming the other day when this last struggle began. I became aware of an old memory, its pain, and how it was interfering with my training, I struggled with it and I worked hard to make it go away — it didn't. It went unresolved. I then tried to avoid it. Avoiding it didn't work any better than the last time. The memory demanded that I stay there and deal with it. I was back to the pain and the wrestling.

The struggle was intense, deep, lonely, isolating, and just plain awful. My brain reached desperately for a solution. There was none. I prayed for one. I wanted one. I wanted to get out of the pain. I felt like Jacob wrestling with the angel. I didn't want ever to surrender to it. It was awful. I screamed, "I'll never surrender! You'll never win. NO! No! No! Never! I'll fight until I have no more energy for the fight." The worst part of not knowing was the fear of what was coming and what I was surrendering to.

When I did finally surrender and allow myself to go into the feelings, there was a peace. At times, it was awful, but there was also a peace, a knowing that I will learn, grow, and find relief from the pain through feeling the feelings. I knew I could handle whatever was coming just as I have handled other struggles. I knew I had to go straight through the process so I could gain *all* that I could from memory. I didn't want to have to repeat this struggle again; there will be enough other ones to deal with in the future.

As I went through it, I cried, got angry, and released a variety of feelings. Part of me still wanted to scream, "Get me out of this." The other part of me said, "Stay, learn, grow, gain strength." I knew it was the only way. As I stayed, I gain wonderful insights into my life and my behavior. As these insights came, the pain eased and the confusion lifted. I then found myself making changes automatically in my life, healthy, wonderful changes that gave me more freedom and an increasing sense of inner power, strength, and energy.

I love the energy and power. It's a sense of "I can handle this world. I can climb mountains, conquer problems and, yes, even go through another growth process."

TRAUMA LAYERS AND HEALING PROCESS

Healing is a process of dealing with the many *layers* of emotional pain caused by traumas. Layers are caused by the actual traumas as well as by the protective barriers created by transcenders to defend themselves. When an individual is not able or allowed to work through a trauma, the experience and all its feelings are stored in the body as a layer. Energy, insights, and learning are lost because the experience cannot be processed. This, in turn, makes living in reality and making appropriate decisions harder, if not impossible.

Let me give you an example of the process of creating a layer. Every time transcenders are abused, they feel pain, anger, rejection, abandonment, suspicion, mistrust, loneliness, and shame. It is not safe to feel these feelings because, if they do, they may be even more severely abused. So the feelings and thoughts from the trauma are held inside in what is called a *layer*. When there is another trauma, more pain is held inside on top of the previous layer, creating another layer. Layers function this way: The more the trauma, the more the stored layers; the more the layers, the more terrifying are the feelings; the more the terror, the greater is the need for protection from the feelings. Our bodies remember each trauma, feeling, and thought about the experience, no matter how early in life the trauma occurs.

Tucked inside with the trauma layers are layers of protection. Transcenders have to figure out not only how to protect themselves physically and emotionally from the family, but also how to protect and keep themselves away from their feelings. They have learned that feeling certain, or any, feelings is dangerous. They believe that, if they feel the feelings, they will be more severely abused. Also, they believe that they will become so overwhelmed, they will not survive. This fear may be so strong that feeling it, or even acknowledging it, triggers terror and thoughts of suicide. Often, the hardest part of releasing a layer is dealing with the fear. The layer is literally surrounded by a powerful ring of fear that protects the person from the feelings and that therefore helps ensure survival.

Protection layers come in many forms: (1) beliefs, such as "My family is perfect and they loved me very much" (denial); (2) extreme overweight, fragile, or super body build (physical barrier); (3) resistant, rebellious, or obnoxious behavior (necessary to keep others away); (4) loving, kind, and caretaking behavior (necessary to have others like them so they won't be abused by them); (5) memory blocks (keeping pain out of awareness); and (6) multiple personalities, created in extreme abuse situations. The "personalities" are really just parts of the same person that hold feelings and pain away from awareness, often in memories blocks labeled with specific names.

To be emotionally healthy, each part of each layer has to be acknowledged, felt, and released from the body. Each layer has to be understood and its learning integrated or our body stores it until we do understand and integrate it. The layer does not just go away. Through the healing process, transcenders often become exhausted by the many layers that keep surfacing and need to be revisited. They wish they could stop the process for even a little while because it has become so painfully difficult. The pain does end when all the layers have been released and healed.

In the active healing process, transcenders work with their many stored layers for what seems to be an eternity. This healing time is put into perspective when it is compared with the many years their families degraded, neglected, and abused them. The more the abuse, the more layers; the more layers, the more healing time is required.

Layers come up in no particular order. They are triggered by the therapy process as well as by life events. Once the layer is released, the transcender feels freer, stronger, more capable, and more relaxed. Transcenders also gain new perspectives (internal frame of reference) as well as changed thoughts, feelings, and behavior.

Paul is able to identify his order of layers. This is not unusual, but not every transcender is able to do this:

 Paul

I first feel anger. After I feel it and release its power, the feeling of hurt predominates. Fear follows the hurt. I become frightened of what seems to be everything: people, traffic, going out, staying in, the dark, everything. Sometimes, for instance, in the beginning of my healing process, the fear turns into terror. I reexperience the terror of my inner child who lived through those awful years. What surprises me is that, after the terror, I experience lack of trust in everyone around me. Somehow, I figured that, once through the terror, I'd be in a nice, more peaceful place. My hoped-for peace is really the feeling of betrayal, deep betrayal. Then comes a layer of "beware" that protects me, the real me. Underneath this protection is the deep original hurt and incredible sadness. Once through this original hurt, I do feel better and I reach a place of peace. I find the only way to get my layers to shift is to feel each thoroughly.

* * *

A healthy method of processing feeling instead of creating a layer goes through the following steps: (1) an experience occurs that triggers feelings; (2) there is an awareness of the feelings; (3) the feelings are felt to their fullest extent; and (4) learning and insight from the experience are gained and stored for later use. The following is the way a layer is created: (1) an experience occurs that triggers feelings; (2) most of these feelings are shifted out of awareness; (3) the feelings cannot be safely expressed so they are denied, buried, and/or transferred; and (4) the feelings create a new painful layer in the body, and little learning occurs.

TRANSCENDERS' HEALING AND GROWTH PROCESS

Transcenders' healing process has two major, powerful components: (1) grieving the past and (2) reclaiming the self. This two-part process is very hard and very intense because grieving and reclaiming are going on at the *same* time.

1. *Grieving the past* consists of feeling the losses from childhood. These losses include what the transcenders *did not* have in childhood (e.g., love, affection, support, and a normal childhood), as well as what they *did* have in childhood (e.g., abuse and neglect). *Everything* must be felt and grieved. Denial, anger, rejection, and intense sadness are among the feelings experienced in the grieving.

2. *Reclaiming the self* includes discovering, developing, and exploring the original package, (i.e., the authentic self). This is the growth part of the process. It contains a range of feelings from intense pain to joy. In childhood, transcenders have usually been given little chance to discover or explore their abilities, let alone develop authentically. Transcenders often view therapy as the first chance to develop their real selves and potentialities. Transcenders work hard to transcend their families. They work to become a whole, functioning person in a life of their choosing. The process is difficult because, as one transcender asked me, "How do you settle down and live a

normal, regular, calm life when you have already lived ten lifetimes? How do you settle down and not want to live on the edge (a place of constant tension, anxiety, and defense, as well as excitement) after living almost your whole life on the edge?" The healing process is a *huge* adjustment in the style of inner living. Some transcenders have few problems; others struggle deeply.

The healing and growth process is *chosen, active,* and *purposeful.* Transcenders choose to overcome their leftovers from childhood and to apply the needed time, effort, courage, determination, and finances. They use psychotherapy, AA-based groups, significant others, spirituality, group therapy weekends, workshops, and anything else that helps them heal of their past. The commitment to healing is the long-term continuation of their growth decision of childhood.

I must emphasize that there are *no quick, easy fixes.* The healing process usually takes years; growth, a lifetime. As part of the healing process, each individual must face her or his own dark cloud full of thunder, lightning, and gale-strength winds from past traumas.

Our natural healing process works to heal the body, mind, emotions, and spirit of the damage caused by abuse and neglect. Each individual has his or her own personal way of recovering from the trauma of a dysfunctional family. Therapy is often needed to help transcenders uncover and develop this process.

No one method, *no one* therapist is ever enough. Healing requires the use of many different techniques as well as many different people in different capacities. In addition, there is no one thought, no one feeling that is "it" in the healing process. No one anything straightens out all the past and its hurts. It takes a concerted effort over a number of years with many feelings, thoughts, therapies, and people.

This process of healing is full of contradictory feelings. It may be so intense and painful that transcenders lose hope of ever making it, and at the same time, the process is so freeing and loving that transcenders experience uplifting, energizing freedom and joy.

Four stages lead transcenders to their goal of healing and growth as adults: (1) leaving home; (2) transitioning; (3) seeking outside help; and (4) healing and growing in a therapeutic setting.

STAGE 1: LEAVING HOME

Freedom at last! The first step in transcenders' healing process is to leave home as early as possible. Transcenders move out through college, marriage, work, and running away. Their childhood technique of getting out and staying away is now used to move them into well-earned personal freedom. In addition, the turning-point decision to be different from their families once again becomes a powerful focal point helping them leave. This leaving is absolutely essential to transcending the family.

The average leaving age is immediately after high school. However, age is *not* important because survival can occur at *any* age. What *is* important is that transcenders leave and realize that their survival now depends on not going back to the old family entanglements, but on going forward into their own long-dreamed-of world.

The experience of leaving is different for each transcender. Leaving can be easy or difficult, depending on the family's dysfunction. Some families try to stop the leaving by playing emotional games, by becoming so dysfunctional that the transcender feels trapped, or by acting out violently. On the other hand, some families welcome the leaving or don't even notice it. However it happens, the transcenders leave.

Adulthood and freedom for transcenders hold a mixed blessing of excitement and fear. The excitement is that they are free, wonderfully free to be themselves and create the life they have been dreaming about for years. The fears include powerful concerns about themselves and the world, for example: "Who am I?"; "What do I do now?"; "How do I handle this world?"; "Am I going to make it?" Some transcenders are very conscious of the excitement and freedom and are also totally aware of what they are doing. Others have no awareness or only a vague knowing. Tiffany and Marie describe their experiences:

_____ *Tiffany* _____

I left for college immediately after my senior year in high school. I was so relieved, so happy and excited. I was finally free of all those people who wanted to control me. Finally! I'd waited all those years, and freedom was finally here. I could try out all those things I had been dying to do. Wow! It was great! I did all sort of things I could never even dream of at home. Sometimes, I just sat and enjoyed the calm in my life. I began to learn how to get along with other people. I talked with other students, discussing the latest topic. I began to learn that I really did have some brains and abilities. That was a big awareness for me because for years I'd thought I was just conning everyone. I really thought I must be dumb.

At the same time, leaving home was terrifying. I didn't have all the skills everyone else had. I didn't know how to relate to others without the dysfunction. I didn't even know who I was, not really. There were so many questions of "How do I do this?"; "What happens if I don't make it?"; "Will I have to go back home?" I had a lot of fear, but I also had a promise to myself to keep going and not be like my family. I learned as I went, but it was a very mixed bag of feelings.

_____ *Marie* _____

Here I was, almost twenty-one years old, living at home, working, paying room and board, and feeling like a prisoner still locked within the crazies of the family. I was not allowed to drive, have my own bank account (Mom took all the money), date, or go anywhere without my mother's approval. And according to my family, the only way a "nice girl" could leave home was to get married.

I had a job I really enjoyed — working for a doctor. However, it became more and more embarrassing to me because my mother kept checking on me. She would even call his wife. My mother thought I must be doing something wrong with the doctor. I couldn't take it anymore. I had to get away, and yet I knew if I left home, my mother would send the sheriff after me. I never prayed so hard in my life as I did for an opportunity to escape. A couple of guys had asked me to marry them, but I didn't love them. I couldn't see trading one prison for another.

I decided to join the air force and get an education after I saw an advertisement on television. I had completed two years of college and really wanted to finish my education — but not half as much as I wanted to get away from home. The doctor I worked for asked me if I had ever thought about joining the service as a way of getting away from home. I confided in him what I was planning. The doctor helped by "firing" me so the air force would look like a great opportunity to my mother. She saw it as a great chance for me to finally become a lady and learn to do what I was told.

I couldn't believe it! I was really going to leave home. I was finally going to get away. Each night before I left for basic training, I'd lie awake thinking, "What have I done" and felt a lot of fear. At the same time, I knew that no matter how hard it was, it could not be as difficult as my life within this prison. At this time, I had no conscious awareness of the sexual or physical abuse, let alone being forced to participate in the horrible satanic rituals. All I knew was that my mother was unable to love me because I was such a "bad girl." I felt responsible for my parents' unhappiness and their divorce, and I even felt guilty for being born. I hoped, in addition to getting away from all my "failure feelings," that my mother would be happier if I wasn't around every day to remind her of what a failure I was. And yet, way deep inside, a part of me questioned whether I was the one who had failed. Regardless, I had given up on the little-girl hope that "Today is the day I'll be good enough to be loved." I could no longer stand the verbal abuse and the putdowns. I was getting out.

I was very aware, largely because of my parents' brainwashing, that even though I was leaving home and getting away from the craziness of my family, I would have to be very careful not to let people get to know the real me. I still believed "if they knew what I was really like, they wouldn't want me around." (Parent tape #1) [Tapes are certain ways of feeling, thinking, and behaving that are learned from others that "click on" under certain circumstances.] I also knew that people couldn't be trusted. I had already learned that in my world, even though I was not conscious of the reality that had given birth to these feelings. I knew I was "bad, dirty, and cheap." Regardless, the free world had to be better. Besides, if I kept up the facade of the smiling, happy, helpful, responsible person, then people wouldn't have a chance to find out what I was really like. And I would be able to lock the bathroom door and have my own bank account, and for the first time in my memory, I could make my own decisions.

Most of the other air force trainees were just out of high school, so I had a little edge on maturity. Many rebelled at the strict discipline. I found great comfort in the structure and in a discipline far less rigid and certainly more logical than the kind I experienced at home. I can't say that basic training was the easiest thing I'd ever been through, but I fell back on my "Let's see what you can learn from this experience" perspective. It had gotten me through so many things in the past.

After several days of testing, I was surprised to find that my test scores were high enough to qualify me for the next officer candidate school — but my parents said I was dumb? A few weeks later, I was told I had the potential for receiving the outstanding-trainee award and was expected to receive this award at graduation. I can remember thinking that the officer didn't know what kind of person I was, but if she thought I was capable, I wasn't going to try to change her opinion. The outstanding trainee is voted on by peers and staff, each vote carrying the same weight. No one was more surprised than I when, on graduation day, my name was called to receive the award. This opened the door to the fact that I was capable.

I was so excited and couldn't wait to call home with the happy news. My mother's reply was "Oh, they didn't find out what you are really like, or I'm sure they would have chosen someone who was worthy of the award." I was devastated. I realize now that my true freedom from my family really began several months after my mother was killed in an automobile accident. After realizing she was really dead, I felt as if I had just been born. I could never have survived if I had not left my crazy family. Her death opened the rest of the door to life for me!

STAGE 2: TRANSITIONING

The second stage in transcenders' healing process is the transition period. The transition is the period of time after leaving home and before formal therapy in which the transcender is adjusting to life without the family. It can last a few months or many years. Transcenders rarely know how to live a normal life in the world, and it is during this time that the learning begins. During this time, transcenders learn through correct decisions as well as mistakes. Tremendous learning occurs. They learn to handle their freedom, set up dreamed-about lifestyles, and begin to really know themselves. Their mistakes include wrong relationships, marriages, and jobs. Transcenders again use their powerful turning-point and personal-growth promises from childhood to push themselves to learn and grow in their adult world. They learn from their successes as well as from their mistakes.

Transcenders do not accept their mistakes as permanent. They work hard, do not give up, and continue to create a life that is more in line with what they pictured in childhood. Some transcenders seek therapeutic help immediately and do anything possible to enhance their life and accomplish their goals. Others work hard with themselves and in significant relationships to create healthy, nurturing lifestyles. However it is done, transcenders work to overcome issues, problems, and dysfunction stemming from childhood, (i.e., leftovers).

The transition time is a unique adjustment period for each transcender. It is a time of experimenting and learning what they want

as well as don't want in their world. Transcenders also begin to learn
how to get along in the world without the family and its dysfunction.
They experience fun, relief, confusion, pain, sadness, joy, fear, and
health, as well as painful relationships. Some find enormous success
during this time, others little.

STAGE 3: SEEKING OUTSIDE HELP

At some point, many transcenders find themselves not living the
way they intended and, instead, living in emotional turmoil and pain.
Leftovers from childhood may also intensify as transcenders experience the world. Transcenders experience emotional pain from mistakes made in relationships, work, and the creation of a healthy
lifestyle, as well as from ghosts of the past. Ghosts are people and
memories of past abuse, pain, and loneliness that seem to haunt
people in their present life, in the present moment. These memories
and their influences on behavior interfere with transcenders' lives,
triggering resentfulness, anger, confusion, guilt, depression, fear, and
discouragement. At times, the emotional pain is so intense that
functioning on *any* level becomes difficult. Transcenders may believe
that they will never have the life they want and dreamed of as a child.
They may even fear that they have turned out to be like their family.
(Sometimes, transcenders have traits like family members' because all
of us are influenced by the people who raise us, *but* these characteristics are not permanent and do change during the healing and growth
process.) It is this combination of emotional pain, mistakes, frustrations, depression, ghosts, fear, the awareness of the leftovers influencing their lives, and the promise they made to themselves as children to
grow that drives transcenders into therapy.

This stage usually occurs around age thirty to forty. There is no
right or specific age for any part of the healing process. All ages are
relative and *not* important. I mention them only to give you an idea of

time. Any individual can choose to be a transcender of childhood at any age.

-------------------------------- *Chris* --------------------------------

Chris, the scapegoat of the family, describes his experience before entering therapy:

I wanted relationships in my life that were healthy and fun. I needed to be accepted and loved. In relationships, however, I always had problems. They always fell apart and became incredibly painful. I was always left lonely and feeling punished.

In one relationship, the woman and I loved each other deeply. We shared wonderful times and could talk forever. It was so good, for a while; then it fell apart. We ended up fighting and soon began to hate each other. I needed to be accepted, but every time she'd get close and offer the love I needed, I'd shove her away. It looked as if I was a bad guy. In reality, I was terrified to be that close. In reality, I needed the love she offered.

This relationship, as well as others, continued to go downhill. I decided I was a total failure. I knew I wasn't worth much. I had so much pain, I couldn't stand it. I also decided that my parents were right: It was all my fault, and I deserved to be punished by people leaving me.

Finally, the pain was so great, I had to do something. My world was falling apart; all my relationships ended up in pain and anger. I knew something had to be wrong with me. It couldn't always be everyone else all the time.

By the time I finally got into therapy, I couldn't maintain any organization. Even my finances were going downhill. I was unbelievably lonely and depressed. I believed I had no friends and knew I didn't have a family. I believed no one loved me.

Therapy came up when a friend and I were talking. He told me how he had been helped. I listened because I knew his childhood had been just as bad as mine. I also saw changes I liked in him, and I wanted the same changes. He was happier and calmer and even beginning to have some good friendships. I went and am glad I did. I now understand my childhood and have changed my pattern of relating to me and others.

In therapy, I learned that I set up relationships to fail. That is, I set the person up to reject and dump me. Just the way my family did! My family did a good job of teaching me how to do it. My family also taught me it was all I deserved; I deserved to be rejected, unloved, and lonely. I now know those were the leftovers from my childhood and have changed most of them. I'm beginning to have healthier relationships and feel better about myself.

* * *

Therapists offer transcenders information about the healing and growth process. They help transcenders know what feelings are normal at different stages in the process as well as give support and help through the process. For example, there is a stage when transcenders believe they have become just like their parents and need reassurance that this is not true. (This belief occurs because, as healing continues, feelings, thoughts, and behavior come up that do look like the family's dysfunction. Transcenders, happily, are able to change them.) There is also a totally confusing, feeling-"crazy" time that occurs when new and old patterns of operating are functioning at the same time. Transcenders need reassurance and guidance during these difficult times. They especially need to know that they are doing well and are going to make it.

STAGE 4: HEALING AND GROWING IN A THERAPEUTIC SETTING

The last stage in the healing and growth process is psychotherapy. Psychotherapy is therapy focused on helping the individual heal and grow mentally, emotionally, physically, and spiritually. Each individual has his or her own unique process within these general steps and needs different healings. The steps are *not rigid*, and as in any process, the steps may mix, overlap, skip, change order, repeat, or occur at the same time. The grieving and reclaiming processes are going on at the *same* time and are detailed in this chapter and Chapter 7.

Developing a Trusting Relationship with the Therapist

Most individuals who grow up in dysfunctional families have problems with trusting another human being. They either can't trust or trust too easily. Thank goodness, appropriate trust can be learned, earned, and developed in healthy relationships. In therapy, it is vital that a healthy, trusting, working relationship be established with a healthy, dependable therapist to promote the learning of trust and the working through of intense feelings and important issues.

Part of a trusting relationship for transcenders is to feel genuinely cared about and supported in their process. What transcenders need to learn from the therapist at this step is "Does what the therapist say and do match?"; "Does he or she really care for me as a person and not just as a paying customer?"; "Does he or she see the pain I am in?" It is *very* important that transcenders work with a therapist who helps develop trust.

Equally important, transcenders need to gain a trust of themselves and their healing process. It is essential that trust in the self develop, because it is either not developed or is severely damaged during childhood. Trust of themselves becomes increasingly important as transcenders heal deep layers.

Developing a trusting relationship with oneself and others takes time. Even minimal trust sometimes takes more than a year to develop with the therapist. A deep inner trust of oneself and others may take years. Patience on the part of the transcender and the therapist in this area is a must.

Exploring the Background

At the same time the trusting relationship is developing, an exploration of the transcender's background is also begun. An infinite number of details about growing up are remembered, described, and examined. Many of these are painful memories that also trigger the very important grieving process. These memories encourage the grieving to start by helping the transcender gain an awareness that "I had a horrible growing up, and I experienced a lot of pain, sadness, and loss." This awareness helps transcenders to stop blaming themselves, and to see the family's dysfunction and destruction more clearly. All of this, in turn, strengthens and helps the healing and growing process to continue.

Reclaiming the Self

Reclaiming is the finding and developing of the original package. Reclaiming of the self begins the day transcenders decide to rid themselves of leftovers, be more themselves, and get into therapy. The process works this way: Everything that transcenders discover and feel about their families releases trapped internal layers. Each layer blocks part of the original authentic self. As the layers are released in the body, the authentic self is unblocked in some way and has a greater freedom to be. Also, as each layer is dealt with, more awareness of the trauma occurs, and the authentic self is acknowledged and can be developed.

Grieving Intensified

As transcenders continue to explore and describe the past, old grief is triggered. Grieving at this stage is extremely intense and painful. It is very important. *Many* hours of intense, painful crying occur. Often, the crying seems as if it will rip the person apart and go on forever. (It doesn't do either.) There are also feelings of denial, anger, fear, and confusion.

Transcenders express it this way: "I feel as if I could cry without stopping for years"; "If I start crying, I'll never stop"; "If I give in to it, I won't be able to function or ever be the same again"; "I just know I'll die." There is no guarantee *when* the crying will stop. There *is* a guarantee that it will stop. When it will stop depends on that particular individual and how many layers have been created over the years that need expression. When the tears are felt fully, they stop. Time off from routine activities as well as a medical leave from work may be very important at this time. This is not a weakness, but an acknowledgment of a powerful time in the healing and growth process. When transcenders question this, I ask them, "Wouldn't you take time off if you had a intense *physical* illness?" They need to learn to take care of themselves.

Internal Clearing and Ending of the Tears

As the intense grief reaches its end, an internal clearing begins to occur. Transcenders begin to see their families as well as their role(s) in the family with less pain and less confusion. What happens is this: As the pain is felt and dealt with, it moves out of the body, leaving the person freer to view the family in a different, clearer perspective. Literally, transcenders' view of their world (internal frame of reference) is more honest, less inhibited, less confused with conflicting emotions, and more in tune with what really is and was in their family. (Emotional pain distorts how we view our world and influences our behavior and decisions.) It is during this step that individuals get a clearer view of the damage their family has done. In addition, understanding, or insights, about past and present functioning—thoughts, feelings, and behavior—is developed. One transcender described this step this way: "I never thought the tears would end. I really didn't believe my therapist. But they did! I now see why I felt so bad! My family really hurt me."

Understanding the Childhood

Understanding their childhood is another essential part of the healing process for transcenders. As adults, transcenders must know what happened to them in order to heal. They work hard to develop an understanding of what happened to them as children and the influences it has had on their adult life. As adults, they go back to childhood traumas to heal that inner part of them that was so hurt and still feels like a hurt child (inner child). They reexperience their childhood with all its grief and reclaim the parts of themselves that are lost in childhood. Transcenders must refeel, reexamine, reclaim, and grieve everything that is part of the traumatic past.

An understanding of the past has to include the mental, emotional, physical, and spiritual parts for transcenders. Understanding their past helps them to accept what happened and to love their inner child, who is so hurt by the past. They learn that they were helpless children who were abused by people who were emotionally ill. They are able to forgive themselves for not being able to stop the abuse or for being "so stupid." Many transcenders believe that they should somehow have been able to stop the abuse and failed. As a result, they are angry at themselves and have rejected their inner child. As adults, they maturely explore this anger, and their relationship with themselves is healed.

Gaining an understanding of the past also includes working hard to sort out family "games." These games include "We're perfect, but crazy"; "You're the crazy one, we're all fine"; "Let's pretend the elephant in the living room is not there"; and "We are all kids, you're the adult." Each game needs to be closely examined and explored. With this understanding comes the choice to continue or stop the games.

Behavioral Changes

Understanding continues as transcenders work in therapy and become more aware of the damage caused by their families. They become better able to make healthy decisions about themselves and their world. At times, changes seem to occur easily and naturally; at other times, old patterns are extremely difficult to change and a concerted effort is needed. Changes occur in all areas of life: relationships, work, play, goals, family of origin, and present family interactions.

Basically, transcenders work to change the patterns they had to develop as children in order to survive. These patterns are no longer needed and now interfere with healthy, productive living. Therapists help sort the patterns that are healthy and needed from the ones from the past that are no longer usable. The final decisions about which patterns to change are always the transcenders', not the therapists'.

Learning to Take Care of Themselves

One of the important changes that occurs is that transcenders learn to take care of themselves appropriately and lovingly. In dysfunctional families, transcenders are not only not taken care of appropriately but, most likely, have had to take care of others in extreme forms in order to survive. Often, they have been taught that they don't count and that their only worth is in caring for others.

Transcenders often need to love themselves in special ways. They do this by doing things just for themselves. This is often difficult and sometimes guilt-producing. The guilt comes from the fear of being abused. The message from the family is usually "Don't take care of you. Only take care of me. If you try to take care of you, I'll hurt you." Or "You don't deserve anything." The transcenders' response is, for example, "If I take care of me, Mom might call me selfish and become angry. If she becomes angry, I could be hit." The guilt that once kept them safe in childhood is no longer needed as an adult.

To deal with the guilt, I have transcenders thank themselves for taking care of them all these years. I tell them to allow the guilt to be and not to fight with it, then to say they now have a better way to keep themselves safe. They have to go on and take care of themselves even if they feel guilty. The guilt lifts.

In the beginning, I recommend starting by doing little things, such as taking a long nurturing bath by candlelight, going for a walk, being with a friend, listening to special music, or even being alone. Bigger things may include taking a special vacation, changing jobs, or even moving to a long-dreamed-of home. Taking care of oneself is *anything* that nurtures and expresses love to the authentic self *and* is not harmful to oneself or others. It is a fun discovery journey because most transcenders have not had a chance to learn about themselves. It's a time to find out what they like as well as what they don't like. If something is liked, it needs to be continued. If something is not liked, it doesn't have to be repeated. The important part of this stage is to make it a *fun*, growthful journey: a journey to discover the self.

Time Off

Another significant part of the healing process is to take time off from formal therapy. This time off may be for a week, a month, a year, or several years. This is *not* an avoidance of issues. This time allows the transcender to think about, explore, experience, and adjust to the many new changes that have occurred in therapy. The break also gives relief and solidifies what has been learned. This is not a break from the healing or growth process, just from formal therapy. Healing and growth always continue.

This break is needed because the healing and growth process is very intense and may take years. Transcenders need to play, laugh, and take a break from the intensity of formal therapy. Also, some transcenders are so determined to heal and grow, that they can create self-abuse with therapy that corresponds to and continues the child-hood patterns of abuse. By self-abuse, I mean pushing oneself so hard for so long that joy and relaxation never occur. There *has* to be a time to relax and praise oneself for what has been accomplished and for doing things differently from one's family. There has to be time for fun and a more "normal" way of living. Transcenders usually know when they are ready for a break. Life feels a lot better, and they are experiencing joy, changed behavior, and a sense of "I feel complete for right now."

Returning to Therapy

A deeper level of healing and growth occurs when transcenders return to therapy after a time off. Not everyone takes time off, and not everyone returns to therapy. Some return more than one time. Again, it is an individual process. Those who do return experience a deeper, more intense healing. There may be a lot of fear surrounding this exploration, but transcenders go after the healing. Transcenders at this point in the healing and growth process gain a different look at their survivorship. Some even see positive traits they gained from their childhood.

Returning to therapy often coincides with a person's midlife transition (or crisis, as some call it). At this stage, transcenders' process sends them as far back as the origin of the hurt and damage. Often, this is as far back as infancy. Grieving and reclaiming the losses of childhood are intensified during this period, with wonderful results that offer more freedom and more authenticity.

There is a powerful surge at this stage to heal all of the hurt at the deepest possible layer. The mind, spirit, and body seem to demand this deep healing to create an integrated, functioning being. Essentially, it is a deep cleansing of everything that is blocking the authentic self. At times, it's like a volcanic eruption with enormous intensity that clears out everything that is blocking the flow of the original package. Without this, it is difficult for transcenders to get through the midlife transition and to begin the second half of life. As in the previous steps, all feelings have to be felt and understood.

Completion

After the previous step, transcenders usually do not return to formal therapy. They have learned to process their feelings and thoughts and to change unwanted behavior. They have learned to set realistic goals and to create positive changes in their world. They have developed healthy relationships with others as well as with themselves. After the completion of formal therapy, transcenders continue their personal self-growth journey. They may take seminars, workshops, group intensives, classes, and so on for the rest of their lives. They never view their development and growth as complete.

Tune-Ups

Sometimes, transcenders go back into therapy for what I call a *tune-up*. A tune-up is one or more sessions that focus on their process of growth. It is a reaffirmation of where they are in their lives and/or a reexamination of old issues. Whatever is explored, it is usually not intense or long-term. Each transcender is different in his or her need for tune-ups.

CONCLUSION

What is left after the above steps are healed scars and twinges of pain when experiences trigger memories of the old feelings and thoughts. There may even be a revisiting once in a while, but it is usually not with the past intensity or duration.

There are no fairy-tale endings: Life is difficult. But life can be good and full, with the full range of feelings, learning, and growth and without the past haunting that at every step influenced decisions and behavior. There can be a deep, inner peace and a true sense of freedom.

The healing and growth process is centered on the self. Many transcenders feel selfish because they have been taught well to care for others and not for themselves. It is definitely not selfish. It is a personal, unique, important process by which transcenders learn to take care of themselves by focusing their energies, time, and money on healing and growing out of past trauma. If you are a transcender, take care of yourself, give to yourself, and explore what you are all about. Take all that you need to heal; it's worth it. The selfish and guilty feelings can be dealt with in therapy. This healing is essential to moving on in your world. Remember, when it does feel selfish, know that unless you take care of yourself first, you will have nothing to give anyone else.

If, during the healing process, you get pressure from well-meaning friends and family to stop the process because it's too painful, because you're not taking care of them, or because the past is over and you should forget it, tell them, very politely, that it is not over for you. Tell them you feel the pain every day and it is influencing your life. Educate them. Teach them how you need them to be your friends. Remember that, as long as it is alive in you and you feel it, it is not in the past. It is in the present moment.

In closing this chapter, I leave you with these thoughts:

> The only way through pain . . . is to go through it, to absorb, probe, understand exactly what it is and what it means. To close the door on pain is to miss the chance for growth . . . Nothing that happens to us, even the most terrible shock, is unusable. And, everything somehow has to be built into the fabric of the personality just as food has to be built in. (Sarton, 1980, p. 21)

Chapter 7

Grieving the Dysfunctional Family

It seems very appropriate that I am beginning this chapter after the death of a dear cousin. It is the day before Easter, and my cousin died on Wednesday night. He died of cancer, an agonizing death with intense struggles. Tom adjusted his life to battle the disease by changing his behavior, living style, and eating patterns and doing anything that had the hope of bringing more energy and life to his dying body.

I am keenly aware of my feelings about my cousin's death. I feel the death. It is an intense, deep pain and longing, a deep missing that nothing and no one can ever change. I grieve the times I will no longer have with my cousin as well as the times I wish had been different. I will miss the times that could have been and weren't. I grieve for what I had and what I didn't have. The missing will be there forever. It may not be at the intensity it is now, but it will always be there.

I feel my whole pattern of living trying to avoid the pain of the missing, loss, and loneliness for my cousin. My old system, my old way of dealing with pain, desperately wants to take over so I can stop feeling the pain. I want to eat more, stay extremely busy, put myself under more stress, and confuse my thinking—anything to stop the pain and to be able to go on with my life as if everything were fine. I want my world to be back to a more innocent age. I am also angry at the world, cancer, doctors, and God for not saving my cousin. I find myself screaming at God and the world with tears and anguish.

The worst part is that I really can't stop the pain; that's an illusion. I must go through it, feel it, and learn from it. Even though it is painful and seems futile, there isn't any other way. That's my new healthy system, authenticity in my feelings. I must own and feel what I am experiencing. Thankfully, my new system wins. But I will never be the same naive person again. I have grown and changed. I have become more patient, more understanding, and wiser. These are my healings and growth from feeling my cousin's death.

Grieving a dysfunctional family is *exactly* like my grieving for my cousin. It is intense, painful, and lonely, with deep longings and missings. Grieving is the part of the healing process that screams with anguish and tears for what *was* in the family as well as what *was not* in the family. There is a missing of times that never were, a longing for times that should have been, and a deep sorrow and rage for the abuse that was. This missing will always be at some level; it will never completely go away. Its intensity will change, but the missing will still exist. It's like a wound that completely heals but leaves a scar that reminds us of the injury. The intensity of the grief changes when all the pain is completely felt *and* every piece of learning is gleaned from it. It may seem futile at the time, but from the process, there is not only healing, but incredible growth.

While one is growing up in a dysfunctional family, one changes many behaviors in order to stop the pain, as well as to gain energy and life as my cousin did fighting cancer. Individuals work to adjust and keep going. One of the primary purposes of the old patterns is to keep feelings out of awareness and the authentic self protected. Neither are safe while one is growing up in a dysfunctional family. The grief is held off, denied, avoided, projected onto others, and handled in any way possible so that one can avoid feeling and keep going. This is survival in its basic form. The grieving process that is part of the healing from a dysfunctional family is the feeling of stored, unfelt feelings. Avoiding the grief supports survival, *but* it is usually dysfunctional in adulthood because grief demands tears, deep, gut-wrenching tears. Stopping the pain blocks this release.

During grieving times, we need to be held and encouraged to cry. We need to be angry, sad, and disillusioned and to express our anguish. It is through our tears that we release the pain and trauma and learn to accept what was and is. Without the tears, there is no cleansing, no release, no healing, and no hope for the future. Without the pain, there is no learning or growth.

TRANSCENDERS' GRIEVING PROCESS

My grieving for my cousin contains many areas of loss for me. I have lost a person with whom I shared over forty years of special memories. I have lost a sense of more innocent times. I have lost a dear friend, someone I knew I could call if I needed help. I knew that he was in my life and that we cared about each other. I have lost part of my family. It feels as if nothing will be fine again, not really.

Transcenders have similar losses because of growing up in a dysfunctional family. There is a loss of never having had a happy, normal childhood. The loss of innocence from their childhood can never be regained, any more than I can regain the loss of my innocence in the death of my cousin. Transcenders have also lost the chance of ever having the loving parents they so desperately wanted and needed. Even if they heal their relationships with their parents in adulthood, their parents of childhood remain dysfunctional.

Other losses in childhood include the loss of closeness with others, the loss of trust with others, the loss of having needs appropriately met, the loss of appropriate dependency, the loss of ever fully being a child, the loss of knowing how to play, the loss of knowing who one is, the loss of dignity as a person, the loss of feeling safe and protected, and the loss of feeling accepted and loved for just oneself.

Also lost are opportunities to excel in certain areas. This does not mean never participating in an area, but excelling in it as a child. For example, if I wanted to be a top gymnast and my parents blocked all my opportunities to do so, I have not lost the chance to participate in gymnastics, but I have lost the chance to excel because of my age.

Not all transcenders have all the above losses. Each transcender has unique losses to grieve. However, *all* losses must be fully grieved for at a deep, intense level and for as *long* as needed. Grieving includes many different kinds of feelings: denial, anger, making deals with God, sadness, and finally, acceptance of and/or forgiveness for what was and is. These feelings occur in no specific order, may occur at the same time, and may also recur. They may also flow from one to another and then back again. For example, with the death of my cousin, I felt intense sadness that shifted to anger, then to denial, and then to anger and sadness again. I still don't accept it. It takes time to work through all the feelings and finally arrive at acceptance.

In essence, grieving a dysfunctional family means feeling all feelings fully, gaining an understanding of what has happened from an adult perspective, learning from the experience, and finally experiencing the end product, the blessing, of acceptance and/or forgiveness.

Some mental health workers consider forgiveness the essential end point of the grieving process. I do not. There are some families, like Marie's, in which the damage was so intense and so awful that *I* can't even imagine forgiving them, let alone expect her to. Forgiveness, to me, is more than letting go of the situation. It is a pardoning or giving of grace to another person. If forgiveness is possible, it aids in the healing. However, acceptance can be enough because it is a letting go of the pain and moving on with one's life.

The process of grieving a dysfunctional family has no specific time line. As described in Chapter 5, a process begins at and takes its own time. The process comes to completion when it is fully experienced. The person needs to allow it to run its course until the tears, anger, sadness, and agony of the losses end. Unhappiness and frustration continue if the individual decides not to do the grieving work. The individual becomes stuck, alters behavior, and cannot grow. This state is called *neurosis* in the mental health field.

HOW GRIEVING BEGINS

There are a number of ways the grieving process can begin. Like the turning point, transcenders' pain and loneliness in adulthood are often the trigger. Incidents in life can also be a trigger. At times, the person resists the process and the therapist must be a guide into the grieving. The guiding can be done by transcenders' describing in detail the experiences of their childhood. From this description comes an awareness of the dysfunction in which they grew up; this awareness is followed by the unfelt feelings. Transcenders can then no longer contain the feelings and maintain the old way of living in the face of the facts. The grieving process is then under way.

Another way grieving starts is by the discovery that old patterns of living and getting along in the world don't work anymore. Transcenders come to a point of saying, "I can't do this any more"; "I'm not going to make it"; "I don't have the energy to keep this up." The "this" is having used all their inner drive and energy to maintain the old, inauthentic, protective way of living. They know they can't continue, but may not know what is wrong and what to change. This feeling may be so intense and so overwhelming that it may feel as if they are going to have a physical or emotional collapse. What is really happening is that the transcenders no longer have the energy to stop the feelings that are surfacing by using the old patterns of being. They also no longer have the energy to maintain the old pattern of living. At this point, transcenders often experience a deep, *inner-core tiredness*. It is a tiredness that sleep does not change or touch. It comes from living and working hard to survive for decades. The only relief is to release feelings and change behavior. No matter how the grieving starts, the losses of childhood must be revisited and grieved.

THE DECISION TO HEAL

At this point, a decision to heal or not to heal is made. Sometimes, the decision is easy. Other times, it is painful and difficult. The fear of the pain and destruction is what prevents transcenders from just surrendering to their grieving. Remember, there is a belief that to feel may cause insanity or death. The greater the abuse, the greater the fear of feeling. The greater the fear of feeling, the more the grief process is held back to protect the transcender.

The decision to heal is made just as was the decision to survive the family. The individual lives with the pain and frustrations and arrives at a powerful decision to heal and continue to grow. Deciding to heal also entails a recommitment to their childhood personal-growth decision. In any grieving process, there is a choice to heal or to block the feelings and continue to suffer. Transcenders choose to heal. The following shows the process of making the decision to heal by Steve, who was the scapegoat of a family that physically, emotionally, and sexually abused him as well as neglected him:

Donna: Steve it's time to do your feeling work from your past. I know the feelings are awful and are triggering intense fear in you. I also know you are feeling suicidal and want desperately not to feel.

Steve: I can't make it. It's too painful. It's too much. Just too much. I am so sad. I just want to die. I *have* to die. I just have to die. There is no other way. My kids would be better off. Their mother then would have to take care of them. They'd have my insurance. There is no other way. I've decided to die. (*Steve did not want to die; he just wanted to get out of the pain and saw no other way.*)

Donna: Sounds as if you see no hope of ever getting through this pain. The pain must be horrible. Tell me about it.

Steve: It's so bad. I can't stand it. I can't live this way. There is absolutely no hope. Not for me or my kids. Suicide is the only way out. I'm crying all the time. All I do is cry. I can't stand it anymore. I just can't do it. I just can't go on. No one cares about me. No one helps me. Not even you. You're just paid to be here. You don't really care. Not really.

Donna: *(At this point Steve wants me to take responsibility for his pain and make me do his feeling work for him. When I hear this, I say and mean the following)*: Steve, I wish I could take the pain away. I would give anything to have the power and ability to end your suffering. I can see you are suffering terribly, and if I could, I would do your healing work for you. But it doesn't work that way. I have to do my healing and feeling work, and you have to do yours. I wish with all my heart I could take the pain away.

This type of dialogue continued for a month. Steve worked harder and harder for me to be responsible for him. He did this by going into crisis and sometimes, running out of sessions. Finally, after much pain, the following dialogue took place over the phone:

Steve: I've finally heard you. I know now you can't do my feeling work for me. I even sort of believe you wish you could. (*Trust builds slowly.*) I have decided to do whatever I have to do to get through this. I want to get through the suicide stuff. I wish there was another way. God, do I wish there was another way. But I know there really isn't. I just wanted to call you and tell you what I have decided.

Donna: Steve, I am so excited for you. You can now fully grieve your childhood and heal. Yes, there will be pain and intense struggles, but there will also be joy, love, and learning.

Steve and I continued to work together, and he was able to work through the pain and to begin to receive love in his life. He also created new ways of relating to and living in the world. The suicidal thoughts and feelings left.

Other transcenders know where they have to go, and the choice is easy and determined. This was the case with Paul:

Paul

I'll do anything to heal. I want to be better. I want to feel normal and healthy. Somewhere I lost it. Tell me what to do to heal, and I'll do it. I never want to go back to the old way again. Never!

* * *

When I am working with clients who are grieving, I feel deeply for them and I wish I could feel the pain for them. I can't. It is theirs, not mine. The grief is deep and ages old. It is scary and very hard to accept, let alone feel. In the grieving process, transcenders become more and more aware of what they did and didn't have in their families. They also become intensely aware of their pain and loneliness. The process consists of the adult grieving the losses as well as feeling the pain from all the experiences in childhood. The feelings have to be felt and understood for changes in life to occur. Here are some descriptions from transcenders about their grieving process:

Sylvia

I just knew I was going to die. I felt as if I had the best case of the flu without really having the flu. My stomach was upset. I had diarrhea and a severe headache. These symptoms seem to take turns torturing me. I was also dizzy and tired. No amount of sleep shifted my fatigue. I walked around in a daze and couldn't think clearly for weeks. My kids complained about my not remembering things they said, and I didn't! I wouldn't even remember them talking to me. I was so inner-focused that I was barely aware of others around me. If they did intrude, I became short-tempered and nasty. I was working hard just to exist with all the pain. I really thought I was going to die.

———————————— *Tiffany* ————————————

Tiffany comes from a strict traditional family where the abuses were harder to pinpoint, so her grieving process began a little differently:

I always felt sad and abused. It took me a long time to figure out where the feelings came from because my family looked great. I had productive parents and siblings who were liked in the community and successful in many ways. I kept asking myself just what was my problem. What was wrong with me, because it wasn't them, or was it? While working in therapy, I finally began to figure it out. It really wasn't me, but the dysfunction of my family. I was never allowed to be me. I had to be the caretaker, traditional girl, and responsible one. I also believe I was a scapegoat for my brothers. I don't ever remember being just me except when I was alone.

What I learned in therapy was that I was still playing the role I had been well trained for in childhood — this time as the adult. However, by this time, there was only a little of the real me left in my life. Before knowing this, I believed that I had to be happy because I had everything a person could want. As an adult, I had a house in the suburbs, an executive husband, two kids, a dog, and a cat. I looked the image of success and happiness. Because I had everything, I thought I had to be happy. Finally, after a lot of hard work in therapy, I knew what to grieve. I then gave myself permission to feel my deep sorrow.

Once the grieving started, it was horrible. I longed for the daddy that was always at work and never there for me. I longed to be held and loved. I desperately wanted someone to see me for me. I wanted my siblings to at least talk to me as a real person, not as just my role or an object to ridicule. I wanted a mother who would break away from her traditional role and be a complete, whole, functioning, loving person. They all wanted a "little girl" who performed like a little, perfect, traditional, caretaking robot. Especially Mom, she wanted and needed someone to take care of her sadness and loneliness. They didn't want me. I felt each and every loss and pain.

I even had to mourn my own death, the death of the child I always wanted to be. I imagined me, putting me in my coffin, and then sent me to a place to regenerate. I literally gave birth to myself as I died. The false me had to die in order to give birth to the real me.

My grieving was at such a deep level that I thought my insides were going to explode. At times, I'd cry, not knowing what I was crying about. Other times, I knew exactly what the loss was. What was neat was that every time I did cry, get angry, and express my feelings, I felt better and more like me — the real me.

Marie

At the time I began therapy, I honestly wasn't aware of a past to grieve. I knew my father had raped me soon after my parents divorced, and I never saw him again. I was aware that, before having children, I had gone into therapy because I didn't have very positive feelings about families in general. I had always felt unloved and unwanted. I also knew there were a lot of gaps in my usually good memory. Nothing, however, could have prepared me for the memories and feelings of the past that were so deeply hidden. The memories began to surface when I was in therapy and felt safe to deal with them.

In my fantasy, I had created a loving, caring, "perfect" family that I had failed. However, as memories began to surface, I couldn't believe the terrors and tortures. In the early stages of therapy, I hypnotized myself to allow the memories to come into awareness. Frequently, feelings would surface before the memory. Sometimes, I could feel the anger of my therapist toward my parents for the tortures they performed on me. I, on the other hand, would try to defend their actions. After all, it must have been my fault; I was there. If I hadn't been present, then maybe they wouldn't have tied me up, urinated on me, locked me out, etc.

Another thing I knew before therapy was that my father was an alcoholic and we moved constantly. From the first to the sixth grade, I never began and ended the year in the same school. As I began to match memories to feelings, I came to realize that not only was the "happy childhood" a farce, but so were the two people I desperately wanted to be good enough to be loved by: my father and mother.

Before any grieving could begin, it was necessary to allow myself to remember what had really happened. Deeply implanted in me was a tape from my parents and their cotorturers that said, "If you ever tell anyone the things that go on, no one will believe you, and you will be put up for adoption for causing trouble. *And* something will happen to anyone that you become friends with because you cause bad things to happen to people." Basically, if I ever told anyone, I would have to be punished and die. I often became suicidal during therapy because of this tape even though I didn't want to die. Sometimes, the pressure was so strong that I had to fight with myself (and sometimes my therapist) to stay alive.

As I listened to the tapes of those particular sessions (we taped sessions so I could go over and over them to learn about me), I felt ice water run through my veins when I heard myself talk about my own suicide. I explained how and why it had to be done just as if I were talking about the weather. In fact, it was a long time before my voice held any emotion when I would talk about being sexually abused by my parents, being locked out in the cold, or listening to my parents plan how they were going to kill me and make it look like an accident.

It wasn't until I was ready to put memories and feelings together that my voice on the tape changed from relaying factual information to the terror and sobs of a terrified child. It was at this point that I truly began to grieve what had never been nor ever could be. At the same time, I began to grieve for what I did have — the evil, satanically warped people who acted out their emotions on an innocent child. No wonder I could never be "good enough" to be loved by them.

I remember my therapist saying I would have to grieve for my past as part of the process of becoming emotionally and physically healthy. I thought she was talking about sad feelings, but I came to know that there were no words that adequately described the horrible, desperate, lonely feelings. I had to relive the past with feelings and memories matching. Each time I did, more garbage came to the surface. I tried very hard to use the old ways of blocking so I wouldn't hurt so bad. Nothing anyone could have told me would have prepared me for the deep, intense pain — both physical and emotional — that was to be a necessary part of my healing as layer after layer was slowly peeled away to reveal the real me.

When I fought the feelings, I discovered two things: (1) I had lost most of my old coping mechanisms and was not able to push the feelings back to stop the hurt as I had before therapy, and (2) the harder I fought not to feel, the more intense was the pain. It was only by feeling the hurt that I began not to hurt quite so much. I would go through several days or even weeks of pure hell, which would usually, thank God, be followed by a real growth spurt. I would think, "Thank goodness it is over," only to have the hurt and grief triggered at another layer.

When this happened it felt as if I was going backward in my therapy, and I would complain to my therapist that "I had done this before." I wanted instant cure. After all, the abuse had occurred over a period of fifteen or sixteen years. Why should it take more than a few months to make everything better?

Just about the time things would start to feel great (that was my own personal indicator of progress), along would come another period of deep sadness and loneliness. Many times, I tried to give my feelings away to my therapist, to get her to do my feeling work for me. Fortunately, she cared enough to give them right back to me, reminding me that they were my feelings and my memories, not hers. She was there for me; she could feel with me, but never for me. That was a very hard lesson to learn. Sometimes, I got angry at her because, before I started working with her, I hadn't had the lonely feelings. Instead, I had had migraine headaches, inflammatory bowel disease, and asthma.

I occasionally have periods of grief and pain, but it will never be as bad as it was. The periods are shorter and less intense. I now know that these periods won't last forever, whereas it felt earlier as if they would never end. I can't say I welcome them, but I'm learning to recognize the painful times as periods of growth. I'm convinced that the only way to get rid of the hurt is to feel it with all the intensity that is locked inside. For me, physical and emotional pain are closely linked. As the emotional pain eases, so does the physical. Freedom from the pain of the past is worth the grief. I am becoming a growing, healthy, fully functioning human being.

Chris

Chris, like many individuals, remembers prebirth experiences such as abortion attempts. We remember everything that has happened to us at a deep inner level. This is not unusual, but it is rarely talked about. In the following description, Chris talks about having two therapists. He had a psychotherapist, as well as a masseuse who helped him to do energy and body work. Here is Chris's experience of his grieving process:

Grieving for me was having the courage to feel and eventually accept the fact that my family did not want or love me. Being blamed for everything that was wrong in my family was horrible to grieve. For years, I worked hard and was successful in avoiding those feelings. I was terrified of feeling the rejection, sadness, and anger because I believed that if I felt them, I wouldn't make it. I also believed that I would become crazy or nonfunctioning like my family. I resisted and resisted until I realized that, to be the person I've always wanted to be and have the life I've always wanted, I had to do my feeling work.

It was horrible. I was terrified and felt crazy — the exact feelings I had tried so hard to avoid all those years. I cried so hard and so long I thought I'd be in pain forever. Once I had actually done some of the grieving, I felt relief and, amazingly, began to feel joy. I also started to understand my family and my role in the family and to realize that it was not really me they hated; they would have hated anyone born at that particular time and assigned that particular role in the family.

I learned this when I regressed emotionally and remembered my mother trying to abort me in the womb. It made me realize that she didn't really know me at all. She was just trying to get rid of *any* next baby.

There was a time during my grieving process when my therapists had to help me stop self-abusing. Because of the past and all its rejection and abuse, I had learned never to be nice to me. If I got something good, I had to punish myself. My way of punishing me consisted of keeping my healing and growth process at such an intense level that I was constantly in turmoil. I never allowed joy into my life.

My pattern went like this: As I grieved, I began to feel better. The better I felt, the more I gained, and the more intense I became in my pursuit of growth. I pursued it with such determination that I was constantly in pain. What I actually did was to stay in pain all the time by creating a supereffort to rid myself of all past pain in a very short time. This punished me by stopping the good feelings. My process became very difficult and self-abusing in the name of growth. I felt a lot of sorrow in this area. Wasn't my parents' abuse punishment enough? Did *I* have to do the abuse also? With the help of my therapists I began to see the pattern and the need to relax and play as I healed. With a concerted effort, I stopped the abusive pattern and began to live and enjoy my life a little more.

Steve

Steve is the transcender who grew up in poverty and neglect. Here is his description of the grieving process:

When I finally began therapy, I was a basket case. I was confused and frustrated, and my life just didn't seem to be going anywhere. The more I tried, the more frustrated I became. I hated me, my world, and everyone in it. The worst part was that I had no idea what was wrong. I had tried everything I knew, and nothing was working anymore.

Once in therapy, I was told that I was in the process of grieving my past. I was also told that I was frustrated because I was fighting and resisting the grieving. My childhood decision to keep going and never, never to go back was now interfering with my healing the past. Because I had decided never to go back and always to go forward, I believed that feeling the past was going backward. That is where I was frustrated and confused. I needed to feel the past, yet my commitment to myself wouldn't allow it. I really believed that if I felt it, I would become like my family: nonfunctioning, unable to support myself, and dirt poor.

Allowing myself to feel was very hard. I had so much fear: fear of being like them, fear of not being able to take care of myself, fear of losing my commitment to never go back, fear, fear, fear. I finally understood that in order to heal, I had to grieve. Once I understood it, I was able to work through all of it and am so grateful I did.

——————————————— *Paul* ———————————————

Paul was severely criticized and ridiculed and felt as if he never belonged in his family. Here are some of his words about his grieving:

I had so much to grieve. So much. I had to grieve all of it. I had to grieve each and everything that happened to me, every critical word, every ridicule. I couldn't believe the memories that kept coming up. I had to feel every feeling about each memory. I remembered things as a two- and three-year-old. I even had an image of being neglected as an infant. I really wasn't sure that the memories or the grief would end.

Donna kept telling me that I would not be overwhelmed or die in the grieving process. I didn't believe her. I knew I couldn't make it. I fought it like crazy. I didn't want to feel it because I believed — no, I knew — that I would not survive if I did. This was one of the ways I had protected the real me. I firmly believed that if I felt the feelings from my childhood, I would lose control and go insane. It took me a long time to give myself permission to grieve. I had been raised not to feel and definitely not to cry. It was tough. I had to make a *definite* decision to grieve and feel. My choice was to grieve and continue to grow or to stop and die at some inner level. The dying was intolerable to me. That would have violated my childhood decision to grow and develop.

My resistance was that if I felt all the old pain, my world would end. And it did. My world will never be the same. I see my childhood as painful and intensely lonely. There is no more illusion that I had "terrific parents." I had parents who did more than their own parents, but who failed to protect me and nurture me emotionally.

I was told I "needed too much." In reality, I did need—I desperately needed nurturance and love at a deep level. The "too much" part came because I had never had it and needed all those lost years' worth. I didn't need "too much." I had just been given "too little."

While doing the grieving work, I just knew the tears would never end. Again, when Donna said they would when all my sadness had been felt, I didn't believe her. It just seemed that all I did was cry for a long time. After a lot of grieving, the tears finally did end.

I still remember the pain of the memories; it was horrible. Sometimes, I felt I was going to be wiped out or die. I did neither, but that's how bad it got some days. Through the grieving I lost my innocence at a deep level. I desperately wanted to believe that I had been cared about as a child on some level. I wasn't. I know now that my parents were just trying to survive while I was growing up. They did not have the patience, time, money, love, or anything else to offer me. This is sad and tragic, but I have come to accept it.

SUICIDAL FEELINGS AND
THE GRIEVING PROCESS

Suicidal feelings, as you may have noticed in some of the transcenders' descriptions, are sometimes a part of the grieving process and usually come from three areas. The first is family tapes, such as "I want you dead!" and "You're bad and need to die." Tapes like these are deeply ingrained and are acted out on some level. In the healing process, the more the transcender feels and the more the layers of pain lift, the closer the transcenders get to the old tapes and the more suicidal they may become. For example, Marie was told repeatedly that if she was worth anything, she would die. Her parents also told her that they didn't understand why she was around and that they wanted her dead. For a while, every time Marie processed a deep layer, she became suicidal. Once the process and the feelings were understood, the suicidal feelings lessened. It's important to remember that transcenders don't want to die but are acting on old well-rehearsed tapes.

The second trigger of the suicidal feelings is the experiences themselves. When children are being abused, there is a real fear that they are going to be killed by the parents. The children push away and bury these feelings of intense fear in order to continue fighting to survive. In adulthood, the fear becomes, "If I feel these feelings, I will die." In the healing process, the fear is felt and owned. As part of the suicidal thoughts, the child may see death as a relief from the brutality of life.

The third area that arouses suicidal feelings is the grieving process itself. Grief may be intense, deep, agonizing, painful, and lonely. It is not unusual that dying is seen as a way out of the pain. Suicidal feelings often occur in the beginning of the grieving process, when the grieving is at its greatest intensity and the person has not yet learned that once the feelings are felt fully, she or he will feel better.

Fear often acts like an electrical fence, putting a protective barrier around the real self. The closer one gets, the more danger is sensed and the more fear is triggered. All the fence knows is to protect the person from the feelings because the feelings mean danger and possibly death. If touched, the fear is so great that the person believes he or she will die. This fear, which protects transcenders from emotional collapse in childhood, is triggered in the healing process by the lifting of layers. The closer one comes to the fence (and the real

self), the more intense is the fear and the more suicidal feelings there
are. Fortunately, this stage usually does not last long.

During this time, transcenders need a strong, available support
system that works to protect them from hurting themselves and to
ensure their safety. Also, transcenders need to know from their
therapist that they are in a difficult stage, but that it will pass and they
will survive. They need to understand the fear and the suicidal
feelings. What I tell transcenders with whom I am working is this:
"The fear kept you safe while you were growing up. It protected you
from emotional collapse and enabled you to survive. It also, and very
importantly, kept your real self hidden and protected from the onslaught. You will survive these feelings even though it doesn't feel like
it. The suicidal feelings will end. I want you safe and alive. You have
come too far to give up now. It is vital that you keep the promises you
made to yourself as a child. You can always choose to die; you can only
choose to live right now. I want you to live, and I know you do, too.

STAGES IN THE GRIEVING PROCESS

Even though transcenders' grieving processes are unique in
content, duration, intensity, and order, there are similar stages. As you
read, be aware that each stage may occur many times and in any order.

Video Tapes

The experience of grieving, as stated before, is a revisiting of the
past as an adult. Memories from childhood are revisited in such a way
that they seem to be relived in the present moment. Old tapes such as
"You'll never amount to anything"; "You're no good"; "Why don't you
just die!"; and "We never did want you" are played back with
incredible intensity and vividness. Transcenders hear or see incidents
as if a video is playing back the scene and they are part of it. These

relived experiences trigger intense, deep, old pain. This pain *must* be experienced fully in the present moment for healing to occur. Because it is so difficult, I often wish I had a magic wand to take the pain away. I can't. Each one of us must do our own revisiting.

Denial

Denial is refusing to accept what is. Memories, thoughts, and feelings contradict the truth, which is often kept out of memory entirely. In denial, transcenders want to deny and not to feel what has happened to them. They may also want to continue the illusion that they had "perfect and loving" parents.

The problem with denial is that it blocks healing. Transcenders must come out of denial in order to heal. This can be done gently and lovingly, but it is often difficult and requires time in therapy before memories surface. The reason it is difficult is that the denied truth often contains painful information and feelings. Additionally, transcenders sometimes fight the surfacing memories because there is intense fear built up around the memory to keep the transcender away from it.

Some transcenders are so successful in denying memories and feelings that they have no awareness whatsoever of the memory. This denial may be so successful that memories are blocked for years and surface for the "first" time during the healing process. The memory block acts as a protection and a survival technique that enables the transcenders to keep going.

When working with the resistance to coming out of denial, I approach transcenders this way:

> "Tom, I know the memories are awful. I know you don't want to remember them, let alone own them, but they are yours. When you have a memory and you are trying to deny it, you must know that is how you survived. Thank yourself for taking care of you so well all those years. Then say 'I now can take care of

myself in a different way.' Know you can transform that energy
used for denial into healing and growth energy."

With this kind of support, encouragement, *and* gentleness, memories and feelings that have been in denial for years or even decades
can surface and be healed.

Feeling the Sadness

The essence of grief is sadness. *All* the sadness of *all* past
experiences must be felt at a deep, intense level. The sadness is not
only for what was, but also for what was not. Transcenders cry because
of abuses, neglect, deprivations, lost dreams, and lost relationships.
The sadness is often described as "tears that seem to have no end"
and that "go on forever." The sadness is so intense that it feels as if
"your insides will burst." Often, the deep sorrow has many layers that
the transcenders must work through. Relief comes when all the
sadness is felt and experienced and all the layers are released.

Shame and Defectiveness

Shame is a deep feeling of guilt, remorse, disgrace, and failure.
During the grieving process, transcenders often uncover a belief or
fear of being terrible and defective like their families. The belief is
often based on old family tapes, such as "You are dumb and stupid";
"You are not good for anything"; "You are worthless"; "What in the
world is the matter with you!"; "Don't you know better?"; "Your head
is screwed on backwards." The shame of the family's abuse and
neglect is often taken on by the transcenders as their shame. The
shame is not theirs. The shame may run deep and is often attached to
deep feelings of sorrow. Feeling defective and feeling shameful
combine to create deep sorrow and a deep hidden secret that they, the
transcenders, are not only not OK, but are so awful that they should
hide their real selves from everyone, including themselves.

Feeling defective and shameful is another loss that must be grieved. Essentially, it is the loss of a grounding of confidence, security, and trust in knowing that they are OK just the way they are. In therapy, it is the therapists' job to gently and firmly help transcenders realize that it is not their but the family's dysfunction that is wrong.

Loneliness

Loneliness seems to be one of the most difficult feelings to feel in the grieving area. Transcenders must reexperience the loneliness of childhood with all of its agonizing tears, fears, sadness, and emptiness as well as the loneliness of the present. Transcenders lock this loneliness away in order to survive. Feeling it means being devastated and realizing that no one—no one—was really there for them.

For the child, feeling loneliness means facing a form of death. We can understand this by looking at the situation of infants. No one there means no caretaking. No caretaking means no food. No food means eventual death. This is known at a deep level but is too terrifying to remember until transcenders are in a safe, nurturing space in adulthood.

Steve gives a description of feeling the double charge of loneliness of both the past and the present:

———————————————— *Steve* ————————————————

In my loneliness, I feel as if I'm always on the outside looking in—as if I never belong. I feel as if I somehow don't fit in. I transcend my "old world" with its awfulness and pain. I like my "new world," which I created, but parts of it don't fit for me either. It's a lonely feeling. It's as if I don't really have any friends. And yet I do.

The loneliness is persistent and pulls me into itself. I'm alone, really alone. I feel its awful fear. It feels as if I'll die if I feel it. I try to run from it and get as far away as possible — but it's always there. When I feel it, it's awful, yet I gain strength.

Going Back

It is essential that transcenders *heal as far back as the hurt.* Going back to only traumas in awareness is not enough. Transcenders need to explore and heal traumas that, in the beginning, may be only felt senses. A felt sense is an awareness of a feeling with no specific identity or memory. Often, something is "sensed" in the body. These senses are then explored and connected to previously blocked feelings and memories. Sometimes, these memories come from as far back as infancy or intrauterine life.

Even though we may not have any conscious awareness of some memories or feelings, our bodies store and remember them. These stored layers cause intense feelings and dysfunction until they are healed. Body-work therapists are wonderful in helping people to explore this area and to bring memories into awareness.

Fear

Fear is another intense, difficult feeling and, like loneliness, is avoided in all sorts of ways. In the healing process, all the old fear of the traumas has to be revisited. The fear sounds like this: "I'm not going to make it"; "She's going to kill me"; "I'm going to be crazy"; "I pray my daddy doesn't come home tonight and beat me"; "I don't know what to do anymore"; "I can't protect myself from her — she always gets me"; "I'm afraid of the real me — I'm not OK."

Actually, fear is a healthy feeling because it tells us something is wrong. Fear signals danger. It works to get us out of danger and tells us to protect ourselves. Fear is a part of every abuse, injury, and hurt that we actually experience or perceive we experience. Think for a moment of the last time you hurt yourself doing a chore around the house, and get in touch with your feelings about that injury. You are probably aware of some fear that says, "Watch out. Be careful." Now, think about a situation in which someone was hurting you on purpose. The fear is intense and terrifying.

In survival, fear is like the protective electric fence that literally surrounds the real self to keep it safe. Every time danger comes near or is perceived to be near, the fence zaps it, either to keep the danger away or to get the individual away from the danger. This fear that protects the authentic self as transcenders grow up interferes with their healing process as adults. This occurs because, as transcenders lift and get rid of layers, they are moving toward uncovering and allowing their authentic self out, and the fence is still fully operational. The fear cannot tell the difference between the healing process and real danger. Its only function is to protect the authentic self and to keep it safe and away from others. The more the layers are removed, the closer one gets to the authentic self; the closer one is to the authentic self, the more fear there is and the more intense the fear is.

At this stage, therapists need to help transcenders feel, understand, and release the fear. Also, transcenders need to be knowledgeable about what is happening to them. This information alone is often enough to ease the fear and help allow the authentic self out.

In addition to the above information, transcenders need to know that their original package is perfect and wonderful and that what they will find is just that: perfect and wonderful. They need to know this because of the shame and dysfunction that comes from a family, they may believe that the reason there is so much fear is that they are terrible, awful, and not likeable. Transcenders are often afraid that they will not like themselves. I have never seen *anyone* not like and love her or his authentic self. Transcenders may have to work through many past and present experiences. They may also have to transform parts of the authentic self, but they always come to a realization that they love themselves. Again, our original package is wonderful and full of talent, life, and love.

The following is Tiffany's description of her fear as she was dealing with her electric fence:

Tiffany

Sadness, deep, intense, unknowing. What's it all about? Fear God, fear life, fear, and more fear. What's the real fear? Don't know. Just know that it's all fear. Fear. Fear. Fear. Fear beyond fear beyond fear. Fear of the next step. Fear of breathing. Fear of smiling. Fear of not smiling. Fear of not knowing and yet fear of knowing. Fear of God — what will He want next? I fear I have given all, and there is nothing left for Him, others, or myself. It's so scary. Nothing left. Help. I'm losing it. I'm sinking. I'm in fear if I move. I'm in fear if I don't. Fear is everywhere, all around me, yet I can't find it.

Anger

Part of the process of grieving is feeling the anger from past traumas. As the sadness is felt and experienced, anger (if not already there) begins to surface. Transcenders, as children, often discover that anger is not an OK feeling in the family. It is either acted out inappropriately (violently), or if expressed by the transcender, it causes more abuse. Therefore, it is changed, avoided, buried, denied, or built up to a rage point. (Rage is built-up anger.) In the healing process, anger involves parents, siblings, relatives, significant others, and God as well as the self. Basically, the anger is aimed at anyone who caused the abuse or neglect or who did not help to prevent it. The anger sounds like this: "Why me? What did I do? I hate what happened. I hate my parents for what they did to me! Why didn't they stop it? Where was God? I want to kill them — no — I want to torture them the way they did me. I want them to know what it was like. I want them to suffer. Where were my teachers? Couldn't they tell? Why didn't they stop it? Why did my parents do it?"

Anger is healthy and important. It tells us that something is wrong in our world and that we need to change something. Anger helps to separate transcenders from the dysfunction in their families. It also helps them clean up confused, clouded areas and gain a clearer, adult perspective of what happened to them in childhood.

Again, therapists need to reassure transcenders that anger is just a feeling and that, like every other feeling, it needs to be understood and expressed. Like every other feeling, it needs to be expressed appropriately. Anger appropriately expressed does not hurt another person or oneself. Some good places to put anger and its energy are breaking dishes (preferably old chipped ones bought at a rummage sale), screaming in cars (not at someone with the intent to destroy that person), pounding with a racket or a piece of hose (pounding pillows, a mattress, etc.), slamming doors (please don't slam refrigerator doors; take it from me, the mess is not worth it), tearing up old papers or old telephone books, or writing *unmailed* letters to people with any language needed to express the feelings fully.

Some transcenders decide to confront a family member about past abuse. Confronting another person about past assaults *has* to be done after the force and energy of the anger have been expressed in another way. That way, the confrontation is not an "I'm going to destroy you" session, but a productive part of the healing process. Confrontation, however, is not always possible or advisable.

There are many ways to release anger appropriately. Remember, don't hurt yourself or another person. Here is a good example from Betty of an unmailed letter to her father describing the hurt, betrayal, and anger caused by her childhood abuse:

——————————————— *Betty* ———————————————

Dear Dad,
I'm not covering up for you anymore. I won't be part of the hideous denial system in our family anymore. You've ruined my life. What kind of monster rapes and sexually abuses his kids? You violated me

to the point where I can't trust anyone, especially men. You abused me when I was so young that I never had a chance to become a person. I grew up hating myself, feeling used, dirty, and crazy. This is the reason I've always been suicidal. There are still many days when I feel as if I have to die to get rid of the pain and the sadness. Your abuse and betrayal ruined all my relationships. I was so used to abuse that I sought out men who would repeat the pattern. I'm afraid to get close to anyone because I can't stand any more abuse and hurt.

You can't hide behind the booze anymore. You had choices and you made them. How could you betray me the way you did? I loved you. I looked to you to keep me safe — to love me. I hate you for what you did to me and all of us kids. Look at our lives! Do you see any of us happy enough to give up our addictions and diseases? All I ever wanted from you was to be safe and valued as a human being. You took away my childhood, my innocence, my trust, and my faith in myself.

My denial system is wonderful. I didn't go into therapy to uncover these outrages. I went into therapy to learn how to function better and to learn how to parent. The first time a memory surfaced, I ran into the bathroom and threw up. Then I thought, "What a horrible nightmare!" Then more and more memories kept pouring out. It was as if a dam had burst. All the poison flooded out. It could not be contained anymore. My life has been a living hell since all this happened. There's been night after night of no sleep. I've been afraid to sleep for fear of uncovering still more torture and abuse. And still it came, it came until every energy in my body was spent trying to push it back into denial. I've spent my life denying it, wondering what was wrong with me. It won't be denied anymore. It won't be silenced anymore. I can't get drunk every night so I can pretend it didn't happen. It *did* happen, and I have to deal with it and what you did to me.

When I was an infant, I remember your penis stuffed in my mouth for me to suck on. I remember trying to breathe, trying not to suffocate, and gagging from the semen. I remember you baby-sitting at night. I remember you taking me into the bathroom for a bath, stripping my clothes off, and forcing your penis into my mouth. We then played "horsey" where you forced me down on your penis. Do you know I can still remember the pain of being ripped open? Do you know how terrifying that was for a baby not even a year old? I can remember the whiskey on your breath and your stinking sweat and your grunting sounds. I can remember how cold it was, the radio programs on at the time, and the location of my brother and sister.

I can remember your drinking buddies taking part in the rapes and what you said to them: "Hey, they're only kids. They won't remember any of it. Besides, everyone does it. They like it." Did you really believe that in your drunken stupor? I remember the attic and the scratchy army blanket, your hand covering my mouth, sweat dripping over me as your raped me anally. It went on and on. There was no safe place in my childhood. You ripped every piece of person I was until there was only an empty shell, a zombie that couldn't scream, couldn't cry, couldn't feel. When the terror started, I learned to separate my body from my mind. I blacked out. It was the only way I could survive.

Remember all the times Ma pulled you off my sister? I was in the same bed; I know you also raped my daughter. The day you baby-sat when I came home from the hospital from having surgery, you were blacked out; she was crying hysterically, clothes falling off. I denied it then, too, like everyone else. What kind of sadistic asshole are you? Is this why you spend your life blacked out from booze? Does it help? You have everyone's support. That should cheer you up. Our entire family collectively denies it all with you, starting with Ma. Our entire lives have been spent denying the outrages that were done to us. But at what price — ruined relationships, heart attacks, obesity, bleeding ulcers, and alcoholism? Not me! Not anymore! I'll not deny my reality anymore. I won't be silent anymore. I refuse to be part of the huge conspiracy of alcoholism, incest, and insanity in our family.

These outrages that were done to me have ruined my life. The silence is not going to ruin any more lives. All my life I knew there was something wrong with me. I hated myself without even knowing why. I blamed myself for the abuse. I thought I was bad. I loved you and idolized you as only a small child can. I looked up to you to keep me safe from Ma's insanity. You didn't. You took my trust and betrayed me. I want to make it all go away. I want to pretend that you're not my father. But I can't.

I want nothing from you now. You have nothing to give. I hate you for what you did to me and my girls. Burning in hell would be too good for you, but I don't have to worry about justice. You've made your own hell right here on earth. You're dead to me. You have been for a long time. I want you to know I will be no one's scapegoat anymore. I will no longer be victimized by you or anyone in our family. I will not listen to putdowns. I will not be terrorized or victimized anymore. I will not pretend we have a wonderful family. I will speak my truth. I will make excuses for no one anymore. There are no excuses for the evil that went on and still goes on in our family. I am totally committed to uncovering and healing the outrages that were done to me. These are my terms for communication with any member of our family: Do not deny what happened. Do not call me with putdowns. Do not tell me I'm crazy. Do not try to minimize the truth and the ugliness. Do not call and ask me to validate your denial and dysfunctional behavior; I won't. Do not call me and try to lay guilt trips on me; I'm not buying it anymore. Everyone alive has choices. I'm choosing health and sanity. I choose to live, not merely to exist. May God give all of us the courage to face the truth about our lives and the courage to heal.

Joy

Once one is through even *some* of the grieving, feelings of freedom and joy begin to be felt. This joy may be after one layer or several, but it always comes. It's as if transcenders get a break from the dark thunderous cloud and the sun peeks through for just a little while. From this break, transcenders gain encouragement and hope that a better way of living is coming. They also gain additional energy and courage to deal with the next layer.

Often, transcenders experience this time as a chance to "catch their breath" and reorganize. They begin to understand at a deeper level the effects of their childhood and realize they have choices, choices more in line with their original package. Gratefully and with relief, they begin to know that they are going to make it through the healing process.

Repetitions

The above steps need to be repeated as often as the layers surface. This is an individual process that depends on the amount of abuse and neglect experienced as well as on the personality of the individual. Basically, the more the abuse, the more the layers, and the more the repetitions. Repetitions often blend and overlap. One layer being worked on and healed will always touch and trigger another one.

Repetitions occur at any time in a person's life. Any incident or experience may trigger a layer, for example, a fight with a significant other, a death in the family, legal problems, a television show, or a trip home. Writing this book, for example, has triggered deeper layers of healing and growth for me. I have learned to use these times for growth. Yes, there are times when I pray, "That's enough. I've had it! I don't want any more." But I am *always grateful* when I have explored and learned from what has been triggered. I find richness and knowledge about myself and the world. I feel freer, clearer, and happier.

Layers that are triggered after the in-depth healing process in therapy are equally important but, thankfully, are usually not as intense, nor do they last as long. Most transcenders learn to see these events as opportunities to clear out more of the past hurt and to gain deeper healing and growth. Here is Donavin's description of one of these events:

———————————— *Donavin* ————————————

When my father died I had so many mixed feelings. Mostly, I was relieved. I also was very angry, but for a different reason than for the childhood abuses. I was angry that he had died because I could never resolve my problems with him and never have the relationship I always wanted with him. He was *never* available to me — and now he had died! It was the ultimate rejection by him — the ultimate rejection of me and our relationship. How could he do that? How could he leave permanently? It was the final ultimate ZAP!

The tears and sadness I had were mostly for the loss of the hope of having a relationship, the finality of the loss of what could have been and what I had hoped for and prayed would be.

What surprised me was all the tears — I didn't think I could cry much more about my father. I also thought I had myself well protected from further hurt from him. What a surprise! I cried as if I really cared. I learned that I did. That was another loss of me, knowing I still cared and could not stop all the pain. I wish I had known this; I might have gone to him and shared my feelings. I guess I had just shut that part off. The whole thing took me by surprise because I thought I was done with the entire relationship.

Acceptance and Forgiveness

At the end of the grieving journey is acceptance and/or forgiveness for the abuser as well as for oneself. As described before, either is acceptable. At this stage, transcenders feel peace, calm, and love. There is no longer the intense anger or deep hurt. There is no longer deep, inner body tension. There is clarity about what happened and a deep understanding of its effects.

This stage is the result of all the hard work of the grieving process. It is the ultimate goal. Transcenders have come to accept who they are and know they are OK and valuable.

Some transcenders have a difficult time accepting and/or forgiving themselves for the many things they haven't liked about themselves in the past. Transcenders have to make a concerted effort to accept and forgive themselves. The list of unacceptable mistakes may be endless; here are a few I have heard:

- Hurting themselves
- Hating themselves
- Hating important special significant others
- Being jealous of siblings
- Hating in general
- Not being superman or superwoman and stopping the abuse
- Being human, with all its frailties
- Overcaring
- Undercaring
- Lack of assertiveness
- Overassertiveness
- Being angry
- Making themselves wrong
- Making others wrong
- Hating their lives
- Being mad at God
- Being afraid
- Not being afraid
- Not being mature enough
- Missing their childhood
- Needing "too much"
- Needing "too little"
- Disappointing themselves
- Not being perfect
- Not taking better care of themselves
- Being manipulated
- Many unspoken transgressions aimed at themselves
- Being too sensitive
- Not being sensitive enough
- Not knowing enough
- Leaving the family

Chris describes acceptance and forgiveness this way:

─────────────────────────── *Chris* ───────────────────────────

I feel acceptance coming in like a peaceful fawn. It is dawning like a lovely sunrise after a storm. It feels as if the war is over. There may still be battles, but now there is a peace and a knowing that all is well.

Regrets

With the acceptance come regrets or sadness that will always be. These regrets are about childhood. Transcenders wish their growing up could have been different. They regret lost relationships, lost opportunities, the struggle to learn a different way to live, working to overcome the past, not having more discipline, and the lack of warmth and caring while they were growing up. Although they accept the experiences, most express sadness that life had to be that way. The following passages give a flavor of this sadness:

─────────────────────────── *Bill* ───────────────────────────

I was unipolar. You are falsely independent, and really dependent. I didn't need anybody else, and made sure I damn well didn't. I needed nobody or nothing. I could make enough money. I would find enough jobs. I could do what I wanted to do. I could pay my own way. And with some anger — I'm not feeling anger, I'm just saying that with some assertiveness now — and a sense of wistfulness, there are sadness and opportunities lost that I can't replace or make up for. It's like, what can I do now to make my life more full, more complete, with more people, with deeper levels of connectedness and attachment? I feel and reflect with some sadness that I don't have any friends from grade school.

Sylvia

My mother didn't want to rock the boat, make waves — Just roll with the punches. And you could walk all over her, and that was fine with her. I wish I'd had a strict upbringing rather than a lenient one like I had.

Chris

In the last few years, my parents and I have given to each other and started a new relationship or friendship. It's still painful to think of those years that could have been so much nicer, so much warmer.

* * *

I close this chapter with a quote from Paul after his intense grieving:

Paul

I have grieved the losses, the missed opportunities. I wished for times that cannot be. I have desperately sought and longed for my mother's arms to hold, nurture, and love me. I have longed for security, caring, and the joy of warm, loving relationships. I have grieved for it all. It is with tremendous sadness that I look at the loss and the emptiness of my childhood. There is still a missing, but now I can let go, let God be in charge, and move forward in my life. I can also let my family go for their better good. I no longer have to hang on and struggle. I am free.

Chapter 8

Reclaiming the Self

The reclaiming process is like being on your very own personal yellow brick road that leads you to Oz. In Oz, you find your authentic self. Along this road, there are many different parts of you that have been rejected, abandoned, or never discovered during childhood. In the reclaiming process, you journey along the road and pick up those precious lost pieces of your original package. Some of these pieces are reclaimed, and some are discovered for the first time. Some of them you have known about, but because of the great need to survive, you could not stop and develop them. In a more normal childhood, your parents work to help you discover, accept, and develop the original package. In a dysfunctional family, parents rarely help and usually damage this process.

Reclaiming of the authentic self is the second part of the healing and growth process. Reclaiming is the process of discovering, rediscovering, owning, reowning, birthing, rebirthing, renewing, and being responsible for your original package. It's a time when the promise "Someday I'll be me!" is kept. It is an exciting, energizing growth time.

Growth occurs in many areas during this time: potentialities, abilities, skills, thoughts, changed behavior, emotions, self-love, and self-liking. It is a time of dynamic learning and insights into your past and present life. Healing and growth demand reclaiming because transcenders, in order to survive, have to hold back, deny, give up, or never discover and develop certain parts of themselves. At this point, it is time to take it all back.

The reclaiming process is a self-discovery journey that is deeply intertwined with and occurs at the same time as the grieving process. The reason for this intertwining is that the authentic self is uncovered, discovered, and freed as grieving lifts the trauma layers. The grieving process forces an examination of the self. This examination leads the way to reclaiming because it forces transcenders to find a way through and out of the grieving. It forces them to find *their* way. The more the grief, the more authenticity must be present to handle the situation. And for a while, the more the discovery of themselves, the more the grief because part of the grieving process is the loss of the authentic self in childhood. A memory in the reclaiming area will trigger feeling work in grieving, and vice versa. For example, if I am dealing with knowing I have an ability to ski and I'm fifty years old, I have to grieve that I have lost my chance to be on the Olympic team and claim the skiing ability I still have.

As this journey continues, transcenders find more of themselves and, maybe for the first time, the real self. The end of the journey is similar to arriving in Oz, where they get to go home and really feel and love what home is all about. On this journey, home is the authentic self. Along the way are "lions, and tigers, and bears" — fears and concerns about what will be found. However, what is found is the original package. Some of the parts discovered fit and feel wonderful. Other parts fit, but feel awful. Transcenders sort through these precious findings, reclaiming and transforming them.

Like the grieving, transcenders have to go back to each memory and be responsible for each feeling, thought, and behavior. It's as if part of themselves is locked back in those experiences. As the memory and all its feelings are revisited, transcenders gain thoughts and insight into their behavior as well as their emotional patterns. They gain a deeper knowing and understanding of themselves. Transcenders glean each experience for every bit of learning about themselves and their world.

Again, like grieving, the reclaiming process occurs while one is doing the feeling work. It is only then the layers lift and one knows what to reclaim. What is reclaimed is personal power, strength, clear thinking, an authentic way of being, and self-love. Also gained is the learning from past experiences that has been lost because of the inability to process situations during childhood.

This reclaiming process often, and amazingly, takes transcenders back to their infancy. Transcenders *have* to go as far back as the trauma and hurt, where the abuse, rejection, and abandonment first began. They have to go back and reestablish a loving relationship with themselves at all ages. Often, it is at young ages that transcenders get a powerful glimpse of their original package. These glimpses are then encouraged and developed. Early decisions are also discovered and explored along with thoughts and feelings about people in the transcenders' world. In essence, they go back to the core, the beginning, and reclaim all that is authentic and process out everything that is not.

This sorting-out includes questions, such as "Who am I as opposed to who my parents are?"; "Which part is me?"; "Which parts are them?"; "What parts of me do I want to transform?"; "Which parts do I want to keep just as they are?"; "Which parts of me are purely survival skills that I no longer need?"; "What are my feelings?"; "What are my parents' feelings?" This sorting is vital to transcenders. This is a period of time when transcenders focus totally on themselves to separate themselves from the family at a very deep level. This time is vital to healing and growing because it means separating and getting rid of the nonbeing, or nonme, and discovering and developing the real or authentic me. It is the authentic self that can be happy, productive, and growing in the world.

Reclaiming the past is work dealing with transcenders' inner child. A poem by a transcender illustrates this process:

This Child

This child yearns to be
to struggle is her destiny
to run
to play
to let unfold
a life
a story
yet untold
of dreams
of songs
of rhythm dancing
of fun
of love
of self-enhancing
ways of being
yet to be
and yet to grow
and yet to show
the magic of a destiny
of childlike
love and energy
bursting forth creatively
This child will always
yearn to be
This child will always struggle
to be free
from all that chains and blocks and stops
the freedom of the child in me
the spirit of the child who's free
the spirit of my destiny
to be
free
to be
me

As transcenders heal and grow, they learn what characteristics, lifestyle, and people they really like and don't like. Most important, they learn who they really are and what they are *realistically* capable of doing and not doing. The reclaiming process includes developing potentialities, abilities, and strengths. Sometimes this is all new learning because, when children are prohibited from exploring, unrealistic expectations and views of the self and the world develop. For example, if I have survived a severely abusive home, I may feel so beaten down that I believe I can't do anything. *Or* I may believe I am superman or superwoman and can do anything and everything. Either way, I am unrealistic. Potentialities are unlimited, but there are limits on how they will develop or be used.

An important area in the reclaiming process is love. Love is the healing power for transcenders. They use love from others and for others as energy to keep going. Love of self is part of healing and growth. Love of self may be there in some form that can be relied on and used for development. Or self-love may have to be uncovered, developed, or healed from past abuses. During the reclaiming process, self-love is healed, deepened, and enriched and brings joy.

Reclaiming is not an easy process. It is confusing, frustrating, and full of pain from the past. Old memories are remembered and have to be revisited. The process is also fun, joyful, exciting, and full of self-love. As the reclaiming process continues, transcenders feel less crazy because they are more themselves and have sorted out more of their families' dysfunction. In addition, they have more of themselves available. Transcenders end up liking and loving themselves. I have never seen a person who ended up not liking and loving herself or himself after working hard in the grieving and reclaiming process. Please remember, the two processes do take time.

Before we continue, the following definitions of *self*, *false self*, and *ring of fear* are given to help you understand the process of reclaiming at a deeper level.

Self. The self is our core, our being. It is our authentic self, our realness, the original package. This core is influenced by family, friends, church, society, and all that is in our world. I believe that our self, or core, is present at conception and that how it develops depends on the environment around us. In the reclaiming process, it is the self that has to be healed and developed. For example, if I am a happy, outgoing child and my world is abusive, I may withdraw and hide the real me. In the healing process, I need to feel and separate the outgoing me from the decisions I made to protect myself from the pain. I can then reestablish my outgoing authenticity. (For further discussion of the self, see Chapter 4.)

False Self. Growing up in a dysfunctional family creates a phenomenon I call the *false self*. At birth, the authentic self is present, and depending on the environment, the authentic self is developed and supported or a false self begins to be created. A false self is developed when an individual senses or knows that the real self is not acceptable or loved and/or is endangered. This is learned through experiences with the family and the world. The false self is a creation of the real self that works to protect and enhance the person and to make him or her more acceptable and lovable to the world, especially the family. It is created to help ensure survival. The false self has parts of the real self in it, but it is not totally the real self.

The false self is what is presented to the world, and the real self is usually hidden away and protected deep inside the person. The false self is also an off-center self. It is usually pictured outside one's body, while the real self is centered within the body. The tragedy of developing a false self is that individuals come to believe that their false self is their real self. This belief creates confusion, anxiety, sadness, and a powerful knowing that something is wrong without knowing what.

When a person is operating in the false self, I often hear the following: "I'm just conning everyone"; "I really didn't make those good grades in school"; "I just fooled everyone"; "I really don't know what I am capable of or what I can do"; "I'm just sort of here"; "Just tell me what to feel and I'll feel it"; "I'll do anything for people to like me"; "I have no idea of what I feel"; "I'm angry, but don't know why."

Uncovering the real self means going through the feelings that first developed the false self. This process is seen in a journal excerpt from Steve:

Steve

There is a secret inner spot where I keep the condemned me. I put it there and keep it contained and hidden. It's the me that's afraid; the me that's not good enough, the me that's judged wrong. The other me tries to keep going and to be what others would have me be, to get the love I want, and to survive. I changed me into something false and not me. I try to be what I could never be — someone else.

The condemned me is the real me. It is buried deep, deep, deep — so deep in my depths, it's almost not real. But there, in the inner being, is me, the real me, the me I love, the me I am. I hide the real me — I don't want to be ridiculed or judged and found wanting. I keep me hidden because I'm precious, and it's not safe for me out there. So I stay hidden and show myself only when I feel absolutely safe, and that's only after a long time. Otherwise, it's only when I am alone that it's safe. It's when I'm alone that I can breathe, move more freely, and feel my feelings more authentically.

*   *   *

Ring of Fear. Since the false self is developed because the authentic self is viewed as being in danger and not being accepted, survival depends on protecting and staying away from the real self. We do this by putting a powerful ring of fear around the authentic self. This fear works in two ways: (1) it protects the authentic self from the outside world, and (2) it stops vulnerability — the exposure of authentic thoughts, feelings, and abilities. The fear acts like a protective electrical fence. Every time someone or even the transcender gets close, it lets out a zap. Transcenders either fend off, attack, or withdraw when this happens in order to protect the authentic self. Here's an example of a transcender's words of fear when someone is getting close to the electrical fence:

> Beware of self. Not OK. Not acceptable. *Cover. Cover.
> Cover.* Cover it up. Keep it hidden. Label it dangerous. Keep
> away. Don't let light into it. Hide it. It's hideous. Don't let it out.
> *Beware.* If you get close, you'll die!

As stated in the previous chapter, the problem with the electric
fence is that it continues to work long after it is needed in childhood.
After transcenders move out of the family and into a safer world, the
fear around the authentic self still operates. It still tells them it's not
OK to be their real self: "Stay away." Depending on the childhood,
this fear may be *very* powerful. Sometimes, transcenders even believe
that they will die if they come in close contact with it. Transcenders
need to know that it is a protection they have placed there and that
they can deelectrify it. They usually do this through an awareness of
what has happened and feeling the fear. From awareness and feelings
come insights and understanding. What often helps transcenders is
thanking themselves for the protection and telling themselves it is
now OK to be authentic. They can also tell themselves that they can
now take care of themselves in a different way.

STEPS IN RECLAIMING THE SELF

The process of reclaiming takes time, effort, and persistence.
Sometimes, it is hard and requires a concerted effort to gain even a
small entrance into the authentic self, let alone a change in behavior.
At other times, entrance occurs almost effortlessly. The following is
Marie's experience of the reclaiming process:

———————————————— *Marie* ————————————————

Who am I? What do I like to do, to eat, etc.? What don't I like
about myself? These are some of the questions that I began to ask
myself, especially following an intense period of grieving and sadness.

I had spent most of my life taking care of and trying to meet the needs of others. To begin doing things for myself, especially at first, felt very selfish, very self-centered. I was so accustomed to meeting the needs of others that I had difficulty choosing food in the grocery store that I wanted. It was as if I wasn't good enough and didn't deserve to have my own wants, needs, and desires met. As I began to do small things for myself and to make more choices based on what I really wanted to do, I also became aware of what my own needs really were. I began to feel my own feelings instead of running away or blocking them out as I had in the past. I began to breathe the fresh air of freedom for the first time.

My feelings were not always happy, on-top-of-the-world feelings, my former facade, but I learned that I really could cry alone and that the tears really would stop. I was surprised to find that, instead of enjoying being by myself, there were times when I felt very lonely and very sad. Although I don't always like being there, I feel an honesty and an orientation to reality that were previously unknown to me. For a while, during the intense grieving period, I felt I had lost my sense of humor. As I grew emotionally, I learned that my laughter had been a cover-up. I was surprised to hear myself on tape, in an earlier session, say, "If I laugh about things, it keeps me from having to feel." My sense of humor is very much intact and certainly used more appropriately. There are times when I still want to block out feelings. When I do, the result is almost always the same: more pain in another way and at another time until the issue is resolved.

I've learned that, for the most part, I like myself. The old fear of "being like my mother" is almost totally gone. In many ways, the reclaiming process has been getting to know me for the first time. I've learned who I really am. I am learning that I can make choices. I'm also beginning to learn that I'll never be perfect—the former parent requirement. With more and more insight and understanding, I understand—no, I KNOW—I was not a "dirty, bad, and cheap" little girl who wasn't good enough to be loved. Instead, I know that I had crazy, evil people for parents. I refuse to acknowledge them as mother and father, as they never were.

In learning who I am, I am learning what I am not. I am not the abuse and torture I endured as a child. I am not guilty because I was there. I am not responsible for the choices my parents made in their own lives. In reclaiming who I really am, I find a child who was a victim and one who will never be a victim again. I had no control over the things that were forced on me as a child. I very much have control over what happens to my life in the present and the future. I can now continue to grow, no longer caged in the past, to take new steps, to invite other people into my life. The self I have come to know has nothing to hide and no secrets to live in fear of someone's finding out.

Is the future frightening to me? Yes, but also very exciting. I work very hard not to continue the abuse begun years ago by my parents. Good times, happy times, although greatly enjoyed, can trigger the old pattern of the "you're not good enough" and "you don't deserve to be happy" tapes. Instead, I allow my newfound self to enjoy and know that it's OK to be happy, really happy, not just acting as if I'm happy.

I lied to myself for years about my life. The quality of my life now, the excitement of my own personal growth, the lifting of the horrible burden of misplaced guilt, laughing real laughter, crying real tears, feeling real feelings, viewing and evaluating the past with the maturity of an adult, giving up old ways of surviving and developing new and more appropriate ways of functioning — these are only some of the things I had gained in therapy when my daughter's therapist said to me one day, "You might want to pursue your own family background further and go back into therapy." Going back, that is the direction I had to travel in order to go forward, to be free and grow.

————————————— *Chris* —————————————

The reclaiming part of my healing was wonderful. Somehow, as I felt the pain, the real me began to surface. I'd find bits and pieces of me everywhere. For example, I found that I really didn't like getting up early in the morning and preferred a job that started later. My mother never allowed us to sleep past 6 A.M. I now have a job where I have to be at work at 6 A.M., but I am taking steps to get trained for other work that starts later. I also discovered that I liked being with other people and need time alone to be with me. Before this, I was always with people, which kept me from feeling.

The reclaiming process was very painful at times. I had to revisit all the old experiences of abuse and take back each piece of me that either I had left there or my parents had raped from me. Each time I did, I felt more powerful and complete. Each time, I saw how they had raped me of me. They decided I could never choose anything, could never make my own decisions. I was to do just as I was told and never, never question anything. Questioning, even one question, meant certain abuse.

What I found was the real me, the true me. I've never really known me. I was this person who needed to survive and was trained to do so. Parts of that survival soldier was me, but so much of me was hidden. I couldn't believe that I could be accepted or OK. I found that I was. Most important, I found I was accepted as OK by me. I actually like me! I always thought I was bad and not OK because I was blamed for everything. Only a bad person could be at fault for so much. Finding out I was OK was wonderful. I felt free and alive.

I now work to develop talents and abilities that are truly mine, like writing and running. I am also becoming more financially stable and organized, something I never thought I could do. I now know who I am. I am on a self-discovery journey of finding and developing more of me.

*   *   *

The following are the steps of the reclaiming process. As in the grieving process, they have no set order, they may overlap, and they may recur many times. The focus is always on discovering one's self and becoming authentic in one's own world.

Discovering Authentic Thoughts, Feelings, and Behavior

As transcenders grieve the past, there is a constant discovery of thoughts, feelings, and behavior that are directly connected to past experiences and that also occur in present life. Transcenders gain powerful learning and understanding of what has happened to them and how it has shaped their self and their world. They become aware that many thoughts, feelings, and behaviors that they thought were theirs are really their parents'. These are old tapes that were ingrained in them at a very young age. (For example, when I discipline my child, I often have one of my parent tapes running. That is, I will say and do exactly what my parents said and did to me.) Once the tapes are fully examined and felt, transcenders have a choice to keep the thoughts, feelings, and behavior, or to change them.

As the grieving and reclaiming process continues, they come to realize, gratefully, that they are not responsible for what happened to them in the family. They know, beyond a doubt, that the dysfunction in the family was *not* their fault. They did not choose to be abused and neglected. They discover that they are *really* not like their parents, which is an old, deep fear, and this discovery brings relief and joy. Transcenders then work hard to uncover and develop what they authentically think, feel, and want in their world. They then make decisions based on these new thoughts and feelings.

The knowledge that they are not responsible for the family's dysfunction gives them permission, energy, and the courage to explore further, even if only to explore one more scary, painful memory. It is enough to keep them healing and growing, gaining insights and learning that are powerful and vital to their living. Growth continues to come as long as transcenders continue to work and are committed to their process.

Going Back

As in the grieving, transcenders need to go back as far as the loss of self. They must go back and reclaim each and every part that was left behind when they were infants, children, teenagers, and adults. This includes everything: feelings, thoughts, behavior, abilities, potentialities — everything that is the original package *plus* all the learning that has been gleaned from experience. Some transcenders go back to birth, infancy, or even prenatal experiences. For example, one transcender remembers her mother beating on the uterus trying to abort her.

When transcenders go back, they must heal as well as develop a relationship with those lost parts of themselves. These parts have often been disowned, rejected, judged, and abandoned not only by the family, but also by the transcender. Transcenders must bring forward in time all the feelings, thoughts, and insights from that age and own them in the present moment. Doing this brings incredible learning about themselves and their world. They learn why they feel, think, behave, and respond the way they do in certain situations. They learn about their original package. From this understanding, they can make changes.

Learning That Feelings Are Normal

Growing up in dysfunctional families, transcenders learn that feelings are not OK. Not only are they not OK, they are horrible, crazy, and terrifying and bring more trauma. In therapy, a *major* learning is that *all* feelings are normal, OK, and very important. Actually, the awakening of feelings is *the most important* element in healing, growing, and getting to know the authentic self. Transcenders also learn that feelings need to be, and that they can be expressed appropriately and healthily without hurting other people. In my sessions with transcenders, one of my *most* repeated questions is "What are you feeling?" Feelings have absolute priority.

Feeling work has priority in therapy because unless transcenders know what they are feeling, they will not begin to find out who they really are and to gain an understanding of themselves or their abilities. Feelings give us *more than half* the information we need about ourselves and our world. As transcenders do their feeling work, they become more aware of themselves, their world, and what they want in their world. They are also able to separate themselves from dysfunction. After the feeling work, decisions can be made with reason, logic, and insights gained from the feelings. Decisions come after feelings, learning, and insights.

Learning that feelings are normal is sometimes very difficult. Transcenders have seen feelings acted out violently and inappropriately. They have feelings locked inside from years ago and must go back to heal the traumas the feelings surround. This means overcoming the fear, acknowledging the feelings, and actually feeling the feelings. This is hard. For example, anger is one of the most feared feelings to feel because it was the feeling most likely to be violently acted out. Transcenders don't feel safe to feel anger. There is often an image of a parent ready to abuse them if they even think anger. Anger may also be the only feeling that was allowed in the family. If this is true, other feelings become fused with anger. That is, if I am hurt and sad, but anger is the only feeling that is allowed expression, then my hurt and sadness will look like anger. It takes diligent detective work to begin to separate fused feelings.

Here is Tiffany's description of how she came to accept her feelings:

Tiffany

In my family, anger and happiness were the only feelings allowed. So, every heavy feeling fused with anger; and the lighter ones, with happiness. I worked real hard at separating my fused feelings and figuring out what I was really feeling. I loved learning about me, and whatever fears I felt, I quickly worked through because I knew my feelings were the "me" I had been looking for, for so many years.

Some feelings I never acknowledged because they were so forbidden by my family. Jealousy was one of those. It took me literally years to admit to feeling jealous. It is still hard for me, especially in competitive ways. I was taught to be a "good sport" and not to want to win. I am involved in a very competitive sport, and sometimes I really just want to blow everyone away. Then I feel guilty and get mad at myself. I can't even own up to the fact that I am jealous at times.

I can still remember hearing about feelings for the first time that really made sense. I was in graduate school, and the professor, a wise, loving woman, described her understanding of feelings. She shared that feelings just were. She went on to explain that feelings are not good or bad, but just part of our humanness. We don't have to judge them, make them wrong, or try to do away with them. We *do have to* accept feelings, and learn about ourselves from them. She further explained that no one can be responsible for anyone else's feelings, but that we are totally responsible for our own.

I felt instant freedom and love. I felt the real me beginning to surface as it never had before. It was the me that has always wanted to be. As I grew and learned, I faced many fears about accepting my feelings that surprised me: "What would my parents think?"; "How would people respond to my having real feelings and having opinions that come from those feelings?"; "Would I still be loved if I didn't take care of others' feelings?" I overcame these fears one by one in ways that were not terrifying. I did it with the help of several people who were mentors and therapists to me. They taught me to work with myself gently and lovingly. The abuse and neglect had been done. I didn't need any more of that. What I needed was to love myself to health and growth through acceptance of my feelings.

Now, when a feeling comes up that I don't want, I may try to avoid it by using the old system and responding with anger, but my new way of being with my feelings takes over. I feel, accept, and learn. I grow with every feeling, and my feelings help me to know what I want in my world.

Establishing Boundaries and Limits

Boundaries, or limits, are extremely important to transcenders. In a dysfunctional family, the normal physical, mental, and emotional boundaries have never been established or have been violated. (More information is in Chapter 1.) Boundaries normally start to develop as the infant grows and begins to understand that the parent, usually the mother, is a separate individual. This concept is usually firmly established in the "terrible twos," when the child demonstrates the separation by being able to say no. When parents do not encourage this separation or violate the physical, mental, and emotional boundaries through abuse, the child can't establish this separation. The child then easily takes on others' feelings and responsibilities and believes they are his or her own.

In the reclaiming process, transcenders work to define and establish their true boundaries. Transcenders must create a clear boundary line between themselves and others, especially with family members. They must get Mom's, Dad's, and siblings' feelings and responsibilities out of themselves. To do this, transcenders go through a confusing time of conflicts and battles: "What if I say no and they hate me?"; "Will they abandon me?"; "What if I fail?"; "What *are* my boundaries?"; "What are *my* feelings?" The process is an evaluation of self and values that leads transcenders to their real selves with real boundaries that are felt when violated. There can no longer be a changing of oneself to be accepted.

Transition: Feeling Crazy

As transcenders continue to heal and grow, new ways of living in the world begin to be created, and a transition period occurs. A transition period occurs when the old ways of living are no longer needed or wanted and new ways have begun to be created. The new ways begin to replace the old, *but* they are not completely known and definitely not solidly in place, to be readily used in every situation.

During this time, transcenders feel that they have absolutely no ground underneath them. They believe that if they take one step in any direction, they will fall into a bottomless pit. When life experiences occur, they don't know whether to use the old way, which they now realize is not healthy because they have grown and changed, or to use a new way that they don't know well enough and that is not a settled part of them yet. The old and new literally clash. Transcenders may find themselves alternating between the old and the new.

During this time, transcenders feel intensely frustrated, fearful, angry, disoriented, and crazy. I hear reports of transcenders feeling totally confused and not knowing who in the world they are! If you were to ask transcenders during this time, "Would the real person please stand up?" no one would stand up because there is so much unsureness of who the real person is. It is a traumatic and scary time. Transcenders often wonder why they even began therapy because it has only made things worse.

In handling the transition period, transcenders need to relax into the fear and continue moving forward. "To relax into the fear," as I am told by professionals, as well as clients, is "absurd." Actually, it means to relax, to know that the fear will be there, but not to let it stop you from your forward growth journey. It means not to struggle with the fear. Have an awareness of it, learn about it, but don't become too excited and upset with it. Accept it as a part of the transition period that will eventually go away.

The best way to handle the transition period is to not struggle, to let the cloudiness and confusion clear on their own. They will do this as the reclaiming process continues. The old ways of being will give way to the new. Transcenders then report feeling better and less crazy. Steve gives us a sample of this confusing time:

Steve

I knew something was going on, but I didn't know what when I was in the transition period. I was so confused that I couldn't figure out if I was going to use the old way of behaving or attempt a new way. If I did the old way, I felt depressed, angry, and just plain awful! If I did a new way, I felt terrified and so unsure of myself.

I had no idea who I was — not wanting the old, but not really having the new. I didn't know that the old was fading and was beginning to be replaced by the new. I was told to "relax." Ha! Relaxing when I felt so scared? How could I? How do you relax in the fear? But the more I struggled — and I really struggled — the more frustrated and scared I became.

My brain was like a white cloud, a cloud that was so thick there was no vision at all. If I'd been at an airport, all planes would have been grounded. In the fog, there were people, things, situations, and feelings floating around. I worked hard trying to figure it out; each time I tried, it became cloudier and I became more tense. I finally listened to my therapist, who said, "Relax into the fear and confusion, and let it alone." It was the only thing that worked. As I let it be, it cleared.

Working through the Layers

Layers are accumulated traumas that have not been dealt with and are stored in the body. (Layers are described in detail in Chapter 5.) The releasing and healing of the trauma layers are essential to the grieving as well as to the reclaiming process. From the layers, transcenders gain valuable information about themselves and their world that is very important to reclaiming the self. When layers are not dealt with and are trapped inside, learning and growth from those layers are lost.

As transcenders work through the layers, learning is gained and their authenticity is uncovered, discovered, and freed. The process is difficult, and with each layer comes pain and struggle, but also, as each layer is healed, comes joy and learning. As more and more layers continue to surface, transcenders often feel as if they are going backward. This is *not* regression! It only feels like regression because the layers seem as if they will never stop. *Each* layer felt and worked through is progress. What is actually happening is the processing of the many old layers and the transcenders' struggling to heal them. Sometimes, the layers come one at a time; at other times, it feels as if a dump truck has backed up and dumped its entire load. Each layer offers learning about the past and about the individual. Each layer is slightly different from the others. The layers continue until the transcenders have healed and released all the layers within themselves.

It has been my experience that layers tend to move out of the body like stacked bundles. The first one to be felt and worked through is the one on top; then, the next. Layers do not necessarily come in chronological order, or in any logical order, for that matter. Usually, they come up in the way they are stacked and can be handled emotionally. The body also seems to have its own agenda in helping to release layers. The direction of the releasing is to deeper layers, to healing, to growth, and to an ever-truer self.

Discovering the Fear and Protection Layers

The process of the layers' moving through the body may trigger intense fear. This fear may be experienced as anxiety or terror, depending on the layer, its memories, and its feelings. This fear is part of the layers of protection that transcenders had to have while growing up. Transcenders set up a system to keep the layers of feelings and memories away so they could survive and deal with the present moment. The more severe the trauma in childhood, the stronger the fear had to be to hold the layers out of awareness. This protection is vital.

I describe to clients the fear while releasing layers in the following terms: "The layers are going to continue to surface until they are done. The fear you feel is part of your old protection system that kept you safe while growing up. You no longer need it, and we will deal with the fear and the layer as they surface and learn from them. This process allows the next layer to surface and more learning and growth to occur.

"Each layer needs to be felt and learned from fully. Each time you do this, you will gain another part of you and reclaim more of your personal power. Know that the fear will be stronger at some times than at other times. The fear is a signal to intensify our exploration, not a signal to stop. It means we are close to your authenticity. It is time to search for and deal with the truth of your growing up."

A second part of the protection fear was described this way by a transcender:

"I had to leave me in my childhood. I had to bury myself and pretend I didn't exist on the surface. I had to conform in order to survive and be acceptable. If I hadn't, I wouldn't have made it because they would have got me. I still won't be acceptable, and they will get me. The real me wasn't safe. I can't be the real me even now. If I let me out, I still won't be liked, loved, or accepted."

The feeling of not being accepted is powerful and often sets up the following belief:

If only I could be better. If only I had taken care of my dad a little more. If only I had talked less. If only . . . then they would have liked, accepted, and loved me. If they had loved me, they would have stopped hurting me.

From these thoughts come a codependency pattern of taking care of others to the exclusion of themselves. What they are doing is protecting themselves *and* trying to get some sort of nurturing in return.

The third part of the protecting fear is the fear of revisiting the past experiences, a fear I well understand. Who, through choosing, would ever want to go back to trauma after trauma and feel all the old pain as if it were happening right now? That is what healing demands. It is painful and difficult.

A fourth part of this area is a fear of what kind of person they will find: "Will I hate me?"; "Will I be acceptable?"; "My parents didn't want me, so why would I?"; "I must not be OK." Some transcenders feel, "If you really knew me, you wouldn't like me and wouldn't want to be around me, because I may not be the loving, caretaking person you see. I'm really an angry person." Of course there is anger; it's anger at what happened to them in childhood and at the loss of self.

As the feeling work is done and the layers are released, transcenders develop an understanding of what happened to them. From this understanding, they learn and grow. Transcenders can then let go of the past, heal, *and* realize not only that they are OK, but that they are someone they like and respect. They learn that they have always been OK and that it was the family dysfunction that made them believe otherwise.

Learning and Discovering

A major part of the reclaiming process is the fantastic learning that contributes to growth. Transcenders learn about themselves and their world with truth and authenticity. The learning is endless. They learn that they are not conning people with their abilities; their abilities are real. (We *cannot* have a skill or be intelligent when we are really not; those are original-package gifts.) In addition, transcenders discover that they have skills they didn't know they had. They may find out they can ski, ride horses, or be good at numbers. They learn the truth about themselves and their families, and this information gives them the freedom to be themselves. They also discover a new, clearer perspective about their world. The reclaiming process is a discovery journey about themselves.

A major learning in relationships is discovering that other people really do like them as their real selves. Because the real self had to be hidden in childhood, transcenders find it very scary to put themselves "on display." As they take the risk and reveal more of themselves, there is more chance of having the authentic self inspected and judged. It is something like showing off a new baby: an important part of you is out there and vulnerable. What if they don't like me? Then what? There is nothing else. Ideally, parents praise and encourage their children to become their authentic selves, and the children develop a strength that carries them through inspections. In a dysfunctional family, this is not true, and the authentic self is made to feel wrong and to hide. For help in this area, transcenders need to surround themselves with caring, accepting, loving, nonjudgmental people who encourage the development of the real self.

Sometimes, transcenders find that they have to change certain situations in their world because they no longer "fit" in them. If changes are needed, transcenders decide through the process of healing and growing what they will change. The changes may be easy or hard, but transcenders choose and are ready to make the changes. For example, Tiffany was working for an organization that was severely dysfunctional. As she healed and grew, she decided she could no longer work for that organization. She had come to realize that the company was very similar to her family and that she was in intense emotional pain while working there. She also came to realize that she had changed and no longer needed the company (i.e., the *family*). When she left, she was leaving the dysfunction of the organization as well as that of her family. She was beginning to create a world of her own choosing.

Changing Relationships

In the healing process, *all* relationships in the transcenders' past and present life are explored and evaluated: Mom, Dad, siblings, significant others, bosses, relatives — everyone. These relationships have to be explored in detail so that the transcenders understand the emotions and meanings of these relationships in their lives. This is especially true of relationships that contain some sort of pain because they are apt to be saturated with the family's dysfunctional system. Often, transcenders find Dad in a lover, Mom in a friend, or a combination of Mom and Dad in a spouse. This happens because there is a duplication of the family's dysfunction. For example, if I need to caretake because of my past experience in my family, I will pick a significant other who is dependent. An extremely dependent person, in return, will pick a strong caretaker. Or if I feel "loved" or relieved only after I have been physically abused, I will get into a relationship that is physically abusive. This is *not* to say that I want to be abused. It is to say that I feel "love," or relief, when I'm abused because that is what happened in my family. Also, the concept of love changes as the person heals and grows. Please note: This is not always the case, and many transcenders refuse to put up with any type of abuse in a relationship.

Transcenders have learned how to act in relationships from past experience in the family. Relationships that simulate the family relationships feel right, or at least familiar, if not comfortable, because this is what they know and have been taught. To change these patterns, transcenders must define the dysfunction in painful relationships and separate it from the healthy, authentic self. They do this by feeling, exploring, and examining relationships to gain a clearer view of why they are attracted and attached to unhealthy relationships. They can then make powerful, healthy decisions about their relationships. It is a difficult process, but it often moves transcenders out of painful relationships.

As reclaiming continues, transcenders find themselves feeling less crazy and confused. They feel better and more relaxed, they learn to play, and they become more authentic. Shifts then occur in relationships almost automatically. Transcenders find themselves attracted to healthier, more authentic people, and they discover healthier people being attracted to them. New, healthier relationships are formed *and* enjoyed.

Some transcenders are already in healthy, growing relationships that are enhanced by the reclaiming process. Others are in difficult relationships that may be healed rather than terminated. There is no set rule about relationships. What is important is the healing, growing, and striving for an ever-healthier, happier life.

Healthy, growing relationships are vital to support the process of reclaiming the self. Without these relationships, transcenders stay in loneliness, isolation, and often depression. It is these healthy relationships that give positive feedback to transcenders: "I like you for you"; "I like your real self"; "You're neat"; "I love you"; "You're not just a role, you're a valuable person" —and very important, "Keep going." These kinds of relationships may already be in place or may be formed during the healing process.

In another important area of relationships, transcenders find other transcenders and share backgrounds. As a result, they gain support and no longer feel that they are the only ones "this has ever happened to." This sharing is extremely valuable in shifting guilt, shame, and loneliness. Through this exchange, transcenders gain thoughts of "If they can do it, so can I."

By support, I mean having people in your life who value, love, help, and give in many ways that show caring for you as a person. An excellent example of supportive, loving relationships working at their best is in my mental health clinic, the Center for Realistic Living (CRL). The CRL is highly unusual as a mental health clinic because its core is love. The clinic has two basic tenets. The first is that, as a clinic, we are dedicated to helping people, with love, caring, and gentleness, to heal and to grow into their authentic selves. We do this with hugs, extra calls, extra time, and a deep personal commitment to each client we work with. We are all aware that the core of healing and growing is love. Second, we are dedicated to our own healing and growing as individuals on the staff. At any time, on any day, I can walk down the hall and get a hug, a listening ear, support, information, help, and feedback. This is love of the most wonderful kind. Often, if I am having a rough day with my own family or with work, a staff member will just come up to me and say, "You look as if you need a hug." I then get at least one hug if not ten. I feel validated, affirmed, supported, and loved. This staff member's energy gives me a boost to keep going and to work through the obstacle. It has been the encouragement and support of CRL staff, family, and friends that have given me the needed encouragement to continue to write this book when life forces worked to discourage me.

Relationships are just as important in healing and growing as they are in surviving the family. Transcenders change relationships by ridding themselves of old dysfunctional patterns. They move out of unhealthy, painful relationships with courage and strength that are impressive. From this entire area, transcenders gain love—self-love and the love of others in healthy, appropriate ways. Love in all its forms is examined and reflected on so that it becomes the essence of relationships.

Exploring Perfectionism

Another stage of the reclaiming process is exploring perfectionism: "If I work a little harder, if I make straight A's, I'll do everything right; I'll be perfect, and then they'll love me"; "I must be better than everyone; then they won't hurt me"; "If I'm perfect, then I'll get through life OK"; "I can't make any mistakes"; "I'll become like his friend; then he'll love me"; "My parents want me to be their perfect little girl/boy for them, so I'll be that, then they'll love me." The belief is that if I try harder and am perfect and do nothing wrong, I'll be accepted and loved. Thus the authentic self is thrown away, and a "perfect," false self is created.

The negative side of this "perfection" means not being yourself, but striving to create a more acceptable, lovable, and, it is hoped, less victimized self. It means living up to or down to authorities' expectations because the false self is based on what a more powerful other(s) wants. It means being the image of someone else's illusion and fantasy. *But* this someone else is almost always dysfunctional. Sound crazy? It is! Crazy and confusing. Sometimes, what the authority wants one minute, she or he doesn't want the next. What brings love one time brings rage the next. One transcender was told to be perfect by driving a tractor in a straight line at the age of five. He could barely touch the pedals, let alone figure out what a straight line was. He was severely punished when he went crooked. This is crazy.

Attempting to be perfect does offer transcenders a type of protection from the world: "If I do everything right, no one will hurt me." So they work very hard to do what is right, or what works to keep them safe from abuse. Perfectionism also helps to maintain self-esteem, even through false channels, so transcenders can function in the world on at least some level. In adulthood, as transcenders heal and grow, they find that they can no longer strive to be perfect. It takes too much energy and too much effort. They may also find they no longer need the illusion of being perfect.

Perfection is an illusion. Perfection does not exist in our world. We can only come close by creating something that is wonderful and appears perfect. In a family that demands perfection, perfect means *never* failing, always doing the "right" thing, and never being wrong. We, as human beings, are not perfect—never have been and never will be. One of the major ways we learn is by experiencing frustration and mistakes. We are designed to learn and grow from all our experiences, not to be perfect in them. What we do have is our humanness and our precious original package. What transcenders discover about themselves is they have always been "perfect." They have always been acceptable and lovable. They discover and confirm that their world was at fault.

Changing the perfection illusion involves feeling the fear and working with the dysfunction that caused the need to be perfect. The fear is "If I stop being perfect, will I be OK?"; "Who am I?"; "Will I be safe?"; "Will I be liked?" The perfectionism fear shows up in things like being afraid to change one's hair style, being afraid to eat new foods, being afraid to change the style of clothes one wears, or being afraid to appear in public unless one is looking absolutely perfect. The change away from perfectionism occurs with healing, support from significant others, and transcenders' courage to be.

Overcoming Tiredness

At some point in the healing and growing process, transcenders experience what I call a *deep, inner-core tiredness*. What happens at this stage in the process is that transcenders, who have been working for decades maintaining themselves by survival techniques, become emotionally, mentally, and physically exhausted by the effort it has taken to survive and to create a different lifestyle in adulthood. The tiredness is deep in the inner being, and regular sleep does not relieve the symptoms. What is needed is getting *all* the sleep and rest required until physical, mental, and emotional energy returns. This rest sometimes takes weeks, sometimes months. Patience and understanding are important from others as well as from themselves.

What I hear during this time is "I can't do this anymore"; "I can't go on"; "I can't seem to get enough sleep"; "I just want to sleep and sleep and sleep"; "No matter how much sleep I get, it's never enough"; "My tiredness feels so old and so deep"; "I don't think it will ever go away"; "I just can't go on this way."

Here is Tiffany's journal entry during this time:

Tiffany

I am so tired. It's a deep, deep tiredness. I don't feel especially sleepy, yet I do. It's not exhaustion, just deep, old tiredness — old, old, as if my struggle has gone on a long, long time. Before all this started, I had the thoughts "I can't keep doing this. I am so tired. I can't keep doing it." I didn't know exactly what the "it" was, but now I do: the "it" is keeping me hidden and keeping all that pain inside, and keeping on pretending I am OK, not sad. I have to hide the sadness. The sadness is the shame I felt guilt about, so I have to hide it or people will judge me as wrong and not acceptable.

Now this tiredness is there — outside. Wave after wave of sadness brings up the tiredness — old, old tiredness. It's not body tiredness; it's eons old; it's inner-core tiredness — tired of battling, tired of being someone else.

Deep — Tired — Old — no words, no physical — just deep, deep tired. Tired of trying to be competent, covering up my vulnerability. My vulnerability is fear of rejection, hurt, ridicule. I'm not accepted. There's game-playing. There's being nice when I feel angry, cover, cover, cover. It's too much now, too much struggle too much, too old. I have to surrender to me. *I have to be me at all costs. I can't go on this way.*

* * *

The deep tiredness does go away when transcenders have got enough rest. After the entire system is rested, growth seems to be accelerated, and transcenders have the energy to implement changes. The learning in this step is the deep realization that they can no longer live the old way and that they have to find a new way. The old patterns of living have to change to healthier, easier, more authentic ways of being.

Learning about Needs

Needs are a very important part of the reclaiming process. A need is defined as a requirement, something necessary for living, something essential. Needs must be separated from desires. A desire is defined as wish, fancy, inclination, liking, or fondness. I may desire a castle, but I don't need one. I need to eat. I need to feel. Desires are important in helping one to create dreams and goals in life.

For transcenders, learning to distinguish their needs from others' needs and to meet them in appropriate ways is important. They have to stop meeting needs inappropriately through dysfunction. *Appropriately* is the important word here and means "in a suitable way without hurting ourselves and/or others." Transcenders often have a fear of meeting their needs because of what they saw when they were growing up. Their families tried to meet needs through abuse, neglect, and making others responsible for their feelings, needs, and desires.

When needs were met inappropriately, transcenders may have been given the responsibility of meeting others' needs, as well as desires, and they lost any sense of their own needs and desires. For example, if my mother is needy and lonely and needs me to feel her feelings early in our relationship, I will have very little awareness of a separation of her needs and feelings from mine. In this kind of relationship, I may feel overwhelmed, confused, and helpless. I may also believe that her needs are really mine. In the reclaiming process, I have to sort out me from Mom in many ways so that I know which needs are mine and which needs are Mom's to satisfy. No matter how hard I try, I can never satisfy Mom's needs; she has to do it for herself. I can only choose to help her satisfy her needs; that is my human limit.

Learning about our needs is vital because needs teach us what we like, what we don't like, and what we need in order to feel loved and OK in our world. Needs help us to know whom to invite into our world to help satisfy us and whom not to invite. When we explore our needs, we discover and enhance our common bond of humanness with other people. As a result, we learn greater love and patience with ourselves and each other.

An important thing that many transcenders learn is that they are human and that their needs are very similar to, if not the same as, everyone else's. They discover that their needs are not out of proportion or "too much." They discover that they were given "too little" as children.

Marie's parents, for example, did not want her and acted out their anger by physically abusing Marie when she was hungry and tried to get some food. She learned that if she tried to satisfy her needs, she got hurt. She learned to be afraid every time she needed. This fear then acted to block even an awareness of her needs. Every time she got close to a need, the fear said, "Don't! Dangerous! Stop! Stop before you get hurt!" Such fear must be felt and understood before one moves on to satisfy one's needs appropriately. In a case like Marie's, it means feeling the awfulness of starving and then eating when she is hungry. She may first have to learn when she is hungry by putting herself on a schedule like an infant's.

Learning to satisfy needs is a journey of trial and error for transcenders, a journey of trying different ways to satisfy their different needs. They discover that different ways work at different times; that some ways don't work at all; and that a normal, growing, ever-developing human being's needs change and evolve. Needs change from day to day and from year to year, depending on the transcender's world and activity. For example, what we need as infants is very different from what we need as teenagers. Needs also depend on what kind of day it's been. I love to ride horses. Depending on what kind of stress I have had, I have different needs in the riding area. On some days, I have a great need for a hard, challenging lesson. On other days,

I just want to take a trail ride. On still other days, I may want to groom the horse more than to ride. Whatever my need is that day, it is OK.

Using the Will Appropriately

The will is the focal point of the self. It's like a librarian who gathers all the available resources and puts the resources in a certain area for use and the accomplishment of goals. The will's strength then takes the resources and works to keep the person focused by screening out and fighting any onslaught or distraction from a goal. For the transcender, the will gathers resources that protect and nurture the authentic self during childhood. (The will is further discussed in Chapter 4.)

Some transcenders, in order to survive, have had to develop a strong will. During the healing process, this strong will often interferes with growth because it has been trained to ensure survival. To be used appropriately and productively in the healing process, the will has to be channeled into promoting growth and healing rather than fighting it.

To change my use of my will I like the process of thanking myself for all of the help I have given myself by using my will and then adding, "Now I need to use my will in another way." With this kind of wording, transcenders treat themselves in a gentle manner and encourage growth rather than having another battle to deal with inside themselves. This way of talking to oneself unites their internal strength and shifts the focus of the will. Transcenders are then able to decide when to use their will "full strength" and when to lessen its effect. They learn this as the healing continues and they develop more trust of themselves and others. The process of shifting the willing is a learning process of trial and error. Transcenders learn how, when, with whom, and with what strength to use their will in "normal" life, now that life is safer and more secure.

Getting Rid of Shame and Secrets

In the reclaiming process, shame and secrets have to be uncovered and disinfected. I view both of these areas as old infected wounds that need to be lanced, cleansed, and aired to promote healing. As with any infected wound the less the airing, the more painful the wound and the more the energy needed to contain it. If one is to cleanse and heal shame and secrets, they must be expressed or aired. Once they are expressed, the feeling work can be done. The inner pain and energy that have held the secrets for so long can then be released, and fresh air can be brought in for healing.

In addition, an understanding of the shame and secrets must be developed. This understanding allows transcenders to gain more insight into what happened to them and to gain an understanding of their parents' behavior. Secrets are often generations old and have been passed down through the years to each new generation. With the understanding comes a choice of continuing the secrets or stopping the generational dysfunction surrounding them.

In my family, a generational secret was my grandmother's deep loneliness. She was from the old country and could not speak English when she arrived. She made few friends and kept to herself most of her sixty-four years. Her children, at some deep, inner level, felt responsible for her loneliness. But the loneliness was a secret and created shame. What would have been healthier would have been to talk about her loneliness and to become clear that it was *her* loneliness and not her children's.

Sometimes, old shame is triggered by trying to blend the family of origin with new, healthier friends. The following is from Chris about his experience with shame in his family:

———————————————— *Chris* ————————————————

There is an awareness of shame and embarrassment about the past in the present. Feelings of hurt and disappointment never seem to dissipate. I still have a gnawing pain when thoughts of my family arise. For example, I never invited my mother to my wedding because I felt embarrassed by her. What would my new friends and family think? I was also secretly happy when my stepdad died so he couldn't come to my graduation. I also couldn't let anyone know that my father committed suicide; they would think that something's mentally wrong with me, too.

*　*　*

The greatest feeling comes from airing secrets and shames: *freedom*! After this airing, transcenders have more energy because they no longer have to hold in the "crimes." They also have more energy to be themselves because they are no longer afraid and shameful, and they no longer have to hide. Once again, they come to realize at a very deep level that they are OK.

Developing Trust

Trust, like respect, is learned and earned in relationships. Trust is a knowing that what a person says, she or he will do. If I say I will be at the clinic for an appointment with a client, that client needs to know I will be there. If I say I will call, I call. When words match behavior trust is built. Trust of the self is vital to the growing self. Trust is supposed to be taught by caring parents from the time we are infants and all the way into adulthood. Infants learn trust when they are hungry and cry, and their parents come to feed and comfort them. From this experience, they learn to trust others as well as themselves and their needs. When appropriate responses don't occur, infants learn not to trust themselves or others. They may even have a hard time knowing when they are depressed because they have rarely been treated with love and respect. They may come to accept being unhappy as normal living.

Think for a moment what abused children do learn from their parents. (It is not trust of others or themselves.) They literally find themselves fighting for their lives with the very people who are supposed to protect and love them. They learn, in essence, not to trust, and always to be on guard to defend themselves.

As adults, transcenders must learn trust, or life will be very difficult and painful. This learning is possible through caring and loving relationships. It can occur in therapy with a good, nurturing therapist who encourages and acknowledges this area of growth. I have often been told by clients that the greatest assets in therapy are love and acceptance, which teach the clients that they are not just the next appointment. This does not mean that the therapist is "perfect" and does not make mistakes. Mistakes, however, are *not* abuse and *not* a lack of trust. They are just mistakes, which need to be acknowledged, discussed, felt, and dealt with in a manner that encourages trust. Many transcenders have an all-or-nothing belief. If the therapist makes a mistake, that's it, and therapy is done. What processing the mistake does is to teach another way to deal with mistakes and to help develop trust. Transcenders learn that they are human and that it's OK to make mistakes.

Trust also builds when transcenders continue to reclaim themselves and to eliminate the betrayal of self. The betrayal of self occurs when the false self is created and the real self is abandoned by the transcender. Reclaiming in this area is going back and forgiving themselves for the abandonment and reowning themselves. There is usually a lot of anger and fear in this area. Understanding that the betrayal and abandonment occurred to ensure survival is important.

Here's one final note on trust: Because they had little from their world, transcenders have adopted what I call a *tyrant*. The tyrant is in charge of making transcenders do what they are supposed to do. If the task is not accomplished, the tyrant usually dishes out some sort of punishment to the transcender. Sometimes, this tyrant is imagined as a troll or a fiendish type of character with a whip that lashes out and drives the transcender unmercifully. The tyrant is a combination of the parent that transcenders carry inside themselves (the internalized parent from childhood) and the drive to survive. Part of the reclaiming is either to eliminate the tyrant or to tame and retrain it. This occurs when transcenders begin to build trust in themselves to handle their world without abuse and dysfunction.

Examining Work

Work is another area that must be thoroughly examined and evaluated in the reclaiming process. Without knowing it, some transcenders find themselves working for companies that are very similar to their dysfunctional families. The similarities include the pattern and style of relating, the neglect of employees, the abuse of employees by overwork or the use of off-hours, rigid rules that are not negotiable under any circumstances, and lack of structure, or rules, so that no one knows what he or she is supposed to do. Sometimes, employees may even "get into trouble" if they take their own initiative.

As transcenders grow, they become more aware of how the dysfunctions of their work and their family compare. It is like a match. Transcenders know it feels OK to be in the organization because it is similar to their family's system of relating. It's familiar, and they know what's expected, how to behave, and what to do. I hear, "I like it, I know what to expect. I'm comfortable there." These are feeling responses and may not actually be true, but they are true concerning the dysfunction.

As transcenders heal and grow, they become more and more aware of the dysfunction in their work place. At some point, transcenders make a decision about staying or leaving their employment. Sometimes, they choose another field entirely; sometimes, they leave on early retirement or move to a new company. In some wonderful instances, transcenders are in healthy, loving places to work.

Learning to Play

Play releases stress, re-creates energy, balances life, develops the inner child, and is fun. Play is very important for everyone, children and adults. Some transcenders, thank goodness, use play as a survival technique and find it a vital escape that helps ensure survival. Others did not play as children and have the disadvantage of not knowing how to play as adults. Play *can* and *must* be learned by those who don't play. Learning to play is an important part of reclaiming the child from the past as well as the adult of the present.

Play can be learned in many ways: watching others; attending play workshops that focus on teaching play to the adult children of dysfunctional families; participating in play with others who do play; and playing with children. One learns to play simply by doing it. In the beginning, it is a little scary and unnerving. Transcenders may feel that someone is about to come and punish them. These feelings usually come from never having been a "real kid" and the guilt of play's not being OK. These feelings pass as play becomes more comfortable and fun. If there is punishment after play, a close examination is needed to stop this abuse. It may be that the transcender is punishing herself or himself, or that the "playmate" is inappropriate.

Learning to play should be an experimental, discovery-filled journey that is fun and creative. We need to give ourselves permission to be carefree and full of life and to take time to discover ourselves. To start, think of things you have always wanted to do, and do them. If you do something and find that you really don't like it, try something else. If you find you like it, continue doing it, and enjoy it. If the activity requires certain skills and you want to develop them, do so. Don't expect to be perfect in the beginning. The goal is fun, not stress or perfection. Some activities you may enjoy, but you may not want to develop those skills. For example, I enjoy walking with our dog. I just walk. Some days, I walk fast, some slow. I don't want to develop a technique of walking or get into walking races. I just want to enjoy walking. However, in my horseback riding, I do want to develop my skill in riding and jumping my horse. I want to become an adequate rider and to show my horse in shows. Both walking and riding are play to me. So are teasing (not critically) and bubble blowing. If I find I no longer enjoy these activities, I will explore and find other things I do want to do. Nothing is permanent, right or wrong. It's up to you. The only rule is don't hurt yourself or others, and don't let others hurt you.

Play is anything you enjoy doing. It may be having dinner out, talking with a dear friend, wrestling with a significant other, or listening to music. It may be playing in the sandbox with your children. Children are great at teaching play to adults; watch them and join in. Play may also, at times, be your work. Whatever it is, play needs to help you shift gears to a more relaxed, carefree, fun state, a state in which you can enjoy and have fun.

Developing Spirituality

Spirituality is the core not only of the healing and growth process, but also of humanness. It's so vital to reclaiming the self that the next entire chapter is devoted to it.

Surviving Dysfunctional Days

Over the years in my work with transcenders, we have both noticed what I have come to call *dysfunctional days*. Dysfunctional days are a throwback to earlier times with the family, but they occur after most of the healing has been done. Transcenders seem to revert to old feelings, thinking, and sometimes even behavioral patterns. Experiencing a dysfunctional day is like reliving a day in your old pattern of dysfunction with the family.

The good thing about dysfunctional days is that they don't last long *and* that, as transcenders continue to grow, they occur less and less often. The bad thing about these days is that they can be unnerving and unsettling, especially, if one doesn't know what is happening. Transcenders honestly believe that they are regressing and losing all their hard work. Neither is true. Once the dysfunctional day is dealt with, the healthier patterns return.

Dysfunctional days may be triggered by stress, loss, anniversaries of important traumas, or other difficult times. They may also occur for what seems to be no reason at all other than waking up. Transcenders need to deal with these days in the same way they deal with other feelings: feel the feelings and work to gain an understanding of what the day is all about. If they are in therapy, they need to explore the day in session. If the dysfunction occurs after the therapeutic process and lasts longer than a few days, an appointment with the former therapist is needed to explore the feelings. Most important, transcenders need to learn from this experience and to remember that these days don't last.

CONCLUSION

The process of reclaiming the self is vital to healing and growing. As traumas of the past are reexperienced and explored, the authentic self is uncovered and developed. There is time in this process for "catching up" with oneself and for no longer having to be mature beyond one's years. There is finally time just to be.

Through this difficult process, joy does return and emotional health is gained that has never before been experienced. Transcenders gain confidence, love, and the ability to love. There is a clearing, a cleaning, and a releasing of the body and the soul into true freedom to be one's own self.

As transcenders grow, they put their families of origin into perspective. They are even able to laugh about certain things that happened to them in their families. They may even remember some good things that happened in childhood. Amazingly, they are even able to list the ways they gained and grew because of their survival. In the process, they go from trauma, anger, and despair to healing, growth, and hope.

Future days are full of challenge. Healing and growth don't mean that the rest of life is totally wonderful. They do mean that transcenders have all of themselves to deal with whatever life brings.

Chapter 9

Spirituality, Healing, and Growth

I just finished a twelve-hour day at work. It is one of many twelve- to sixteen-hour days I put in between work, writing, and family responsibilities. Today, I had a meeting with the staff, picked up the kids after school for an appointment, functioned as a clinic director, worked with clients in therapy, and met with two attorneys and discussed a very difficult, emotional case. Yesterday, I coached my daughter's high school equestrian team. With this responsibility, I get up at 4:30 A.M. and run around with horses and riders until at least 6 P.M. Sound like fun? Actually, it is. I love the kids, clients, work, and, especially, the variety in my life. The only problem with my schedule is that there is little time to rest, and I sometimes become exhausted.

When I finally arrived home tonight, all I wanted to do was to crash. I didn't want to move or talk to anyone about anything; I just wanted to vegetate. However, our dog just got loose and has decided to have one of his biannual excursions into the neighborhood. On these excursions, he believes he must, like my two teens, stay out most of the night visiting everything around. I am contented to let him roam and greet him in the morning. However, my daughter, who works for a veterinarian, has seen many dogs that have been hit by cars and is refusing to go to bed until he is home and safe. She isn't feeling well and is exhausted. So I, not wanting to be a "bad mommy," have promised to stay up until he safely arrives home. It is now midnight, and my wonderful husband has just taken over dog-watching duty for me.

I'm so tired that I'm not sure who I am anymore. I climb into bed *anxiously* looking for my head and pillow to meet. *Just* as I climb into bed, I feel that God is telling me to pick up the pen and write. After many years of having a relationship with God, I know to follow such feelings because it is the best for all concerned. So, I pick up the pen and start to write. As I write, the words come in spite of my tiredness — God and I are working together.

My relationship with my spirituality, that part of me that relates and is connected to God, enables me to use my resources whenever and wherever they are needed. This is true in giving to others as well as to myself. My spirituality has given me the ability to write this chapter in spite of being tired. Actually, the more I write this, the less tired I feel and the more energy and strength I feel. Energy, power, strength, wisdom, understanding, and love that are beyond human limitations — that's spirituality. These are available to me at any time, in any place, whether I or someone else needs them.

My personal relationship to God enables me to balance the many facets of my life. God loves me, nurtures me, strengthens me, and gives to me wisdom and abilities beyond my human limitations. It is my spirituality that helps me to help others find and develop their original package. In my work, I have seen many miracles — things that happen beyond the human-sighted, concrete, world understanding. It is God who creates miracles by using me and others as a channel for His love and power. I find that miracles are common when we are connected to God's power and love.

I define spirituality as that part of us, our life essence, that is connected to and relates to God. Others may use terms such as *higher power*, *higher consciousness*, or *universal energy*. For simplicity in this book I use *God*. Whatever we call our spirituality, it is the relationship between our essence, the spirit or soul, with the living, loving power that created us. It is through our spirituality that we are connected to our higher power. It is through our spirituality that we can love. We human beings are spiritual beings first, then physical, mental, and emotional beings. It is this core that is our power and the prime influence in action and life. As our core, our spirituality must be nurtured and developed. It is an amazing, needed power that helps us navigate through life as well as through the healing and growing process. It is vital to everything we do.

By spirituality, I do not mean organized religion. Organized religion may be part of the expression of our spirituality, but it is not itself spirituality. Our spirituality may be expressed by communing with God in the woods; meditating; worshiping in our homes, in a church, or in a temple; or sharing our spirituality with people who believe the same way that we do. However we relate to God, we always gain healing, growth, understanding, love of self, love of others, and direction for our lives.

Do we need our spirituality? God? Absolutely! I remember a time in my life when I was without a deep relationship with God. I describe myself during that time as an angry, depressed women in a deep, dark slime pit. I was a young mother with two children. My daughter was two and my son had just been born. I was recovering from his birth, a caesarean section. I was tired, exhausted, lonely, and unbelievably depressed. I *truly* did not know who I was. No one could have prepared me for what it was really going to be like to be a mother. I hated it (hate is a strong word for intense anger, nothing more). At that time, no matter how hard I tried to rest to gain energy, or to do better, or to be less angry, or to be a more loving mother, I couldn't. I felt as tired as I do tonight, with one major difference: Tonight, I can function — not be in hate — and know, really know, that tomorrow I will regain my strength. Tomorrow, I will be fine and will have whatever I need to handle the day. I have a power, my spirituality, beyond my humanness because my humanness is limited.

As I work with clients, there are times (as in everyone's work) when I don't know how to help or what to offer next. At these times, all I have to say is, "God, help!" I then feel Him working through me to offer what that person needs. Sometimes this is a thought or intuitive feeling. Other times I may confront a continuing dysfunctional behavior. Whatever form the help comes in, it always encourages healing.

How does this healing occur? Basically, the self, the soul, and the free will join God to develop the original package, the ultimate human who is both spiritual and human. One flows with and through the other, each nurturing the other, each contributing to our lives and the world with God's power and love. In this way, we are combined and enmeshed with God to help heal individuals and our world.

Because God created the original package of the self and the soul, we need to be in a relationship with Him. We will feel incomplete and sense something is missing without it. Without God, there is often an empty spot or void inside us that only He can fill and nurture. Usually no one and nothing else fits, fills, or satisfies this emptiness. This void in us is connected to God by what I call a *spiritual umbilical cord*. The umbilical cord connects soul to creator. It is there when God creates us, and we need to have this connection throughout our life. It is through this connection that we receive His energy and love.

Feeling abandoned is really feeling our separation from God. This separation is often felt as a deep, gnawing, lonely feeling. Philosophers sometimes call this feeling *existential loneliness*: We essentially come into this world alone, live our lives alone, and die alone. However, it is more than a feeling of loneliness. It is a spiritual need. God has given us this need to help us unite with Him at a deep level because He knows we need Him to get through life. We all feel a form of abandonment and are spiritually hurt and crippled until we find and develop our relationship with God. Once this union occurs, the void is filled, and deep soul healing can occur.

Does it make a difference? Yes! I am able to accomplish all I do because I gain energy, strength beyond human limits, and wisdom from my spirituality.

THE TRANSCENDER AND SPIRITUALITY

Spirituality is important to most transcenders. They need to believe in and rely on a power greater than themselves while working to survive the abuses they endured. Their spirituality helps to guide, energize, nurture, and develop the transcender's authenticity through childhood and adulthood. Many transcenders find their relationship with God the core of the survivorship that enabled them to transcend their family. It is this power that enables them to continue and feel focused on a positive path. In addition, formal worship at churches and temples supplies transcenders with a sanctuary as well as relationships with nurturing people. Marie and Tiffany were two of the transcenders who found in their spirituality the essence of their survivorship and healing. I relate their sharings with you:

--- *Marie* ---

When I was a small child, I decided God was really my father. He would take care of me and keep me safe by teaching me how to take care of myself.

Looking back over the years, I see that this adoption of God as my father at an early age was a strong influence along the path of growth and the development of my own value system. The facade of the upstanding Christian life my parents showed the outside world "took" in my young life. As a child, I was forced to be involved more in the dark, evil world of Satan than in God's warm, caring love. I knew the difference. God's love fed and nurtured me and protected me, my spirit or soul, from the cold, satanic life of my parents.

I was so alone that it was very easy for me to look to God for direction. Fortunately for me, the bad was so bad that the only direction was away from the lifestyle of my parents, and the only other direction I knew was that of God. I certainly could not claim credit for trying to be a "good person," for the alternative was too horrible.

One of my coping mechanisms, which began in my early teens and which I still use today, involves thinking through whatever situation I am in. I search for the answer to the question "What does God want me to learn from this?" I never felt that God wanted me to be hungry, lonely, terrified, or hurt, but because I was in that situation, it was my responsibility to learn something positive from it and then to use the knowledge to help myself or someone else.

I have always felt sorry for people who say they don't know how to pray. If God ever took a vacation, I would be in trouble because I talk to Him all the time. How many times in my life, especially in my adult life, I have found myself in situations where I've had to say, "Okay, God, you are going to have to get me through this," and He always does.

I have been through periods of doubt, even anger at God, but it is through this doubt that my faith in God has been strengthened, and I know He is quite capable of handling my doubt and anger. As much as I love God, His watch and His calendar are rarely the same as mine. It is when I try to do things in my own time frame, without regard to His, that He lovingly brings me to my knees to wait for Him, much as a lion swats at his cubs when they get a little carried away with their own importance.

Without God's love, His very real presence, I do not believe I could have survived my childhood as I can now see it. I feel a very strong debt to God, one that I can begin to pay back only by sharing whatever I have with others. Sometimes, I forget that this is to be done for His glory, not mine, and He gets my attention.

I cannot imagine being strong enough to survive in this world without a sense of God. I know that I could not. Without God's guidance and direction, I would be lost and only marking time in life.

In many ways, God was all I knew as true, safe love. As my healing continues, I am learning the joy of receiving safe love from other people, and this safe love is usually God-based to some degree.

Because healing has necessitated returning to my childhood, I don't think I would have had the courage to do this without God right beside me. I have no doubt in my mind that He chose my therapist because of her commitment to Him, just as I also know that He continues to direct my process through both of us as well as others He chooses to enter my life. My therapy, my healing, has been one of the most demanding tasks I've ever undertaken. For me, my surviving and healing from the past would not have been possible without a strong faith in God.

Tiffany

I don't know how I knew to be connected to God. I just knew it was important, very important. I attended church. Sometimes, I attended with my family, but most of the time I attended without them. My family would give me rides, but they were too busy to go themselves. I am grateful that they valued church enough to take me every week.

I didn't go to Sunday school; I felt that what they were studying was dumb. I can remember going once and deciding that I got more out of sitting in church than out of being in Sunday school. Being in church was a powerful experience for me. When I went into church, I usually felt beaten, demoralized, stupid, and a bad person. As I sat there and took in the service, with its prayers, singing and nurturing atmosphere, I would begin to feel close to and nurtured by God. I prayed intensely and deeply about my life, my loneliness, my problems, and anything else I needed to talk to God about. I also prayed about my "badness." As the service continued, my mood would shift, and I would feel lighter, a good person and happier. I felt I could go on again.

After I attended church, the week went better for me because I had had this intense, uplifting, nurturing experience. I felt that God loved me, and that was all that mattered. Also, I attended church with a good friend. Her family never went, so we became buddies in the process of surviving by attending church together. We both knew that we needed it; we didn't really understand why or how it helped, but we knew we had to be there. We were both still very lonely, but not alone in our loneliness.

In my adult healing and growth process, my relationship with God was my stabilizing, nurturing, sustaining core. It enabled me to get through the pain, turmoil, struggles, confusion, and deep grieving. My relationship with God also guided me to all of the steps of my process. Without it, I would have been lost and unsure of the direction I was going in and terrified to do the feeling work I had to do.

During the worst part of the healing, the intense grieving, I could feel God supporting and loving me. With this knowing, I never felt alone and knew I would not only feel better but would also become more of the real me. Without God, I would have had a much more difficult time. One of the best things I have learned over the years is that I can express all my feelings and thoughts to God. I have been intensely angry at Him and have screamed and yelled at Him. After these sessions, I feel Him holding me, loving me, and sort of saying, "Now doesn't that feel better?" I have learned that what He wants from me is my love and my sharing with Him. It's the not talking to Him that really messes up the relationship.

Again, I don't think I would have made it through childhood or the healing process without Him. I was still messed up emotionally and needed to do a lot of healing as an adult, but I found the ability to do it because of God's love for me.

HEALING AND SPIRITUALITY

My spirituality has been the core of my healing and growing from past wounds. God's power has taken me from the slime pit, with all its dysfunction, anger, and pain, to amazing healing, growth, and joy. For example, my body used to get sick when I wanted to retreat from my world. I now have a body that rarely gets sick. I used to have few friends. I now have many vitalizing, growing, exciting, wonderful, spiritual people in my life. Healing, under God's guidance, is nothing short of amazing. I still battle in some areas, but I see those areas as opportunities for growth.

God's purpose in healing is to develop the original package, the authentic self. The authentic self is like the kernel of a seed. Growing up in a dysfunctional family forces the kernel to create a hard outer covering to protect it from the world. This protective covering is the behavior and patterns that we develop to fend off painful experiences. Sadly, the behavior is mostly dysfunctional and not authentic.

Like maple seeds with their propellers, we are sent forward to have many life experiences. These experiences offer a chance for healing, learning, and growth. As we are propelled forward and experience life, we have a choice of shedding the hard exterior of the seed by healing and becoming authentic, or of staying in old, dysfunctional behavior. If we choose to heal, the wonderful kernel, the authentic self, is then exposed and free to be. Through healing, the authentic self becomes ready to meet the world openly, without the tough protective covering. We then learn to be free and to grow like the seed, which produces new life: vulnerable, yet strong; strong, yet vulnerable; open, strong, and illuminating—illuminating the truth of ourselves in relationship to God.

This illumination is spiritual light. Spiritual light, God's light, always overcomes darkness. It gives joy where there is sorrow, happiness where there is pain. Through the healing and growth journey, we are personally called on to develop our authentic selves and to reach out to others on their journey. The process of healing means growth and learning not only for ourselves, but also to help bring peace and love to our troubled world.

We get to this healing and light by developing our spirituality, by seeking God. The process is one of healing deeper and deeper to the essence of our being, to our truth and integrity. This healing can occur in two ways: (1) we begin to heal from our emotional hurts and then develop our relationship with God, or (2) we unite with God and then heal from emotional wounds. Either way, or a combination of the two, leads us to healing, growth, and a spirituality that sustains us through life.

Spirituality commands us to live our lives with integrity — the truth of our essence, our original package. Integrity is being our truth, speaking our truth, and living our truth. We are commanded to develop ourselves to the fullest extent possible. As we venture forth and develop ourselves, God helps us take care of others in our world. It's really His job to take care of all the significant others in our lives, not ours. It's His job to take care of the alcoholic spouse or parent. It's His job to heal the abusive sibling. It's His job to tell us how to help with the healing. Our job is to heal, grow, and love ourselves and others in the fullest way possible, sending God's light and love to all things and people we are in contact with as well as ourselves. Healing, growing, living in the light of God — that is our integrity.

God loves each and every one of us deeply. No person ever walks this life alone. God is always there — helping, touching, connecting, and healing. He gives us obstacles in our lives to help us grow. The obstacles are to toughen, teach, develop, and encourage us to be everything we authentically are — the self created by God.

Healing personally has given me the wisdom of profoundness, an ability to say, "I know what it's like, I've been there." I've been where the pain is — the deep sorrow. I can tell you of its pain and torment. I can tell you of its growth and giving. I can tell you of the joy that follows. I can say in all truth that healing is not only possible, but absolutely wonderful. Let nothing stand in the way of your healing. Nothing. You are everything to God. He will lead you to your essence. He will love you and others in your world through the healing process. Above all, He loves. His intention is not to destroy, but to restore, repair, heal, and bring peace and love to you and the world.

PERSONAL MISSION

All of us have a purpose or mission that we must accomplish in our world. It's an important part of our healing and growth process. This mission is of ultimate importance because it coordinates with the mission of others working to heal our world. If we reject this mission or fail to develop it, the world has one less healing and helping person. Also, we lose an important part of ourselves and may become unhappy, discontented, and angry. We cannot be fully content, happy, productive, or joyful until we are working to accomplish our personal mission.

The core of everyone's mission is to support and love each other through our shared humanness. We all need support in our struggle to be authentic as well as in our struggle to love and be loved. Because we are human, we share and know this experience, with all its turmoil, pain, and joy. We can also identify with each other's spiritual struggles. We need to encourage each other's spiritual development and share our need for God. This is true regardless of our sexual preference, food preference, career choice, or lifestyle.

We need to commit ourselves to keep loving, healing, caring, growing, and accomplishing our missions. This is vital in order to stop the abuse and dysfunction in our world. We need to heal so that we can love each other fully, and we need to love each other in order to heal the world. We must love, love, love, and when we are tired, we need to love some more. We *can* heal our world through our love and spirituality.

DEVELOPMENT OF SPIRITUALITY

Spirituality can be explored and developed by praying, reading, meditating, talking with others, and trying different types of organized religions. The only objective is the development of a relationship between ourselves and God. Development of this relationship, like growth, takes a lifetime. As our spirituality develops, we gain deeper strength, freedom, understanding, and trust of ourselves and others.

The earlier spirituality is developed, the sooner it can be a power used during the healing and growing process. Some individuals have developed their spirituality from early childhood. Others need to start from scratch in their explorations as adults. Either way, it's a vital power for all of living.

In your explorations, if you find yourself in a group feeling stifled, controlled, abused, and/or frustrated, you are probably in the wrong place. God is love. Keep looking, and trust your spirituality to help guide you to the right place.

Some people, including many transcenders, have difficulty exploring and developing their spirituality because of a strict religious upbringing. These religions often teach that God is a strict and punishing God, that human beings are totally bad, and that they will go to hell if they do not do everything right. Individuals raised in these religions often experience intense fear and guilt just at the thought of exploring their relationship to God.

Spiritual exploration does not necessarily mean throwing childhood religion out the window. It does means exploring it, evaluating it, and figuring out what *you* believe as opposed to what the religion believes. Some people embrace their childhood religion; others leave and discover a different way. Again, what is vital is the development of the relationship with God.

In exploring spirituality, there is one *major* word of caution. Be alert for satanic-based cults. These cults are very real in our world. As the story of Marie testifies, they are dangerous and severely abusive. There are also many cults that are not abusive in this manner, but that seek to have us believe that their way is the only way and that we will be damned if we don't do things their way. I don't believe this. I do believe that God deeply loves us and is committed to helping us to heal and to develop our original package. His love far outweighs *any* rules or regulations. He just wants us to talk to Him and love Him.

DIFFERENT RELIGIONS

Spirituality is love: love of self, of others, of the world, and of God. God's love is for everyone in the world, and He offers it in many ways. There is no one way. There are many different religions because we are all different and have different needs. It's the kernel God is after, the authentic self that is able to love the self, others, and the world.

In healing and growth, all areas come together in the authentic self: rules and limits, growth, enlightenment, and love. It is in this way that the world, as well as the individual, is fulfilled and healed. God wants us to heal, grow, and enlighten ourselves in His love. That is what *all* individuals who come into this world are directed to do.

In closing this chapter, I leave you with those thoughts: Spirituality is our human essence, our realness. Through our spirituality, God's love, wisdom, and guidance are given to us for all of life. Because of our spirituality, we are never alone.

Chapter 10

Where Are the Transcenders Now?

Transcenders work long and hard to create the world of their dreams. Do they succeed? What are their lives like in adulthood after healing? Are there benefits in transcending? In general, their lives are wonderful in many respects, but they don't have fairy-tale endings. They have gained special learning from their lives even though most of them would trade this painful learning for healthy, loving parents. Often, their present lives, compared with their past, look like Utopia. In this chapter, five previously mentioned transcenders share their present lives and what they have gained from becoming transcenders.

Marie

Looking back at all those painful, horrible times, I can't believe I have such peace and joy today. I believed in the existence of the light at the end of the tunnel, but I had no way of knowing how bright that light could be! I see my recovery as a daily process and one that I continue to work out.

Do I feel successful? Yes! I am continuing to heal, feel, and grow with the help of newly learned ways of working with myself. I am proud of what I have been able to accomplish. I am not proud of the things that happened in my past, but for the most part, these things are over. I see now that I had no control over them and am not responsible for them. I am not the abuser. I was the victim and have chosen to be a transcender. I have worked hard to survive.

Until recently, the past ten years of my life have been very physically painful. Numerous surgeries, including a bowel resection and a colostomy, did not alleviate the pain of inflammatory bowel disease. It was as if each painful memory was stored inside, still producing pain, with the cause unknown to me. For years, I was given injections of Demerol and morphine to help control the pain. Looking back, it's no wonder that the medication was of little help. The pain was the result of an infection known as abuse. To date, no medication has been found to be successful in dealing with that type of pain.

Before, any feeling I refused to acknowledge was immediately turned inward and converted to pain. Now, after more healing, I have learned to own, to feel my feelings and express my emotions rather than to swallow them. The frequency and intensity of physical pain are much smaller than in the past. I am still capable of inflicting pain on myself, but I choose not to! Besides, I don't feel now as if I need to be punished, as I once did. I know I'm not to blame for everything negative.

One of the sad things about growing up in a family where you learn to insulate yourself in order to survive is that, in trying to protect yourself from the bad things, you also keep out the good. I realize now that there were people outside my family, especially in my teen years and beyond, who loved and cared about me. However, because of my background and a well-learned distrust of people, I was unable to take in what these people offered me. The door of fear that protected me was locked on both sides, but I held the key to this door within me. Now, I have unlocked the door and have realized that there are people who really do care about and love me. This is an important discovery and one that I am thoroughly enjoying.

I have always enjoyed working with people. I love to teach, and my years as an educator have been very significant to me. I am particularly skilled in helping others deal with their fears. My own personal background of having to deal with my terror has provided excellent training.

One of my joys in life is being able to provide for others what I did not have myself. Whether I am teaching preschool or community college, guiding my students in the labeling and the appropriate expression of emotions has always had high priority for me; yet I was over fifty years old when I internalized for the first time the idea that anger is a normal, healthy emotion.

Another joy in my life is giving to others and doing things for others. I have always been sensitive to the needs of other people — an outgrowth of the need to read others around me in order to survive. It has taken me longer to learn how to get my own needs met, but I am learning how to receive from others. Recently, a group of newfound friends surprised me with my very first birthday party, complete with balloons and cake. I loved it. It feels so good to be cared about.

Because I have walked in the black darkness of evil, the light of freedom shines even brighter for me. I am free to be myself. I am no longer terrified of beds, as I was for so many years, and am now able to sleep six hours a night; before my healing, I could sleep only three. I no longer live in fear, waiting for that "bad man" to find me. Instead, I laugh with friends I have grown to know and love, friends who know all about me and accept me for who I am. I see freedom as a special gift from my growing up.

I see transcenders as very determined souls. My determination has sustained me in the past and continues to provide me with the perseverance necessary for me to reach toward future goals. I know I can do it, whatever "it" is. From very early childhood, I was exposed to circumstances that engraved on my soul the challenge that I would not be like my mother. I have kept that promise to myself. I know I am nothing like her.

My love for nature has also come from my childhood trials. I am very close to nature because nature provided me many lessons. A walk through the woods, a sunrise, even the lightning during a storm were my teachers. This ability to look for guidance in the symbolism of my world still continues to nurture and sustain me.

Another gift that surviving has given me is God. God has had a very important influence throughout my life. He was the only security I really knew. Very early, I decided that God must think that I was able to handle whatever I had to deal with and that He expected me to turn stumbling blocks into stepping-stones. Many times I would pray, "God, please help me deal with this; show me what I should do," and without fail, God would make His presence known.

I have been asked if I was ever angry with God for allowing the abuse to take place. I don't believe He allowed it as much as He expected me to learn from it. Because of this expectation, I understand the "whys" behind adults who are abused as children and become abusers themselves, and this area is the key to the direction in which God is guiding my life in the present and for the future. There has to be some reason, some purpose, for the torture that I endured. I have a responsibility to use the knowledge and the experiences from my own life in a way that will help others who have experienced similar traumas.

I am now taking the required coursework for admission to graduate school. Within the next two years, I will begin my work as a therapist. I will be very surprised if God does not lead me to a position in which I will be working with survivors — a responsibility for which He has been preparing me for many years. I have gained so much in my life. I want to share what I have gained with others, not as a victim of abuse, but as a conqueror of it.

─────────────────── *Chris* ───────────────────

My life is just as I pictured it as a child. I have a family who loves me, and I love them. We don't scapegoat each other and never blame each other for anything. We work it out. We work at communication and at changing the old dysfunctional patterns, which sometimes surface, to healthier ways of relating. The love I have is so wonderful. There are times when I can't believe it's really mine. When I do get upset and have an old-type day (a dysfunctional day), I handle it. I try to work through it and learn from it. In this way, I gain.

I feel so free, so free to be just me. I'm not carrying my family's guilt, shame, and blame anymore. It's not mine. They still try to get me to take it, but I refuse. I don't even let it go inside me, because it's not mine and never was. I never thought I could say that and mean it. Wow! I'm really the real me. I am lovable, creative, intelligent, energized, and happy. I like my job, my family, my life. If I ever come to a place of not liking part of my life, I know I have the ability to change it. If there were problems with my children or with my wife, I know we'd just work on them and work them out.

Yes, I feel successful and happy. Yes, I have bad days, down days, but they don't last. I see them as part of life, not *as* my life, as I once did in childhood and early adulthood.

Life still holds many obstacles for me. My father is critically ill, and I'm having to face all those feelings. I hate the idea that he is still blaming me for everything, even his illness. But I know it's not my stuff. You'd think he'd give up or change when he is facing death. He'll never stop. There is part of me that still wishes he'd change and hopes he'll change so I can have at least one serious, loving conversation. I'd love to be able to talk about the past and try to heal the relationship. It would feel so good to settle all of that before he dies. I know it's a dream.

I do feel sorry for him, yet, not really. I do feel bad that he is in so much pain; yet he's caused so much pain. He's created his own world. One minute I cry, the next I get angry at him, and the next I pity him. I accept the way he is doing his life, but I don't like it. It's his life and his choices; I wish they were different.

I have gained from my childhood even though I wish it had been different. I wish I had had caring parents, but I have come to accept the fact that I didn't and still don't. I also realize I have gained from my growing up in ways that I would not have if I had had a normal childhood.

I think the biggest gain for me is the wisdom and understanding I now have as an adult. I better understand not only me, but also other people and the world. My past has helped me see that our world is made up of hurting people who need to be understood and loved. Many times, I can offer something to someone who looks as if he or she feels the way I used to feel because I've been there. I think I'm more patient, gentler, and kinder because of where I have been.

It's a good feeling to know that I can handle all sorts of things and continue to learn and grow. I don't feel helpless any more. I am confident and love my life.

Steve

My life now is more stable, less painful, and more fulfilling than my childhood. I never go hungry. I can't say it's always wonderful; it's not. I still have my struggles. I have two children and have a hard time balancing my work, my family, and my growth commitment to myself.

I had an accident recently that disabled me and triggered old emotional stuff dealing with the fear of having to go back to the old way of living. Just the thought of it terrifies me. I put myself back in therapy to work on some of the fear and to help me adjust to the disability. I'm dealing with its effects in my life and the losses it has caused. I'm slower and emotionally stressed. The disability has affected my whole life. I just can't do everything I've set out to do, at least not yet. I'm still working and still hoping.

I'm trying to work with the disability and adjust to it by rearranging my work and family schedules. I need more rest now, and it's hard to get it. Sometimes, my wife becomes upset with me, and I feel as if I'm going backward and will have to go back to that awful poverty again. I dread that so much. I just can't ever do that again, ever! Therapy is helping, but I still have the disability to deal with and the issues it's triggering from childhood.

Do I feel successful? Until the accident, I could have said I felt very successful. Everything was going fine. My wife and I had no major struggles, and I really enjoyed being with my children. We worked out the issues that came up and communicated well. We just handled it all. Now, since the accident, there have been stresses and struggles. We are still working to communicate and to deal with them; it's just harder. I'm not sure anymore if I feel successful. Some days, I know I am doing well and recovering. Other days, I feel set back and very disappointed. I keep trying, though. I won't give up. Giving up means going back to the old stuff; I'll never do that.

Did I gain from my survivorship? Yes and no. I hated the pain, the hunger, the cold, the neglect, the dysfunction, the struggle to be me. I wouldn't wish my growing-up and healing process on anyone. But, yes, I did gain. I learned things I would never have learned any other way. I'm not saying I would want to grow up the way I did; I'm just saying it did teach me some valuable lessons. It's not all a waste.

I have gained strength, a knowing that I can handle many difficult situations. I don't think I would have known what I could handle and live through if I had had nice, wonderful parents. I also gained a deep understanding and knowing of me. Having to heal from my childhood forced me to learn about me. That in itself is a wonderful gift. From learning about me, I gained an understanding and knowing of others, of humanity in general. I wouldn't wish my parents on anyone; yet I wouldn't want to give up my growth either.

Paul

The fighting, criticism, chaos, and all the pain are all that I remember from childhood. Now, I refuse to allow any of that in my house. I don't allow unfair fighting or name calling in my house. I make sure I praise and encourage friends, acquaintances, and relatives. I will never live that way again or allow anyone I care about to live that way.

That's why I seem to be a doer, an accomplisher. Some people call me an overachiever. I call me a motivated, caring person. I'm involved in local and state organizations that work to help children in abusive families. I'm especially interested in helping the parents change. I'm driven to do something more than just living an average life.

I get anxious if I'm not being productive. By productive, I mean accomplishing something that makes a difference. I'm saying I need to give and help. Thank goodness, I have learned to take care of myself and not to overextend my energies, but the giving is a very important part of my transcendership.

My friends understand this drive in me. They see that it makes a difference. They see that things change. That is one of the things I learned from my childhood and the healing process—that I can change things. I learned that I didn't ever have to live that way again, *and* that, if I can change, so can others. For example, a recent career change caught me off guard and sent me back to some old stuff. I know from past experience that I have to feel it and learn from it. I did, and I know my direction again.

Some people call me a crazy optimist. I call me a hard worker who believes in the ability of people to heal and change if given the chance. The hardest part for me is working with people who do not want to change. That's discouraging. The neat part is that a lot of people do want to change, and it's a tremendous high for me to be part of the change.

Do I feel successful? You bet! If I stopped feeling successful, I'd figure out what is going on and then change something. I will never be stuck again. I have learned too much about me to ever let that happen again. I have dear friends who love and and whom I love. I'm healthy, happy, and alive. I will never again accept dysfunction as part of my life.

---------------------------- *Tiffany* ----------------------------

I would describe my life as being just the way I want it. I have my family, friends, a new semihealed relationship with my parents, and love everywhere. The best part of my life is knowing that, if I don't like a part of it or have a clash with someone, I have the power to change it. I can create what I need. This doesn't mean leaving my family or destroying someone else. It means being in charge of my life and having the power to work with important people in my life to make changes that feel good to everyone.

I am no longer the victim. I'm no longer the trapped, helpless little girl who could do nothing to change her world. I really like me, my world, my career, and my family. The problems I have are like every other working mother's problems. I have a difficult time balancing the different aspects of my life with the available time in the day. I get torn between my needs, the family's needs, and career demands. But I wouldn't trade it. I'm challenged, loved, and happy.

I have regrets. I wish I had got into therapy sooner. That way, I would have felt better sooner. But I'm so glad I didn't wait any longer. I pray my children are not too affected by my struggles, especially my anger. I used to really want to hurt with my anger. I'm so grateful I'm healed.

I still have rough days, when I feel I have regressed. I work with my feelings and learn from them. Usually, the rough days are caused by not having the time to feel the feelings or wanting to avoid them. Once I work with the feelings, I feel better, learn from them and get on with my life. Actually, the rough days are part of my living cycle — feeling, learning, and using the growth I gain.

I learned many things from growing up in my family. I would trade the pain I went through any day for loving, adoring, normal parents and brothers. I didn't have them, but it wasn't all a waste either.

The biggest part is knowing I can live through anything. It's a strength I don't think I would have if I hadn't been subjected to all those trials — severe ridicule, criticism, emotional neglect, and not having anyone there to guide me and help me figure out life. I lived through long, never-ending loneliness, when I worked just to get through the minutes, let alone the hours, days, months, and years. My isolation, in turn, has given me a special relationship with myself and a knowing that I can survive.

There are very few situations in my life that I wouldn't be able to handle somehow. Now, my main decision is to find out what I do want to handle. The power is mine. I'm in charge, and I decide what goes and what doesn't. There is a working together with others. I have surrounded myself with individuals who care and listen, many of whom have dysfunctional family backgrounds, who have chosen to heal, and with whom I share a deep understanding.

This strength I have is wonderful and constantly reassures me. It's ever there, ever constant, saying that no matter what happens, "I will make it."

Equally important is my relationship with God. I know He is there for me in every situation. I have often wondered whether I would have turned to Him as much as I did if I hadn't grown up in my family. My spirituality is a prized possession and part of my knowing I can handle everything. God gives me love, guidance, and joy that is beyond descriptions.

My growing up and my healing process have taught me what I would venture to call wisdom. It is an understanding of myself, others, God, and the world. It's a sense of how we all fit. I have a truth about the world and about myself. This doesn't mean I have all the answers; I'm far from that. I do have the answers for me as I need them. If I don't know, I know how to find the answers.

Chapter 11

Practical Applications

Our world is close-knit. How often have things happened that made you say, "What a small world it is"? When one person moves, the next person feels it. When one nation makes a decision, another nation across the ocean takes the consequences. Individuals as well as nations must make healthy decisions to help change our hurting world into a peaceful, loving world. The material in this book can be used in many ways to help individuals and, in turn, to help our world. To close this book, I offer some of these ways.

As individuals, we must heal and continue to grow in order to heal our world and maximize its potential. It is no longer an option or a luxury. Individual healing and growing are necessary to create a healthy world. It is only in this way that we will gain a lasting, loving peace. Just think for a minute of the problems we could solve if we all developed our abilities and spirituality and worked with each other through love.

Collectively, we have the potential to care for, love, nurture, shelter, and feed all the people who inhabit the earth in a way so that *everyone* wins. This cannot be done by governments, laws, or regulations. It must be done by individuals. Each individual must heal, grow, and give love back in many forms. At the moment, we have too many individuals and nations that believe that they have only to take by way of robberies, murders, unfair trade, and major debts and game-playing by governments.

As human beings, we need to care and to take our personal share of the responsibility for helping create the love and peace we so often talk about in our world. This means helping all humankind: people we like as well as people we don't like. Let's care enough to start a chain of healing and growth that will eventually encompass the world. It starts with our healing.

I believe that the healing and growing process documented in this book can help. The essence of transcending, whether by a dysfunctional family or by a prisoner of war, may be universal. It may be the way to overcome all obstacles in our lives. The process can be and has been consciously taught to adults and children. The individuals with whom I have had the privilege of working have given me a change to see the process at work in almost every circumstance: family, relationships, and work place.

Our society has become ready to give back to the world. The generation that grew up in the sixties was termed the "me" generation. The "me" time has been an important growth time in our history. We took the time to learn about the being called a human. This exploration helped us find authentic individuals with abilities, feelings, and potentialities. It has been called "selfish" and, yes, it is, to some extent. However, as in the individual healing and growth, our society needed to discover and develop itself. Without the "me" time, we couldn't fully know the true "we" times. Without the "me" time, there would be nothing to give to others. The "me" generation has served its purpose in helping us to focus on ourselves and to develop a sense of me and the abilities I can contribute to the world. Now, however, it is time for us to unite as human beings on this earth and contribute our part without losing our individual authenticity. It's time for all of us to say, "I can and will make a difference in the world."

This helping is not a codependency type of help, in which I give all and don't take care of myself. We must still take care of ourselves while giving to others. Caring doesn't have to be given as a big offering or only when we feel like it. An example of this caring happened this morning when I was swimming at a nearby health club. My swim time is my "selfish time." I usually go into a state of isolation as I do my laps. If I could, I would put a sign on me that says "Do *not* disturb or enter my lane." With the exception of a few smiles, I rarely communicate with anyone. To share even a "Good morning" seems like an intrusion and too much.

This morning, as I was swimming in "my" lane, I realized that I was sending out more than my usual leave-me-alone signal. I was also sending anger and a hate attitude. I decided I was just in one of those moods and needed to do my laps and go to work. So I hurried up my pace. Something, though, drew my attention to the woman swimming next to me. She seemed down and lonely. I smiled and said, "Good morning." As we swam and took some rest breaks, we chatted a little. By the end of our swim, both of us felt better. In addition, I felt an uplifting energy from our contact. It didn't take from my time; it added to my life.

It's this kind of contact I am talking about. If we can give of ourselves in healthy, loving ways, we all gain. We can do this by running a errand for someone, taking time to listen, or taking a child for a day so an exhausted parent can get some rest.

SPECIFIC WAYS TO USE
THE TRANSCENDING PROCESS

The following are specific ways that the healing and growth process can be used in our world. I'm sure there are other ways and I would love to hear about them:

1. *Help children who are in dysfunctional families.* All through our world, we have *many* children growing up in dysfunctional families. We need to take responsibility for helping them grow up with love. At present, we have many social organizations: foster care, protective services, mental health programs, school counselors, mental health clinics, ministers, rehabilitation programs, juvenile homes, and special education. What we need is more individual involvement. We need each individual to be loving and caring enough to do something personally. This is how we will stop dysfunction and create healthier individuals and societies.

Individuals such as neighbors, relatives, friends, ministers, and teachers can offer a great service. We need to notice that a child is hurting and do something, anything. It doesn't take much. It can be a small or large giving. Here are some ways:

- Teach them the survival techniques described by transcenders
- Listen, above all else; take the time and listen
- Give a special compliment; send a card
- Create a special time doing anything that is fun, such as going to the movies or visiting a playground
- Report abuse to the authorities in your county; help stop it.
- Support the parents, because they, too, have had a difficult past; they are the previous generation's abused children
- Be there for the children in any way that offers love
- If you have a dysfunctional past, share it and how you transcended it; this is supportive and encouraging for everyone
- Keep telling the children that they can make it
- Help others make it by giving your time, energy, and/or money
- Help without judgment, criticism, or ridicule; each of us has our own specific way of healing that is right for us, but that may not be right for others.
- Offer a sanctuary or shelter during rough times
- Be patient and loving

If you are a therapist and working with a child from a dysfunctional family, I offer these suggestions.

- Work with love; above all, the child needs love and may even experience it from you for the first time — helping a child feel love is done by feeling genuine love for them in session no matter how "unlovable" they appear
- Gently help the child to understand that he or she has choices in life
- Help the child to know that he or she *can* create another kind of life
- Offer tons of support and encouragement
- Listen
- Teach survival techniques

2. *Teach survival and transcending techniques* to people who are in dysfunctional situations.

3. *Teach healing, growth, and transcending.* I believe strongly that these can be taught to individuals of all ages. Teachers, ministers, counselors and so on can all offer help. Individuals can be helped to make turning-point decisions. For example, one teenager I was working with became very upset because her birth parents would not release her to be adopted by her foster parents, whom she loved and who wanted to adopt her. Her family situation was abusive, and she had been taken out of the family years before. When her birth parents refused their permission for her adoption, she became extremely upset and began acting out. I gently, but firmly, informed her that she had only three more years to put up with the family (she was fifteen) and then she could do anything she wanted to, including being adopted by anyone of her choice. When she understood this, her face brightened up, and she transcended the situation through the remaining years.

4. *Heal from your dysfunctional past.* Just one person who is healing touches *many* other lives. There are ripple effects, as when a stone is thrown into the water and creates many ripples that continue to move out. The ripples are incredible to watch because we never, ever, really

know where they will go or whom they will touch. It's a wonderful feeling just knowing you had something to do with helping others heal.

5. *Grow as an individual and give your specialness to the world.* It may be a smile, a helping hand, a listening ear, talent, or an object you create. My horse trainer is a good example of a person who gives of her specialness. She has a way of letting me know that I can learn and progress at riding. I don't thing she has ever given up on anyone. When I have a problem, she works hard with me to figure out a way to deal with it. This kind of support kept me riding when I could have become very discouraged and given up a sport that I love.

Another wonderful woman in my life is the woman who cleans our house. Her cleaning is a special gift to me because it frees my time for work, *and* she does it with such love, doing many extra things for me and my family. I also have a dear friend who, at a moment's notice, will drive my teenagers to their destinations when I am unable to do so. I can't do what I do without any of them. Their ripples are enormous because they are combined with many others ripples, all working together. Their ripples affect me, which affects others,which affects . . . What is your specialness? Give it to our world.

6. *Choose to love.* Love is a commitment to caring. It's a commitment to looking for and focusing on the good in ourselves, others, and our world. Love is a choice, not a feeling. I can love others in many ways. I can love our world.

7. *Work for acceptance and forgiveness in your life.* They free you as well as others. Again, they have a ripple effect.

8. *Help others to make the decision to become transcenders.* It is never too early or too late to make the decision. Seventy-year-olds have done it, and so have children. Many individuals need to see that there is a choice, a hope, and a way of creating a different world.

9. *Help transcenders realize what they have accomplished and what a wonderful contribution it is to our world.* Because of their healing, there is one less dysfunctional person in our world, which may mean one less abused child and one more healthy family. Through the generations, who knows how many ripples there could be!

I have experienced much joy in watching and being a part of others' healing and growth. What I see is a gaining of strength that could be gained in no other way. There is a depth in people who have taken the time to heal and to continue to grow. They gain an understanding of themselves and the world. There is also a deep sensitivity within this understanding, a deep compassion not only for themselves, but also for others. Such people enable all of us to battle the disease of dysfunction that ravages the body and the soul. It is destroying our world, and we must stop it.

Afterword

Transcenders provide the world with hope for the future, hope that, no matter what the circumstance, life — full, authentic life — can prevail. They live a life with all its elements: feeling, growing, working, healing, thinking, behaving, and loving.

The journey involves pain, loneliness, and disappointment, as well as happiness, joy, and love. The journey demands from them a decision of life or death. Transcenders decide for life, life with all its challenges and heartbreak, a life full of the courage to be.

> To the Transcender
> May you always be —
> Strong of will
> Strong with courage
> Strong in heart

Resource Section

Psychotherapy, therapy that focuses on the mental health of individuals, is one of the major tools used in the process of healing and growing. It facilitates knowing and understanding yourself at a deep, wonderful level. I strongly believe that therapy is essential to creating a healthy life if you have grown up in a dysfunctional family. Its core strength is that a trained mental health professional gives you an outside view of you, your family and your role in the family. This point of view offers a new perspective as well as knowledge and insight into dysfunctional families, specifically yours. It also offers an understanding of how you function and about human existence, that is, the science of humanity.

I personally am greatly indebted to the therapists and mentors who were committed to helping me on my healing and growth journey. They have helped me establish the life that I long dreamed of, without past hurts, emotions, and dysfunctional behavior. Most important, they assisted me in finding the authentic me. When I now have a difficult or dysfunctional day — and I do — I know how to deal with it because others have helped me to know, really to know, myself. I realize now that those days are there to teach me and that I am to learn from them. Thus, I have learned how to deal with obstacles as part of the flow and growth of my life.

I am writing this section as if you, my reader, are a close friend, and I want you to have the very best. Much of this information is basic and well known to therapists and to clients who have already been through therapy, but it is not well known to the general public. Its purpose is to clear up some of the confusion and misunderstandings about the mental health field. Most important, it's to help you find an effective therapist.

Effective means the kind of therapist and therapy you need at your particular stage of healing and growing. As you heal and grow, the type of therapy, technique, and therapists you need will change because you will change. I have found that one therapist or one type of therapy is never enough, and I personally ask my clients to become involved in different types of therapy while working with me.

One therapist, therapy, or technique is not enough because healing requires different things at different times. You may find one therapist who is able to facilitate your healing all the way through, but don't be disappointed if this doesn't happen. Therapists can be "outgrown." I personally have had "official" therapists and countless other therapists through friends, groups, seminars, and workshops. I have grown and learned with each of them and am grateful.

Outgrowing a therapist, a therapy, or a technique is *not* regression; it's growth. An important note about ending therapy: When you feel you are outgrowing a therapist, it is important to bring *closure*, that is, to talk about the work you have done with the therapist and to make sure you are not avoiding any issues. If you are, stay and work with that therapist. If not, try to leave on good terms. Some therapists are open to helping you find the next step in your process. Others are not.

The following sections answer basic questions about locating an effective therapist and handling the logistics of the process.

WHAT IS THERAPY?

The more I work in the mental health field, the less I know what therapy is. What I do know, though, is that it is love that facilitates healing and growing. I know that it is a process that helps you to face, to get to know, and to develop your authentic self. The therapeutic process helps you seek your truth, your vision, your integrity, and your authenticity by helping to sort you out from your family and your significant others. Therapy is a way of being in a relationship with another person and using special techniques that enable an individual to heal and grow. It can be emotionally painful and wonderfully joyous. It needs to be gentle and loving. By gentle, I do not mean that it is not painful at times. By gentle, I mean that it is not violent to you in any way.

Therapy is a reparenting, an evolution of you. You face and heal from traumas that you have experienced in life to find and learn all about you. It is a process that offers an opportunity finally to become what you have always wanted to be: the authentic you. The work is hard and requires a major commitment to oneself to develop the original package, but it is a joyful reuniting of you with you.

Therapy provides a safe, nurturing, nonjudgmental, nonabusive environment where you can feel secure in exploring all aspects of you — even the parts you are afraid of or don't like. It is the opportunity to focus on you with no judgment, abuse, criticism, or ridicule. And if a therapist is abusive, it's a signal that you need to leave and find a healthier therapist.

Today, therapy is no longer just for those who are considered mentally ill and who have to be institutionalized or on medication for life. Today, most therapy occurs with "regular" people who want to heal and grow. Therapeutic techniques have also changed in recent decades from harsh interventions, such as electroshock and insulin shock, to techniques that are full of love and gentleness, without drugs and horrible side effects.

Finally, therapy needs to go at your pace, not the therapist's or the insurance company's. Please note: many insurance companies believe that short-term, goal-directed behavioral therapy (ten to twenty sessions), is the only effective therapy. This type of therapy usually offers only symptom relief. For deep healing from a dysfunctional family, I believe long-term therapy (two or three years) is needed. If you need a year or more to gain trust in your therapist, take it. If your process moves fast, go for it. If you alternate between slow and fast, that's fine. Whatever your pace, it is perfect for you, and you need to be supported at your rate, not the therapist's or the insurance company's.

WHAT ARE THE BENEFITS OF THERAPY?

The following is a list of benefits experienced by individuals who have been in therapy:

1. Decreasing emotional pain
2. Increasing emotional well-being
3. Increasing self-esteem
4. Healing from traumas of the past
5. Changing painful dysfunctional behaviors in the present life to healthy functioning
6. Becoming your authentic self
7. Developing your skills and potentials
8. Having more happiness in life
9. Having healthier, more satisfying relationships
10. Finding more real friends and significant others
11. Developing a true and healthy support system
12. Finding more personal freedom, power, and success
13. Feeling loved and being able to love
14. Learning your process of healing and growing that lasts a life time

WHY DO YOU NEED THERAPY—
WHY CAN'T YOU DO IT YOURSELF?

Therapy occurs in a relationship with a trained professional who is totally focused on you and your life. As stated before, this relationship is vital to you because it gives you an outside, professional perspective on what has happened in your life. Therapists are trained to help people heal from dysfunctional backgrounds. This individualized time is *your* time. It is not shared with a sibling, a mother, a father, or anyone else who has taken from you in your life. Most important, it's your time to be with you.

In therapy, the therapist helps facilitate exploring all areas of your life. There will be lots of areas. Therapy is not like sharing and griping with a friend who is willing to listen. It is a professional helping you to explore, with meaning and purpose, what has happened to you, in order to promote your healing and growth.

In this relationship, you get feedback based on who you are, not on what your parents or siblings need or needed. When I am in sessions with clients, my focus is on understanding how *they* feel, what has happened to *them*, and what *they* are all about. What is always important is the client's world and perspective. It is only in the client's understanding of this perspective that healing and growth occur. I need to know how Mom felt and what she needed only as these things affect my client.

The professional feedback in therapy helps you to separate from your family and to heal emotionally in a healthy, appropriate way. Once feelings are felt and understood, behavior changes can occur more easily. For instance, one client was convinced that he was stuck forever with his extremely demanding family of origin. As he healed and grew, he came to *know* that he had choices. Once he saw that he had choices, he was able to make changes.

Another reason for therapy is that we have often blocked our feelings to such an extent that we have to be taught how to feel. Or we may never have been taught to identify our feelings, so we don't know how we feel. The people in this category often say, "Tell me what to feel, and I will feel it!" Teaching about feeling is something therapy does well. In the beginning, learning about your feelings can be frightening. A safe, supportive place in which to identify, explore, and feel your feelings is essential.

Another thing that therapy does is to aid you in knowing beyond a doubt that you are not only OK but are the wonderful, original package God created. You usually do not learn this when you grow up in a dysfunctional family. It is very important that you receive this feedback from another human being to affirm, support, and help you heal.

The therapeutic process also helps you uncover and know your needs and wants as an individual, and most important, you learn how to meet them appropriately and not with dysfunction. Finally, therapy helps you learn your natural process of healing and growing. This knowledge lasts a lifetime.

WHEN DO YOU NEED THERAPY?

When should you seek outside help? My general response is: Does it hurt to be you? Does your world feel awful or painful? Are you feeling stuck, discouraged, or depressed? If your answer is yes, seek help. The following is a detailed list of symptoms that help identify when therapy is needed by a child or an adult.

Are you feeling:

1. Confused about you and/or your world?
2. Anxious and afraid so that it's painful or uncomfortable to be you?
3. Guilty to the point where the guilt interferes with your life on any level?
4. Ashamed about you and/or your past?
5. Angry, so that the anger sabotages your life and hurts others?
6. Numb and/or few or no feelings?

7. Dread about not living the way you have always dreamed of living and see little hope for change?
8. Dislike or hatred for yourself?
9. Constantly sad and depressed?
10. Helpless in your life and world?
11. Like a victim, as if everyone is out to get or hurt you?
12. Lonely and isolated from everyone and everything?
13. Detached from yourself and/or others?
14. That you don't belong anywhere?

Do you:

15. Abuse yourself physically, emotionally, verbally, or sexually or neglect yourself in any way?
16. Abuse others (children or adults) physically, emotionally, verbally, or sexually and/or neglect others in any way?
17. Devalue yourself as your family did or does, putting yourself down, and thinking less of yourself than of others?
18. Come from a childhood of abuse and/or neglect?
19. Have few childhood memories?
20. Have little trust in yourself and/or others?
21. Block your creativity?
22. Have any kind of addiction — work, alcohol, drugs, food, anger, sex, etc.?
23. Have difficulties with authority figures?
24. Have continuous health problems?
25. Have trouble sleeping?
26. Avoid living in the present moment?
27. Hate the past?
28. Live constantly in the past?
29. Have a sexual dysfunction?
30. Have a poor self-concept or low self-esteem?
31. Have eating disorders?
32. Have memory gaps or time losses?
33. Constantly wash your hands or behave compulsively in other ways?

34. Have painful, difficult flashbacks from the past?
35. Have suicidal thoughts and feelings?
36. Caretake your friends and family to the exclusion of yourself?
37. Have a fear of being crazy or insane?
38. Have constant turmoil in your life?
39. Constantly worry?

If you have any of these symptoms, or multiple symptoms (usually we have more than one or two), seek help. If you come from a dysfunctional family, seek help.

If the following symptoms are happening to you, seek help immediately:

1. Suicidal thoughts, feelings, and/or plans.
2. Living in an abusive relationship.
3. Abusing others.
4. Abusing yourself in *any way*.
5. Feeling out of control and "crazy."

WHAT ARE THE DIFFERENT TYPES OF THERAPY?

There are many different types (modalities) of therapy: individual, couples, family, play, groups, and education. Each modality has special focuses, such as twelve-step, body-processing, structured, unstructured, relationship, spiritual, and peer. Each type may be either outpatient or inpatient (residential) therapy. When you are deciding on a modality and a special focus, it is important to choose what you need for your stage of healing and growing. What may work for a friend may not be what you need. Sometimes, the only way to find out is to educate yourself and try it. You may have to try different kinds of therapy to make your decision. The following are brief descriptions of therapy modalities or focus:

Inpatient and Outpatient

Outpatient therapy refers to therapy that is done when the client does not live on the site of the mental health facility for any length of time. The client arrives for the appointment and then goes home. Outpatient therapy is done at community mental-health clinics, private clinics, and hospitals.

Inpatient or residential therapy occurs when the client stays at the mental health facility. Residential treatment provides individual, group, family, couple, educational, and milieu therapy. *Milieu therapy* is therapy that occurs during the course of living, in which every moment entails some sort of learning for living. The length of the stay may be a few days or several months. In previous years, there were only inpatient programs for alcoholism, depression, and severe mental illness; now there are programs for codependency, eating disorders, and adult children of alcoholics. One of the benefits of residential treatment is that it provides a sanctuary from life and a time to focus on healing without the interference of outside stresses. This reprieve from the outside world often rekindles hope, relieves intense stress, and dramatically aids in healing. It is always important after residential care to continue therapy as an outpatient.

Modalities

Individual therapy occurs when an individual meets face-to-face with a therapist and focuses on personal issues. The goal in individual counseling is to explore the past and present of the individual in order to gain healing and growth. This kind of therapy explores relationships from the client's perspective, not from that of the family or significant others, and without outside interference. Individual therapy for a young child should occur in a playroom setting with a specially trained child-play therapist.

Couples therapy occurs when a couple meets face-to-face with a therapist. This type of work focuses on the relationship between the two individuals. Its intent is to heal the relationship and to help the couple grow in the relationship. Each person's perspective is important because of how it affects and pertains to the relationship. The past and present of the individuals are explored as needed to help the couple heal and grow.

Family therapy occurs when an entire family meets face-to-face with the therapist to explore the interactions among the family members. It is preferable to work with all members of the family. However, if all members can't attend, important work with those who do attend can still be accomplished. The goal of this therapy is to help the family unit heal and grow. Again, past and present are explored, along with each person's perspective, as needed, to create healthy relationships in the family.

Group therapy occurs when nonrelated individuals meet face-to-face with a therapist. The goal of the group is to help the individuals learn how to relate to others in healthy ways. Individuals in the group share life experiences, and this sharing encourages healing. Group therapy offers a chance to share at a supportive, safe, deep level while working on relationships. Clients get feedback from the therapist as well as from other group members. The goals of group and individual therapy work well together, and many individuals benefit by participating in both modalities at the same time.

Play therapy occurs when a child meets face-to-face with a specially trained child-play therapist in a playroom setting. The playroom is equipped with toys that have been selected for their therapeutic value. As the child plays, he or she works out emotional issues. Sharing with the therapist occurs at the same time. This type of therapy is extremely effective for children. Adults may also go into the playroom to work on childhood issues and to learn to play.

Educational therapy occurs whenever individuals learn anything about themselves, perhaps from reading, workshops, classes, seminars, television, or radio.

DIFFERENT TYPES OF GROUPS

Many types of groups are available in today's therapy market. Again, you pick the one that best fits you and your needs at the moment. A group that is perfect in the beginning of your therapy may not be as appropriate two years later. Groups, like therapists, may be outgrown as you get to know yourself and heal at a deeper level. This is not a failure to fit into the group, but a positive statement about your growth. Also just as you check out any therapy, check out how the group is run and the therapist who runs it. Here are a few examples of groups:

Peer and support groups are groups run by nonprofessionals. The members of the group share problems and help each other by offering support and encouragement. The leader of the group offers only structure and not advice or therapy. These groups are usually free or require only a donation.

Twelve-step groups are groups with a variety of focuses but with a common base in the twelve original recovery steps of Alcoholics Anonymous. These groups also follow those steps. Types of twelve-step programs include Alcoholics Anonymous, Al-Anon, Alateen, Alatot, Adult Children of Alcoholics (ACOA), Overeaters Anonymous, Codependents Anonymous (CoDA), and Emotions Anonymous. Others are being created on a regular basis. These groups are peer-group organizations. The fee for these groups is a donation only.

Therapy groups are run by mental health professionals and focus on healing and growing by having members of the group share experiences and interactions with others. Therapy groups may have many special focuses. Fees for these groups are based on standard professional rates in the area.

Spiritual groups focus on members' relationship to God and their growth as spiritual beings. Professionals and nonprofessionals run these groups. Among them are prayer groups, spiritual growth groups, and specific religious-study groups.

Structured groups have a therapeutic process that follows set, predesignated steps.

Unstructured groups have a therapeutic process with few or no set steps and allow each group to create its own direction.

Body-processing and bio-energetic groups are groups that use techniques that focus on releasing stored memories and feelings through the body. Most feelings are stored in our bodies, not our brains. This is the reason that these techniques work so well. Examples of the techniques are releasing energy by beating a pillow with a racket and specific breathing techniques.

WHAT ARE THE STEPS IN STARTING THERAPY?

Most individuals are frightened when they think about starting therapy for the first time. To help reduce your fear, please know that therapy, your therapy, is all about *you*. Also keep in mind that therapy is a process that helps you discover your wonderfulness. It does this by helping you to reduce pain, to heal, and to discover all your specialness. In addition, most therapists have been in therapy and know how difficult it is to make the first call. The receptionist at the therapist's office will also know that it's a difficult call to make and will help you through it. It takes courage to make the first call to the first therapist, let alone to walk in the door for the first appointment.

Starting therapy is generally the same no matter where you go. First, call the clinic or the office to set up an appointment. A receptionist will usually answer and ask for general background and insurance information. If you have the name of a specific therapist, ask for that therapist. If not, the receptionist will assign you a therapist on the basis of the background information that you shared with him or her. You may also ask for a therapist specifically trained in the area that you need, such as depression, substance abuse, inner child, or dysfunctional families. It is important to work with a therapist who has training in the area you need to work in. If you do not know what area you need to work in, don't worry. Just be honest with the receptionist and the therapist.

During this initial telephone contact, it is appropriate to ask about office hours, fees, insurance eligibility, and the services provided. Also ask any other questions you need answered.

After the initial call, the therapist will call you to set up an appointment, usually within twenty-four hours of your call. Occasionally, the receptionist will set up the appointment. This telephone contact is your chance to ask other questions, such as: How does the therapist work? Does he or she believe in the ability of the clients to find their own direction? Does he or she know the dysfunctional family area? If you are unsure about the therapist after this call, ask for a fifteen-minute interview. Most therapists give such an interview free; some will charge a small fee. Please understand that most therapists cannot afford to give you an entire hour for an interview without charging. Therapists make their living by selling their time. More than fifteen free minutes is more than they can usually handle financially.

Once you are satisfied, or fairly satisfied, make an appointment. You may still have anxieties about therapy. This is normal. Once the appointment is made, and it is usually set within a week of your calling, think about things you want to share about yourself in that hour. Most therapy sessions last forty-five to fifty minutes. The last part of the hour is for the therapist to write notes and get a chance to get ready for the next client. Like everyone else, therapists need breaks.

OK, so now your first appointment has come. Plan to arrive twenty to thirty minutes early so that you can fill out all the forms required. These forms include a general personal history questionnaire of three or four pages, a consent to treatment, a consent to release information if you need the therapist to share information about you with anyone else, an insurance and financial arrangement sheet, and any other policy and procedure forms needed by the clinic or the therapist. These forms vary, but they usually cover the same basic information. You will fill out these forms in the waiting room.

After the forms are filled out, the therapist, your therapist, will come to the waiting room and take you to her or his office. Once "in session," ask any additional questions you have left about therapy, the forms, the insurance, the therapist, the procedures and techniques, and the therapy process. If the therapist resists answering your questions, be aware that she or he may not be very open in other areas either. You should be allowed to ask any questions you need to about procedures and therapy. Questions about the therapist's personal life are generally not the subject of *your* therapy. However, there are therapists who do relate certain aspects of their own lives if they believe it will help you in your therapy. For example, they may share what their own healing and growth have been like in order to help you understand the process better. Other therapists never talk about themselves. The choice depends on the therapist's orientation and personal preference.

Confidentiality is extremely important and must be maintained at all times for you to build trust in the relationship. *Confidentiality* means that the therapist cannot, by law, share anything you say in session with anyone else unless you have signed a consent to release information. This law ensures you a safe place to do your healing work. If you are suicidal or homicidal, however, the law requires that the therapist break confidentiality and take action to keep everyone safe.

After all the initial questions are answered, the therapist will generally ask you, "What has brought you here?" or "What has been going on in your life that makes you want to seek therapy?" At this point, formal therapy begins.

In therapy, the primary technique is talking—talking about you and your world. You will focus on your background, traumas, thoughts, feelings, relationships, behavior, and anything else that is important to you. It is your chance to get to know all about the authentic you. Your pace in therapy is just right for you. There is no right or wrong way to do therapy, just your way. What you are seeking in therapy is your special way of being with yourself, not someone else's. This special way helps our world to have individuals in it, and not clones.

HOW DO YOU PAY FOR THERAPY?

Therapy can be paid for through insurance or private pay (cash). Before your first call to the clinic or therapist, I advise checking your coverage so you know what your insurance will cover and what you will have to pay. In addition, you may have the clinic check it for you. In this case, be ready to give the numbers of your insurance coverage to the office staff. Most insurance covers some part of the per-session rate. The rate at which insurance reimburses varies so much now, that each insurance policy must be checked individually.

When you call about your insurance coverage, here is what you'll need to know:

1. Who is covered under the policy? You? Your children? Your spouse?
2. How much will it cover per year? Per visit?

3. How many visits per year will be covered?
4. How much will you have to pay (copay)?
5. Whom will the insurance pay? A master of Social Work? A master's level psychologist? A doctoral-level psychologist? A psychiatrist?
6. Where will it cover treatment? A special outpatient clinic? A doctor's office? A hospital? Anywhere?

Most clinics and therapists require that you pay as services are rendered, as in a medical office. If you don't have any insurance coverage and do not have the money to cover the fee per session, some clinics and therapists will see you for a lower fee. On rare occasions, some therapists will arrange a payment schedule so that you can pay part of therapy costs after therapy is finished. At my clinic, we usually have at least one intern at the master's level who sees low-fee clients. There are also community-supported agencies, such as mental health agencies (look in the phone book under county agencies), that charge lower fees. Payment at these agencies is based on income and ability to pay.

At a private clinic, therapists are paid only as you pay, and they need to earn a living and pay bills just as you do. At the community mental health agencies, therapists are paid a salary, part of which comes from special state and county funds. Other special funds may be available in certain areas. Do some research to find out what is available in your area.

If the rate of the therapy hour in a private clinic shocks you, please know that therapists have to take the paid amount, give a large portion of the fee to the clinic for rent and services, and then pay taxes on it. Believing all therapists make "big bucks" is an illusion. So, if you have chosen a therapist and can't afford the fee, don't become discouraged or believe that he or she is terrible and an "unfeeling" person, when in reality he or she is working to support a family. Ask for the name of another therapist who may be willing to see you at a lower fee.

HOW DO YOU PICK A THERAPIST?

There are many different kinds of therapists who come from many different orientations. The most effective therapists have been in therapy themselves, have done their healing, and are working on growing. The orientation I present to you in this book is what I call *spiritual humanistic psychology*. Basically, it is a belief that you, the client, have everything you need to go forward in your life. You are an integrated being that consists of body, emotions, mental ability, and spirituality. I, as the therapist, am a facilitator. I help guide my clients, give them feedback, and teach them techniques that encourage the healing process. I can't do the healing or play God in anyone's life. Also, I believe that our spirituality is the human life core and that we must develop it. The humanistic orientation is also called *client-centered* or *holistic psychotherapy*.

There are other orientations, such as therapist-directed therapy. In this orientation, the client is guided more by the therapist and is seen as a patient more than as a client able to do for herself or himself. Included in therapist-directed-therapy is psychoanalysis.

Most effective therapists are eclectic. *Eclectic* means the use of many techniques from many different orientations. These are used at different times as needed by clients in the healing and growing process. *Techniques* are specific ways of helping you heal. Among the techniques are talking, creative visualization, hypnosis, rebirthing, massage, role playing, psychodrama, music therapy, art therapy, journaling, body release work, guided imagery, interventions — the list goes on and on. Techniques work together in the healing process. No one technique seems to work all the time for any one person. One is never enough to release all the layers that have been trapped for so long.

You, as a client, have the right and the ability to read about the techniques and to learn which of them will work for you. You also need to read books that have been written about dysfunctional families.

Your therapists won't know everything that you will need on your journey. Some books and techniques you will love and use a lot; others you may try and may choose not to use again. The choice is very individual, and only you know which ones you like and which ones are effective.

Most important, find a therapist whom you like and with whom you can develop a healthy, trusting relationship. You are going to need the trust to get through the tough issues and feelings. If you can't relate to or don't like the therapist, you'll probably become stuck. Personality clashes can happen between therapists and clients. The therapist you pick needs to be someone you trust to help lead you to the next step and eventually to your truth, your authenticity. The therapist needs to challenge you to go forward, yet not be in conflict with you and your healing and growing process. He or she needs to be supportive of you and your process, yet not create dependency on him or her.

Here are some of my suggestions for finding an effective therapist:

1. Ask for recommendations from people whom you know and trust, and who have been in therapy. Question them about what they liked and disliked about these therapists. Ask what kind of orientation and expertise areas these therapists have. If you can, get two or three recommendations.

2. Call the therapist(s) to get some preliminary questions answered. Set up a fifteen-minute interview with each one if necessary.

3. Ask the therapist about his or her approach to therapy, education, training, and view of the client and what he or she sees as the role of the therapist in therapy.

4. Get answers to the questions: Does the therapist hear and understand you? Does he or she know the healing and growing process? Does he or she know about dysfunctional families?

5. Make sure you like and get along with the therapist because you're going to be spending a lot of time, effort, and money. There should not be personality clashes.

6. If you start with a therapist and after two or three sessions you

find a definite personality clash, talk to the therapist about it. The clash may be resolvable. If it's not, it's OK to seek out another therapist.

7. *However*, and this is a very important however, if you find that you are therapist *hopping* (trying many therapists and finding no one who is OK), the issue may not be finding a therapist as much as what you are trying to avoid in therapy.

8. Check out the therapist's credentials through state and school organizations.

9. If in therapy you begin to feel devalued or misunderstood (a lot), discuss it with the therapist. If this doesn't work, find another therapist.

10. If you are abused or sexually approached, get another therapist *immediately* and report the therapist to the licensing board in your state. This behavior is not normal and not OK. You had enough abuse as a child; you don't need more.

11. Remember, the choice of therapist is yours. You always have the power to hire and fire.

WHAT ARE THE DIFFERENT TYPES OF THERAPISTS?

There are three basic types of psychotherapists:

1. *The psychologist* is a person who primarily studies people from the perspective of the individual and how healing and growth occur. He or she also studies how society affects the individual. There are two levels: master's (M.A.) and doctoral (Ph.D.).

2. *The social worker* is a person who primarily studies the individual from society's point of view. He or she also studies how healing and growth occur. There are two levels: bachelor's (B.A.) and master's (M.S.W.).

3. *The psychiatrist* (M.D.) is a medical doctor who studies psycho-

analysis in his or her residency program. He or she can dispense medications.

WHAT IS THE THERAPIST'S ROLE?

I strongly believe that the therapist's role is being a facilitator; that is, one who helps you find your answers and is not an authority on your life. I believe that *each* of us has what she or he needs to succeed in life. Therapists do not have our energy, our abilities, our experiences, our feelings, our thoughts, or anything else of ours. They can't make our decisions, feel our feelings, or grow our growth. They can't heal for us. Therapists are neither gods nor superhuman. They are human and have obstacles to deal with in their lives just as you do. They have no magical cures. Disappointing, isn't it? What they do have, however, is the training to help people recover, heal, and grow. They offer a vital, caring, objective, trained, professional perspective of what has happened to you in your life. They help you find your way to a healthier, happier, productive life.

The therapist's role includes: (1) being with you through your healing and growth process; (2) helping you identify, clarify, and learn about your feelings; (3) helping you learn techniques that encourage and aid your process; (4) helping you develop healthier relationships; (5) sharing information about dysfunctional families and their effect on your life; (6) supporting you in sessions with difficult feelings; (7) being available in crisis situations by phone or for extra crisis sessions (or having another therapist cover for her or him if she or he is not available); and (8) being a supporter, guide, and encourager.

Therapy is only a *part* of your healing and growth. You must work and develop all aspects of you: physical, mental, emotional, and spiritual. Therapy by itself will never be enough. A lot of therapy occurs between the end of one session and beginning of the next and not in the therapist's office. Sessions are used to support and facilitate your healing. The therapist also helps you learn techniques and gain an understanding that will last you a lifetime.

Sometimes during therapy, there is emotional confusion about the identity and role of the therapist. Freud called it *transference*. Transference occurs when the therapist takes on many faces from the client's past as the client works to heal. The client may treat the therapist as mom, dad, sister, brother, and so on. I have even seen sibling rivalry among clients who had the same therapist. This transference is normal, but it needs to be resolved in therapy. The object is to heal and not just to shift parental issues to the therapist. So when transference does occur, sharing with the therapist and confronting it are important.

The therapist's role is to be with you and to provide guidance through the healing process. It is not, however, to be there every time you have a feeling that upsets you. It is not the therapist's role to be on call twenty-four hours a day, seven days a week in case you need her or him. In case of a true emergency, your therapist, or another therapist who is on call for your therapist, does need to be available to you. This kind of availability is usually arranged through the clinic clerical staff and/or answering service. In an emergency, call the clinic, or answering service, state that it is an emergency, and ask to speak with your therapist as soon as possible. The clinic or answering service will then contact your therapist, who will then call you. If your therapist is not available, the clinic or answering service will contact the person on call or ask someone to talk to you. Some clinics refer all emergencies during off-hours to public crisis numbers. Find out how your therapist handles emergencies.

Please remember, therapists need time off and have families of their own. Most therapists do not like and cannot handle being therapists all the time. Most therapists, after talking to and being with clients most of the day, go home to be with their families and to relax just as you do after work. Therapy is very demanding, and time off is essential for therapists' health and well-being. It is essential to their performance at work. So, if you call after hours, make sure it is an emergency. You can call to make or change appointments during normal office hours; this is not considered an emergency. Suicidal feelings and thoughts are *always* an emergency.

In general, I tell my clients the following: "You are in charge of your life, healing process, and growth. I am here as a facilitator and road sign consultant to help you in *your* process. If I offer something that does not match your knowing of you, tell me. In that way, we can keep exploring to find out what does fit. You are the one who ultimately knows. I am not God, nor do I play God in your life. Your decisions are yours, not mine. We need to work in areas you choose that are important to you. Your natural healing process is perfect for you, and you know it best. I'm here to help you recognize it."

WHAT DOES A THERAPIST NOT DO?

Sometimes clients expect a lot from their therapists. They expect them to be always available, all-knowing in wisdom, and psychic; to play every role that they require (sister, brother, father, and mother); and to be perfect in doing all this. These clients often expect therapists to do their healing work for them. No one person — mother, father, sister, brother, spouse, child, or therapist — will ever be able to fulfill all our expectations. Let me say very strongly that most of us wish we could do this.

When we see pain, we want to change it. That is probably the major reason we come into the mental health field to start with, along with needing to heal and find ourselves. If we could do your feeling work for you and you would heal, we'd probably do it. However, doing your work for you would only give us more pain that is not ours, and you would gain nothing. What we can do is to help you release pain and to heal. That is where our power stops. We cannot heal for you. Therapists cannot feel for you, think for you, or change your behavior for you. You have to do it yourself, just as I and many others have done. Your growth is based on the work *you* do, not the work I do for you. It may be painful, difficult, hard work. But the work is intensely worthwhile.

WHAT ARE SOME WARNINGS ABOUT THERAPY?

There are definite things that should *not* happen in therapy:

1. Abuse of any kind — physical or verbal abuse, criticism, ridicule, sexual abuse, and so on
2. Sexual harassment of any nature — verbal, physical, critical, and so on
3. Manipulations by therapists to use you for their needs; you are hiring them to help *you*
4. The therapist's being inattentive to you in sessions — sleeping, taking long telephone calls, and so on

These are two warnings about techniques:

Techniques that are abusive and/or painful need to be carefully examined. Techniques should help you feel your feelings, not cause more pain.

Body work usually creates a type of altered consciousness: body consciousness. My warning is this: Be careful of how many times a month you do it. Going into body consciousness can be extremely helpful during the healing process because it helps you physically to release stored body memories and feelings while bypassing the intellect.

When there has been too much body work, clients experience the following symptoms: (1) short-term memory loss; (2) spaciness; (3) floating feelings; (4) confusion; (5) feeling ungrounded in the present moment; (6) impaired ability to focus on tasks or other people; and (7) a feeling of not wanting to be in life and preferring to avoid all feelings and problems. If any of these symptoms start, stop the body work immediately, and work on integrating what has already been uncovered. Use only talk therapy until you understand more and the confusion and other symptoms lift. This may require a number of weeks.

In summary, when selecting a therapist, seek a healthy relationship. The relationship should help you build trust as well as help you to find your original package and wonderfulness. The techniques used should aid you in releasing layers, healing, and growing. They should never be abusive. Healing needs to be done with love and gentleness.

Bibliography

This bibliography includes many books covering different areas of dysfunction and healing. It lists more than just references that pertain to the information in this book. These books are offered to help you with your reading selection in the healing and growth process. Many of these books may be purchased as paperbacks or found in libraries. This listing is by no means a complete list of all the pertinent books available. It is sufficiently long and of enough variety to help you on your journey.

When selecting a book to read, use your inner sense, your intuition, and your spirituality to guide and help you choose. When I am picking a book, I go inside myself and allow myself to be "attracted to" one whether it's on a bookstore shelf, mentioned by a friend, or listed on a reading list. For me, this method rarely fails to uncover just the *right* book for me to read next. Occasionally, I buy a book and don't read it until much later, sometimes years later. When I do get around to reading it, it is exactly the correct time.

If I buy a book that doesn't fit, I soon know it as I try to read it. I'll start it only to find that I am soon bored and not understanding what I am reading. I then set it aside until later; I don't feel guilty or say, "You dummy, you should have known better." I know there will be a time when the book will be important to me or someone else in my life. When I read books in my right time, I gain and learn enormously from them. When reading books, give yourself permission to read *parts* of books. Just because our teachers taught us to read *all* the book from front to back, that is no reason to keep doing it. If only certain chapters appeal to you, read only those. If you start a book and find it awful, stop and find another. It may truly be an "awful" book or it may not be your time to read it. Trust yourself. Be good to yourself. And most of all, gain and learn from your reading.

One last word on reading books written by professionals in the mental health field: Don't believe everything you read! Each book, like this book, is written to relate information to the public. This information is what this one particular author has learned. What the author has learned and believes may not fit your situation. Your experience may be totally different, and you may not agree with the author at all. Don't leave your intelligence and education out when you read. Process the information and try the suggestions. *Then* evaluate the information and its effects on you. You are the last word in your life, not someone who decided to write what he or she knows in book form.

Many of the following books are available on cassettes and have work tapes that go with them. Work tapes can be a great help in the healing and growing process; use them.

Al-Anon Family Group. *One Day at a Time in Al-Anon*. New York: Al-Anon Family Group Headquarters, 1974.

Al-Anon Family Group. *Al-Anon: Faces Alcoholism*. New York: Al-Anon Family Group Headquarters, 1977.

Al-Anon Family Group. *Al-Anon: Is It for You?* New York: Al-Anon Family Group Headquarters, 1983.

Al-Anon's Twelve Steps and Twelve Traditions. New York: Al-Anon Family Group Headquarters, 1981.

Alcoholics Anonymous: The Big Book (3rd ed.). New York: Alcoholics Anonymous World Services, 1976.

Anderson, Louise. *Dear Dad: Letters from an Adult Child*. New York: Penguin Books, 1989.

Anthony, E. J. *The Child in His Family* (Vol. 3). New York: Wiley, 1974.

Assagioli, R. *The Act of Will*. New York: Penguin Books, 1973.

Axline, Virginia M. *Dibs: In Search of Self*. New York: Ballantine Books, 1964.

Bach, E. *Heal Thy Self: An Explanation of the Real Cause and Cure of Disease*. Bend, OR: Sun, 1985.

Bach, George, and Herbert Goldberg. *Creative Aggression*. New York: Avon, 1974.

Bach, Richard. *The Bridge across Forever*. New York: Morrow, 1984.

Bach, Richard. *Illusions*. New York: Delacorte Press, 1977.

Beattie, Melody. *Denial*. Center City, MN: Hazelden, 1986.

Beattie, Melody. *Codependent No More*. San Francisco: Harper & Row, 1987.

Beattie, Melody. *Beyond Co-dependency and Getting Better All the Time*. New York: Harper & Row, 1989.

Beaver, W. R. *Psychology and Growth: A Family Systems Perspective*. New York: Brunner/Mazel, 1977.

Benson, H. *The Relaxation Response*. New York: Avon, 1976.

Berne, Eric. *What Do You Say after You Say Hello*. New York: Bantam, 1971.

Bettelheim, Bruno. *Love is Not Enough*. London: Collier, 1950.

Bettelheim, Bruno. *Paul and Mary: Two Case Histories from Truants from Life*. New York: Doubleday, 1955.

Bettelheim, Bruno. *The Empty Fortress: Infantile Autism and the Birth of the Self*. New York: Free Press, 1967.

Bettelheim, Bruno. *The Children of the Dream*. New York: Macmillan, 1969.

The Living Bible. Wheaton: Tyndale, 1971.

Black, Claudia. *It Will Never Happen to Me*. New York: Ballantine, 1981.

Black, Claudia. *Repeat after Me*. Denver: MAC, 1985.

Black, Claudia. *Repeat after Me: Workbook for Adult Children*. Denver: MAC, 1985.

Bleuler, M. "The Offspring of Schizophrenia." *Schizophrenia Bulletin*, 8 (1974):93–107.

Bloomfield, Harold H., and Leonard Felder. *Making Peace with Your Parents*. New York: Ballantine, 1983.

Boom, Corrie Ten. *The Hiding Place*. Old Tappan, NJ: Fleming H. Revell, 1971.

Bradshaw, John. *The Family*. Deerfield Beach, FL: Health Communications, 1988.

Bradshaw, John. *Healing the Shame That Binds You*. Deerfield Beach, FL: Health Communications, 1988.

Branden, Nathaniel. *The Disowned Self*. Los Angeles: Bantam, 1971.

Branden, Nathaniel. *How to Raise Your Self-Esteem*. New York: Bantam, 1987.

Briggs, Dorothy Corkille. *Your Child's Self-Esteem*. New York: Doubleday, 1967.

Briggs, Dorothy Corkille. *Your Child's Self-Esteem: Step by Step to Raising Responsible, Productive, Happy Children*. Garden City, NY: Dolphin, 1970.

Briggs, Dorothy Corkille. *Your Child's Self-Esteem: The Key to Life*. New York: Doubleday, 1975.

Briggs, Dorothy Corkille. *Celebrate Your Self: Enhancing Your Own Self-Esteem*. New York: Doubleday, 1977.

Briggs, Dorothy Corkille. *Embracing Life: Growing through Love*. Garden City, NY: Doubleday, 1985.

Brooks, Cathleen. *The Secret Everyone Knows*. San Diego: Kroc Foundation, 1981.

Bowdan, J. D., and H. L. Gravitz. *Genesis: Spirituality in Recovery from Childhood Traumas*. Deerfield Beach, FL: Health Communications, 1988.

Buber, Martin. *I and Thou*. New York: Scribner's, 1958.

Bugental, J. F. T. *The Search for Existential Identity*. San Francisco: Jossey-Bass, 1976.

Burke, S. O. "The Invulnerable Child." *Nursing Papers: Perspective On Nursing*, 12 (1986): 48–55.

Burke, T. *I've Heard Your Feelings*. Suttons Bay, MI: Delafield, 1976.

Burke, T. *Loving Who You Are Where You Are*. Suttons Bay, MI: Delafield, 1982.

Buscaglia, Leo. *Love*. New York: Fawcett Crest, 1972.

Buscaglia, Leo. *Living, Loving and Learning*. New York: Fawcett Crest, 1982.

Buscaglia, Leo. *Loving Each Other: The Challenge of Human Relationships*. New York: Holt, Rinehart, & Winston, 1984.

Calhoun, M. *Are You Really Too Sensitive?* New York: Dolphin, 1987.

Canfield, J. *Self-Esteem*. Pacific Palisades, CA: Jack Canfield and Self-Esteem Seminars, 1985.

Canfield, Jack, and Harold C. Wells. *100 Ways to Enhance Self-Concept in the Classroom: A Handbook for Teachers and Parents*. Englewood Cliffs, NJ: Prentice-Hall, 1976.

Cantril, A. "Perception and Interpersonal Relations." In A. E. Kuenzli (Ed.), *The Phenomenological Problem*. New York: Harper, 1959.

Capucchione, Lucia. *The Creative Journal*. Athens, OH: Swallow, 1979.

Carnes, Patrick. *Sexual Addiction*. New York: CompCare, 1983.

Carnes, Patrick. *Out of the Shadows: Understanding Sexual Addiction*. Minneapolis: CompCare, 1985.

Carnes, Patrick. *Contrary to Love, Understanding Sexual Addiction, Part 2: Helping the Sexual Addict*. Minneapolis: CompCare, 1988.

Carter, Steven, and Julie Sokol. *Men Who Can't Love: When a Man's Fear Makes Him Run from Commitment*. New York: Evans, 1987.

Casey, Karen, and Martha Vanceburg. *The Promise of a New Day: A Book of Daily Meditations*. New York: Harper & Row, 1983.

Cermak, Timmen L. *A Primer for Adult Children of Alcoholics*. Pompano Beach, FL: Health Communications, 1985.

Cermak, Timmen L. *Diagnosing and Treating Codependency—A Guide for Professionals*. Minneapolis: Johnson, 1986.

Cermak, Timmen L. *Evaluating and Treating ACAs—[Adult Children of Alcoholics] A Guide for Professionals*. Minneapolis: Johnson, 1988.

Cermak, Timmen L. *A Time to Heal: The Road to Recovery for Adult Children of Alcoholics*. Los Angeles: Tarcher, 1988.

Clausen, J. A., and C. L. Huffine. "The Impact of Parental Mental

Illness on Children." *Research in Community and Mental Health*, 1 (1979): 183–214.

Cohen, Allen. *The Dragon Doesn't Live Here Anymore: Loving Fully and Living Freely*. Atlanta: New Leaf, 1981.

Cohler, B. J., D. H. Gallant, H. U. Grunebaum, and J. L. Weiss. "Child-Care Attitudes and Development of Young Children of Mentally Ill and Well Mothers." *Psychology Reports*, 46 (1980): 31–46.

Colazzi, R. R. "Psychological Research as the Phenomenologists View It." In R. S. Valle and M. King (Eds.), *Existential-Phenomenological Alternative for Psychology*. New York: Oxford University Press, 1978.

Colgrove, Melba, Harold H. Bloomfield, and Peter McWilliams. *How to Survive the Loss of a Love*. New York: Bantam, 1976.

Combs, A. W. (ed.). *Perceiving, Behaving and Becoming*. Washington, DC: National Education Association, American Society of Curriculum Directors Yearbook, 1962.

Combs, A. W., D. L. Avila, and W. W. Parkey. *Helping Relationship: Basic Concepts for the Helping Profession*. Boston: Allyn, 1971.

Combs, A. W., A. C. Richards, and F. Richards. *Perceptual Psychology*. New York: Harper & Row, 1949.

Corke, Jean Illsley. *Self-Esteem: A Family Affair*. San Francisco: Harper & Row, 1978.

Cousins, Norman. *Head First: The Biology of Hope*. New York: Dutton, 1989.

Covington, Stephanie, and Liana Beckett. *Leaving the Enchanted Forest*. San Francisco: Harper & Row, 1988.

Cowan, Connell, and Melvyn Kinder. *Smart Women — Foolish Choices*. New York: Signet, 1986.

Crawford, C. *Mommie Dearest*. New York: Morrow, 1978.

Crum, Tom. *The Magic of Conflict*. New York: Simon & Schuster, 1987.

Davis, Laura. *The Courage to Heal Workbook: For Women and Men Survivors of Child Sexual Abuse*. New York: Harper & Row, 1990.

Davis, Laura, and Ellen Bass. *The Courage to Heal: A Guide for Women Survivors of Child Sexual Abuse*. New York: Harper & Row, 1988.

Davis, M., E. R. Eshelman, and M. McKay. *The Relaxation and Stress Reduction Workbook*. Oakland, CA: New Harbinger, 1982.

Decker, Sunny. *An Empty Spoon*. New York: Scholastic, 1970.

Deutsch, C. *Broken Bottles, Broken Dreams: Understanding and Helping the Children of Alcoholics*. New York: Teachers College, 1982.

Diamond, Jed. *Looking for Love in All the Wrong Places*. New York: Putnam, 1988.

Dobson, James. *Hide and Seek: Self-Esteem for the Child*. Old Tappan, NJ: Revell, 1971.

Drever, J. *A Dictionary of Psychology*. Baltimore: Penguin, 1961.

Drews, Toby R. *Getting Them Sober* (Vol. 1). South Plainfield, NJ: Bridge, 1983.

Drews, Toby R. *Getting Them Sober* (Vol. 2). South Plainfield, NJ: Bridge, 1983.

Dwinell, Lorie. "Working through Grief: The Essential Elements." *Focus on Family* (May–June 1985): 18–19.

Dwinell, Lorie. "Working through Grief: The Pain that Heals Itself." *Focus on Family* (Jan.–Feb. 1986): 24–28.

Dwinell, Lorie, and Jane Middleton-Moz. *After the Tears*. Pompano Beach, FL: Health Communications, 1986.

Eastman, Philip D. *Are You My Mother?* New York: Random House, 1960.

El-Gruebaly, N., and D. R. Offord. "The Competent Offspring of Psychiatrically Ill Parents." *Canadian Journal of Psychiatry*, 25 (1980): 457–460.

Elkind, David. *The Hurried Child: Growing Up Too Fast Too Soon*. Reading, MA: Addison, 1981.

Elliot, David. *Listen to the Silence*. New York: New America, 1969.

Emotions Anonymous International Services. *The Enormity of Emotional Illness*. St. Paul: Emotions Anonymous International, 1973.

Fadiman, J., and R. Fragen. *Personality and Personal Growth*. New York: Harper & Row, 1976.

Farmer, Steven. *Adult Children of Abusive Parents: A Healing Program for Those Who Have Been Physically, Sexually, or Emotionally Abused*. Chicago: Contemporary, 1984.

Ferguson, M. *The Aquarian Conspiracy: Personal and Social Transforma-tion in the 1980's*. Los Angeles: Tarcher, 1980.

Fishel, R. *The Journey Within: A Spiritual Path to Recovery*. Pompano Beach, FL: Health Communications, 1987.

Fisher, Bruce. *Rebuilding: When Your Relationship Ends*. San Luis Obispo, CA: Import, 1981.

Flaherty, F. *The Odyssey of a Film-Maker*. Urbana, IL: Beta Phi Mu, 1960.

Forward, Susan, and Craig Buck. *Toxic Parents*. New York: Bantam, 1989.

Forward, Susan, and Craig Buck. *Betrayal of Innocence: Incest and Its Devastation*. New York: Penguin, 1978.

Forward, Susan, and Joan Torres. *Men Who Hate Women and the Women Who Love Them*. New York: Bantam, 1985.

Fossum, M. A., and M. J. Mason. *Facing Shame: Families in Recovery*. New York: Norton, 1986.

Frankl, V. E. *Man's Search for Meaning*. New York: Beacon, 1963.

Frankl, V. E. "Self-Transcendence as a Human Phenomenon." *Jour-nal of Humanistic Psychology* (Fall 1966): 97–106.

Frankl, V. E. *Psychotherapy and Existentialism: Selected Papers on Log-otherapy*. New York: Simon & Schuster, 1967.

Fraser, Sylvia. *My Father's House: Memoir of Incest and of Healing*. New York: Harper & Row, 1987.

Freud, A. *The Ego and the Mechanisms of Defense* (rev. ed.). New York: International Universities Press, 1966.

Freud, S. *General Introduction to Psychoanalysis*, (J. Riviera, Trans.) Garden City, NY: Garden City Co., 1938.

Friel, John, and Linda Friel. *Adult Children: The Secrets of Dysfunctional Families*. Deerfield, FL: Health Communications, 1988.

Friends in Recovery. *The 12 Steps, A Way Out: A Working Guide for Adult Children from Addictive and Other Dysfunctional Families*. San Di-ego: Recovery, 1987.

Fromm, Erich. *Escape from Freedom*. New York: Avon, 1941.

Fromm, Erich. *Man for Himself: An Inquiry into the Psychology of Ethics*. Greenwich, CT: Fawcett, 1947.

Fromm, Erich. *Psychoanalysis and Religion.* New York: Bantam, 1950.

Fromm, Erich. *The Art of Loving.* New York: Harper & Row, 1956.

Fromm, Erich. *You Shall Be as Gods: A Radical Interpretation of the Old Testament and Its Traditions.* Greenwich, CT: Fawcett, 1966.

Fromm, Erich. *The Revolution of Hope: Toward a Humanized Technology.* New York: Bantam, 1968.

Garfield, C. A. *Peak Performance.* New York: Warner Books, 1985.

Garmezy, N. "Competence and Adaptation in Adult Schizophrenic Patients and Children at Risk." In S. R. Dean (Ed.), *Prize Lectures in Schizophrenia: The First Ten Dean Awards.* New York: MSS Information Center, 1973.

Garmezy, N. "Children at Risk: The Search for the Antecedents of Schizophrenia. Part II: Ongoing Research Programs, Issues and Interventions." *Schizophrenia Bulletin* 6 (1974): 96.

Garmezy, N. "The Study of Competence in Children at Risk for Severe Psychopathology." In E. J. Anthony and C. Koupernich (Eds.), *The Child and His Family (Vol. 3).* New York: Wiley, 1974.

Garmezy, N. "Vulnerable and Invulnerable Children: Theory, Research and Intervention." *Catalog of Selected Documents in Psychology,* 6 (1976): 96.

Garmezy, N. "Observations with Children at Risk for Child and Adult Psychopathology." In M. F. McMillan and S. Henao (Eds.), *Child Psychiatry: Treatment and Research.* New York: Brunner/Mazel, 1977.

Garmezy, N., L. Nordstrom, A. Masten, and M. Ferrarese. "The Nature of Competence in Normal and Deviant Children." In M. W. Kent and J. E. Rolf (Eds.), *Social Competence in Children.* Burlington, VT: University of Vermont, 1979.

Gawain, Shakti. *Creative Visualization: Use the Power of Your Imagination to Create What You Want in Your Life.* San Rafael, CA: New World, 1978.

Gawain, Shakti. *Creative Visualization Workbook.* San Rafael, CA: New World, 1982.

Gawain, Shakti. *Living in the Light: A Guide to Personal and Planetary Transformation*. San Rafael, CA: New World, 1986.

Gawain, Shakti. *Reflections on the Light: Daily Thoughts and Affirmations*. San Rafael, CA: New World, 1988.

Gawain, Shakti. *Return to the Garden*. San Rafael, CA: New World, 1989.

Gendlin, E. *Focusing*. New York: Everest, 1978.

Gerber, Richard. *Vibrational Medicine: New Choices for Healing Ourselves*. Sante Fe: Bean, 1988.

Gil, E. *Outgrowing the Pain: A Book for and about Adults Abused as Children*. San Francisco: Launch, 1984.

Ginott, Haim G. *Between Parent and Child*. New York: Avon, 1956.

Giorgi, A. "Phenomenology and Experimental Psychology." In A. Giorgi, W. Fischer, and W. R. Von Eckartsberry (Eds.), *Duquesne Studies in Phenomenological Psychology* (Vol. 1). Duquesne, Pittsburgh: Duquesne University Press, 1971.

Glenn, Stephen H. *Raising Self-Reliant Children in a Self-Indulgent World: Seven Building Blocks for Developing Capable Young People*. Rocklin, CA: Prime, 1989.

Goldberg, Herb. *The Hazards of Being Male: Surviving the Myth of Masculine Privilege*. New York: New American, 1976.

Goldberg, Herb. *The New Male-Female Relationship*. New York: Morrow, 1983.

Goldberg, Herb. *The Inner Male: Overcoming Roadblocks to Intimacy*. New York: New American, 1987.

Gordon, R. *Your Healing Hands: The Polarity Experience*. Berkeley, CA: Wingkow, 1984.

Goulding, Robert, and Mary McClure Goulding. *Changing Lives through Redecision Therapy*. New York: Brunner/Mazel, 1979.

Goulding, Robert, and Mary McClure Goulding. *The Power Is in the Patient*. San Francisco: TA Bookstore, 1987.

Gravitz, Herbert. *Children of Alcoholics Handbook*. South Laguna, CA: National Association for Children of Alcoholics, 1985.

Gravitz, Herbert L., and Julie D. Bowden. *Recovery: A Guide for Children of Alcoholics*. New York: Simon & Schuster, 1987.

Grosz, George. *Love above All*. New York: Shocken Books, 1985.

Harris, Sydney J. *The Authentic Person: Dealing with Dilemma*. Niles, IL: Argus, 1972.

Harris, Thomas A. *I'm Okay—You're Okay*. New York: Harper & Row, 1967.

Hay, Louise L. *Heal Your Body: The Mental Causes for Physical Illness and the Metaphysical Way to Overcome Them*. Santa Monica, CA: Hay, 1982.

Hay, Louise, L. *You Can Heal Yourself*. Santa Monica, CA: Hay, 1984.

Hay, Louise L. *You Can Heal Your Life*. Farmingdale, CA: Coleman, 1985.

Hayden, Torey. *One Child*. New York: Avon, 1980.

Hazelden Educational Materials. *Teen Drug Use: What Can Parents Do?* Center City, MN: Hazelden, 1970.

Hazelden Educational Materials. *No Substitute for Love: Ideas for Family Living*. Center City, MN: Hazelden, 1973.

Hazelden Educational Materials. *Step Four: Guide to Fourth Step Inventory for the Spouse*. Center City, MN: Hazelden, 1976.

Hazelden Educational Materials. *Setting Boundaries*. Center City, MN: Hazelden, 1982.

Hazelden Educational Materials. *Learn About Families and Chemical Dependency*. Center City, MN: Hazelden, 1985.

Hazelden Meditational Series. *Each Day a New Beginning: Daily Meditations for Women*. San Francisco: Harper & Row, 1982.

Hazelden Meditational Series. *Twenty-Four Hours a Day*. San Francisco: Harper & Row, 1985.

Hazelden Meditational Series. *Day by Day*. San Francisco: Harper & Row, 1986.

Health Communications. *Codependency: An Emerging Issue*. Hollywood, FL: Author, 1984.

Heidegger, Martin. *Being and Time*, (J. Macquattie and E. Robinson, Trans.) New York, Harper & Row, 1952.

Hendix, Harville. *Getting the Love You Want: A Guide for Couples*. New York: Harper & Row, 1988.

Hendricks, Gay. *Learning to Love Yourself: Workbook*. New York: Prentice-Hall, 1990.

Hendricks, Gay, and Russel Wills. *The Centering Books: Awareness Activities for Children, Parents and Teachers*. New York: Prentice-Hall, 1975.

Herman, Judith. *Father-Daughter Incest*. Cambridge: Harvard University Press, 1981.

Hollis, Judi. *Fat Is a Family Affair*. San Francisco: Harper & Row, 1986.

Hollis, Judi. *Hope and Recovery: A Twelve-Step Guide for Healing from Compulsive Sexual Behavior*. Minneapolis: CompCare, 1987.

Hora, T. "Transcendence and Healing." *Journal of Existential Psychiatry*, 1 (1961): 501–511.

Hornik-Beer, Edith Lynn. *A Teenager's Guide to Living with an Alcoholic Parent*. Center City, MN: Hazelden, 1984.

Howe, LeLand W., and Mary Martha Howe. *Personalizing Education*. New York: Hart, 1975.

Husserl, E. *Ideas*. New York: Collier Macmillan, 1962.

Ihde, E. *Experimental Phenomenology*. New York: Putnam, 1977.

Jacobson, E. *Progressive Relaxation*. Chicago: University of Chicago Press, 1974.

Jaffe, Dennis T. "Self-Renewal: Personal Transformation Following Extreme Trauma." *Journal of Humanistic Psychology*, 24 (1985): 104–122.

James, W. *Talks to Teachers on Psychology and to Students on Some of Life's Ideals*. New York: Holt, 1962. (Original work published 1899)

Jampolsky, Gerald. *Love Is Letting Go of Fear*. Berkeley, CA: Celestial, 1979.

Jampolsky, Gerald. *Teach Only Love*. New York: Bantam, 1983.

Jampolsky, Gerald. *Good Bye to Guilt: Releasing Fear through Forgiveness*. New York: Bantam, 1985.

Jay, W. Brugh. *Joy's Way: 6 Maps for the Transformational Journey*. New York: St. Martin's Press, 1979.

Jeffers, Susan. *Feel the Fear and Do It Anyway*. New York: Fawcett, 1987.

Johnson, Lois Walfrid. *Either Way, I Win: A Guide to Growth in the Power of Prayer.* Minneapolis: Augsburg, 1979.

Johnson, Robert A. *He: Understanding Masculine Psychology.* New York: Harper & Row, 1989.

Johnson, Robert A. *She: Understanding Feminine Psychology.* New York: Harper, 1989.

Jourard, Sidney M. *Disclosing Man to Himself.* New York: Van Nostrand, 1968.

Jourard, Sidney M. *The Transparent Self.* New York: Van Nostrand, 1971.

Joy, W. B. *Joy's Way.* Los Angeles: Tarcher, 1979.

Kauffman, C., H. Grunebaum, B. Cohler, and E. Gamer. "Superkids: Competent Children of Psychotic Mothers." *American Journal of Psychiatry*, 136 (1979): 1398–1402.

Keen, A. *A Primer in Phenomenological Psychology.* New York: Holt, 1975.

Keen, A. *Doing Psychology Phenomenologically.* Unpublished manuscript.

Kelly, Dan. *The Peter Pan Syndrome: Men Who Have Never Grown Up.* New York: Dodd, 1983.

Kelly, Dan. *The Wendy Dilemma: When Women Stop Mothering Their Men.* New York: Arbor, 1984.

Kelly, E. C. *Urban Educator.* Detroit: Wayne State University, 1980.

Kierkegaard, S. *Concluding Unscientific Postscript,* (D. F. Swanson and W. Lowrie, Trans.) Princeton: Princeton University Press, 1941.

Kimball, Bonnie-Jean. *The Alcoholic Woman's Mad, Mad World of Denial and Mind Games.* Center City, MN: Hazelden Educational Materials, 1978.

Kopp, Sheldon. *If You Meet the Buddha on the Road, Kill Him! The Pilgrimage of Psychotherapy Patients.* New York: Bantam, 1972.

Kopp, Sheldon. *Raise Your Right Hand against Fear: Extend the Other in Compassion.* New York: Ballantine, 1988.

Koupernik, C. "The Bled Discussion: A Review." In E. J. Anthony (Ed.), *The Child in His Family.* New York: Wiley, 1974.

Kübler-Ross, Elisabeth. *On Death and Dying*. New York: Macmillan, 1969.

Kübler-Ross, Elisabeth. *Death: The Final Stage of Growth*. New York: Touchstone, 1988.

Kuenzli, A. E. (ed.). *The Phenomenological Problem*. New York: Harper, 1959.

Kushner, Harold S. *When Bad Things Happen to Good People*. New York: Avon, 1981.

Kushner, Harold S. *When All You've Ever Wanted Isn't Enough: The Search for a Life That Matters*. New York: Pocket Books, 1986.

Lane, Harlan. *The Wild Boy of Aveyron*. Cambridge: Harvard University Press, 1976.

Lankton, Stephen, and Carol Lankton. *The Answer Within: A Clinical Framework of Ericksonian Hypnosis*. New York: Brunner/Mazel, 1983.

Larsen, Earnie. *Stage II Recovery—Life Beyond Addiction*. San Francisco: Harper & Row, 1985.

Larsen, Earnie. *Old Patterns, New Truths: Beyond the Adult Child Syndrome (WorkBook)*. San Francisco: Harper & Row, 1988.

Larsen, Earnie, and Carol Larson Hagarty. *Days of Healing, Days of Joy: Meditations for Adult Children*. Harper & Row, 1987.

Leonard, Linda Schierse. *On the Way to the Wedding: Transferring the Love Relationship*. Boston: Lord, 1986.

Lerner, Harriet. *The Dance of Anger: A Woman's Guide to Changing the Patterns of Intimate Relationships*. New York: Harper & Row, 1986.

Lerner, Harriet. *The Dance of Intimacy: A Woman's Guide to Courageous Acts of Change in Key Relationships*. New York: Harper & Row, 1989.

Lerner, Rokelle. *Daily Affirmations*. Pompano Beach, FL: Health Communications, 1985.

Leshan, L. *How to Meditate: A Guide to Self-Discovery*. New York: Bantam, 1984.

Lew, Mike. *Victims No Longer: Men Recovering from Incest*. New York: Nevraumont, 1988.

Lidell, Lucinda. *The Book of Massage: The Complete Step-By-Step Guide to Eastern and Western Techniques*. New York: Simon & Schuster, 1984.

Lindberg, Anne Morrow. *Gift from the Sea*. New York: Pantheon, 1975.

Lindquist, M. *Holding Back: Why We Hide the Truth about Ourselves*. New York: Harper & Row, 1988.

Lofland, J. *Analyzing Social Settings*. Belmont, CA: Wadsworth, 1971.

Luke, Catherine Ann. *Linking Up: How the People in Your Life Are Road Signs to Self-Discovery*. West Chester, PA: Whitford, 1988.

MacClean, Charles. *The Wolf Children*. New York: Hill and Wang, 1977.

Marlow, Mary Elizabeth. *Handbook of the Emerging Woman: A Manual for Awakening the Unlimited Power of the Feminine Spirit*. Norfolk, VA: Whitford, 1988.

Maslow, Abraham. *Toward a Psychology of Being*. New York: Van Nostrand, 1968.

Maslow, Abraham. *Motivation and Personality*. New York: Harper & Row, 1970.

Maslow, Abraham. *Farther Reaches of Human Nature*. New York: Viking, 1971.

May, Rollo. *Man's Search for Himself: Finding a Center of Strength within Ourselves to Face and Conquer the Insecurities of This Troubled Age*. New York: New America, 1953.

May, Rollo. *Psychology of the Human Dilemma*. New York: Norton, 1967.

May, Rollo. *Love and Will*. New York: Laurel-Dell, 1969.

May, Rollo. *Power and Innocence: The Search for the Sources of Violence*. New York: Norton, 1972.

May, Rollo. *The Meaning of Anxiety*. New York: Norton, 1977.

McConnell, Patty. *Adult Children of Alcoholics: A Workbook for Healing*. New York: Harper & Row, 1986.

McGinnes, Kathleen, and James McGinnes. *Parenting for Peace and Justice*. New York: Orbis, 1983.

Mellody, Pia. *Facing Co-Dependency*. San Francisco: Harper & Row, 1989.

Mellody, Pia, and Andrea Wells. *Breaking Free: A Recovery Workbook of Facing Co-dependency*. San Francisco: Harper & Row, 1989.

Middleton-Moz, Jane. *Children of Trauma: Rediscovering the Discarded Self*. Deerfield Beach, FL: Health Communications, 1989.

Miller, Alice. *The Drama of the Gifted Child*. New York: Basic Books, 1981.

Miller, Alice. *For Your Own Good*. New York: Farrar, Straus & Giroux, 1984.

Miller, Alice. *Pictures of Childhood*. Toronto: Collins, 1986.

Miller, Alice. *Thou Shalt Not Be Aware: Society's Betrayal of the Child*. New York: New American, 1986.

Millonan, Dan. *Way of the Peaceful Warrior*. Tiburon, CA: Kramer, 1980.

Misiak, H., and V. Sexton. *Phenomenological, Existential and Humanistic Psychologies: An Historical Survey*. New York: Grune & Stratton, 1973.

Morris, V. C. *Existentialism in Education*. New York: Harper, 1966.

Moustakas, Clark E. *Psychotherapy with Children: The Living Relationship*. New York: Ballantine, 1954.

Moustakas, Clark E. *The Self: Exploration in Personal Growth*. New York: Harper & Row, 1956.

Moustakas, Clark E. *The Child's Discovery of Himself*. New York: Ballantine, 1966.

Moustakas, Clark E. *Creativity and Conformity*. New York: Van Nostrand, 1967.

Moustakas, Clark E. *Personal Growth: The Struggle for Identity and Human Values*. Cambridge, MA: Doyle, 1969.

Moustakas, Clark E. *Loneliness and Love*. Englewood Cliffs, NJ: Prentice-Hall, 1972.

Moustakas, Clark E. *Finding Yourself, Finding Others*. Englewood Cliffs, NJ: Prentice-Hall, 1974.

Moustakas, Clark E. *Individuality and Encounter: A Brief Journey into Loneliness and Sensitivity Groups*. Cambridge, MA: Doyle, 1974.

Moustakas, Clark E. *The Touch of Loneliness*. Englewood Cliffs, NJ: Prentice-Hall, 1975.

Moustakas, Clark E. *Who Will Listen?* New York: Ballantine, 1975.

Moustakas, Clark E. *Creative Life*. New York: Van Nostrand Reinhold, 1977.

Moustakas, Clark E. *Turning Points*. Englewood Cliffs, NJ: Prentice-Hall, 1977.

Moustakas, Clark E. *Loneliness*. Englewood Cliffs, NJ: Prentice-Hall, 1981.

Moustakas, Clark E. *Rhythms, Rituals and Relationships*. Detroit: Harlow, 1981.

Moustakas, Clark E., and Cereta Perry. *Learning to be Free*. Englewood Cliffs, NJ: Prentice-Hall, 1973.

Newman, M., and B. Berkowitz. *How to Be Your Own Best Friend*. New York: Ballantine, 1987.

Norwood, Robin. *Women Who Love Too Much: When You Keep Wishing and Hoping He'll Change*. New York: Tarcher, 1985.

O'Gorman, P., and P. Oliver-Diaz. *Breaking the Cycle of Addiction: A Parent's Guide to Raising Healthy Kids*. Pompano Beach, FL: Health Communications, 1987.

Oliver-Diaz, Phillip, and Patricia A. O'Gorman. *12 Steps to Self-Parenting: For Adult Children of Alcoholics*. Deerfield Beach, FL: Health Communications, 1988.

Otto, H., and J. Mann. *Ways of Growth*. New York: Grossman, 1968.

Paul, Jordon, and Margaret Paul. *Free to Love*. Los Angeles: Evolving, 1983.

Paul, Jordon, and Margaret Paul. *Do I Have to Give Up Me to Be Loved by You?* Minneapolis: CompCare, 1984.

Paul, Jordon, and Margaret Paul. *If You Really Loved Me*. Minneapolis: CompCare, 1987.

Paul, Jordon, and Margaret Paul. *From Conflict to Caring*. Minneapolis: CompCare, 1988.

Paulus, Trina. *Hope for the Flowers*. New York: Newman, 1972.

Peck, M. Scott. *The Road Less Traveled*. New York: Simon & Schuster, 1978.

Peck, M. Scott. *People of the Lie: The Hope for Healing Human Evil*. New York: Simon & Schuster, 1983.

Peele, Stanton. *Love and Addiction*. New York: Taplinger, 1975.

Peele, Stanton, and Archie Brodsky. *Love and Addiction*. New York: New American Library, 1976.

Perls, Fredrick S. *Gestalt Therapy Verbatim*. New York: Bantam, 1969.

Phillips, L. *Human Adaptation and Its Failures*. New York: Academic Press, 1968.

Pietsch, William V. *Human Be-Ing: How to Have a Creative Relationship Instead of a Power Struggle*. New York: Signet, 1974.

Pogrebin, Letty Cottin. *Growing Up Free: Raising Your Child in the 1980's*. New York: Bantam, 1980.

Polansky, Norman. *Damaged Parents: An Anatomy of Child Neglect*. Chicago: University of Chicago Press, 1981.

Polanyi, M. *Personal Knowledge*. Chicago: University of Chicago Press, 1958.

Polanyi, M. *Science, Faith and Society*. Chicago: University of Chicago Press, 1964.

Powell, John. *Why Am I Afraid to Tell You Who I Am? Insight into Personal Growth*. Chicago: Argus, 1969.

Powell, John. *Why Am I Afraid to Love?* Valencia, CA: Taber, 1972.

Powell, John. *The Secret of Staying in Love*. Valencia, CA: Taber, 1974.

Powell, John. *Fully Human and Fully Alive: A New Life through a New Vision*. Valencia, CA: Taber, 1976.

Powell, John. *Unconditional Love: Love without Limits*. Valencia, CA: Taber, 1978.

Powell, John. *Will the Real Me Please Stand Up?* Valencia, CA: Taber, 1985.

Powell, John. *Happiness Is an Inside Job*. Valencia, CA: Taber, 1989.

Prather, Hugh. *Notes to Myself: My Struggle to Become a Person*. Moab, UT: Real People, 1970.

Privette, G. "Transcendent Functioning: The Use of Potentialities." In H. Otto and J. Mann (Eds.), *Ways of Growth*. New York: Grossman, 1968.

Provence, S. "Some Relationships between Activity and Vulnerability in the Early Years." In E. J. Anthony (Ed.), *The Child and His Family*. New York: Wiley, 1974.

Rainier, T. *The New Diary: How to Use a Journal for Self-Guidance and Expanded Creativity.* Los Angeles: Tarcher, 1979.

Rank, O. *Will Therapy and Truth and Reality.* New York: Knopf, 1950.

Ray, Sandra. *Loving Relationships.* Berkeley, CA: Celestial, 1980.

Robin, Lillian. *Intimate Strangers: Men and Women Together.* New York: Harper & Row, 1983.

Rogers, Carl R. *On Becoming a Person: A Therapist's View of Psychotherapy.* Boston: Houghton Mifflin, 1961.

Rogers, Carl R. "Toward a Science of the Person." *Journal of Humanistic Psychology* (Fall 1963): 72–92.

Rogers, Carl R. "Some Thoughts Regarding the Current Philosophy of the Behavioral Science." *Journal of Humanistic Psychology*, 5 (1965): 182–194.

Rogers, C., and W. R. Coulson. *Man and the Science of Man.* Columbus, OH: Merrill, 1968.

Rogers, John, and Pete McWilliams. *You Can't Afford the Luxury of a Negative Thought.* Los Angeles: Prelude, 1988.

Rosellini, Gayle, and Mark Worden. *Of Course You're Angry.* San Francisco: Harper & Row, 1986.

Rosellini, Gayle, and Mark Worden. *Here Comes the Sun: Dealing with Depression.* San Francisco: Harper & Row, 1988.

Rothman, Esther. *The Angel Inside Went Sour.* New York: Bantam, 1970.

Rubin, Theodore I. *The Angry Book.* New York: Macmillan, 1969.

Rubin, Theodore I. *Reconciliations: Inner Peace in an Age of Anxiety.* New York: Viking Press, 1980.

Rush, Florence. *The Best Kept Secret: Sexual Abuse of Children.* Englewood Cliffs, NJ: Prentice-Hall, 1980.

Russell, A. J. *God Calling.* Old Tappan, NJ: Fleming, 1984.

Russianoff, Penelope. *Why Do I Think I Am Nothing without a Man.* New York: Bantam, 1982.

Rutter, M. "Sex Differences in Children's Responses to Family Stress." In E. J. Anthony and C. Koupernik (Eds.), *The Child and His Family* (Vol. 1). New York: Wiley, 1970.

Rutter, M. "Protective Factors in Children's Responses to Stress and Disadvantage." In M. W. Kent and J. E. Rolf (Eds.), *The Primary*

Prevention of Psychopathology, Vol. 3: Promoting Social Competence and Coping with Children. Hanover, NH: University Press of New England, 1979.

Sanford, John A. *The Invisible Partners: How the Male and Female in Each of Us Affect Our Relationship.* New York: Paulist, 1980.

Sanford, Linda Tschirhart, and Mary Ellen Donovan. *Women and Self-Esteem: Understanding and Improving the Way We Think and Feel About Ourselves.* New York: Penguin, 1986.

Sarton, May. *Recovering.* New York: Norton, 1980.

Sartre, Jean-Paul. *Existentialism and Human Emotions.* New York: Philosophical Library, 1957.

Satir, Virginia. *People Making.* Palo Alto, CA: Science and Behavior, 1972.

Satir, Virginia. *Your Many Faces.* New Orleans: Celestial, 1978.

Satir, Virginia. *Conjoint Family Therapy: Your Many Faces.* Palo Alto, CA: Science & Behavior, 1982.

Satir, Virginia. *Meditations and Inspirations.* New Orleans: Celestial, 1985.

Scarf, Maggie. *Unfinished Business: Pressure Points in the Lives of Women.* New York: Ballantine, 1980.

Schaef, Anne Wilson. *Women's Reality: An Emerging Female System in a White Male Society.* Minneapolis: Winston, 1985.

Schaef, Anne Wilson. *Co-Dependence: Misunderstood-Mistreated.* San Francisco: Harper & Row, 1986.

Schaef, Anne Wilson. *Women's Reality: An Emerging Female System in a White Male Society.* San Francisco: Harper & Row, 1986.

Schaef, Anne Wilson. *When Society Becomes an Addict.* San Francisco: Harper & Row, 1987.

Schaef, Anne Wilson. *Escape From Intimacy: Untangling the "Love" Addiction: Sex, Romance, Relationships.* New York: Harper & Row, 1989.

Schaef, Anne Wilson, and Diane Fassel. *The Addictive Organization.* San Francisco: Harper & Row, 1988.

Schaeffer, Brenda. *Is It Love or Is It Addiction: Falling Into Healthy Love.* New York: Harper & Row, 1987.

Schmitt, R. "Husserl's Transcendental Phenomenological Reduction." In J. J. Kockelmand (Ed.), *Phenomenology: The Philosophical of Edmund Husserl.* New York: Anchor, 1967.

Schreibner, Flora Rheta. *Sybil.* New York: Waren, 1974.

Schuller, Robert. *Be Happy — You Are Loved.* Nashville: Nelson, 1986.

Schwartz, S. R. *Visualization: Breaking through the Illusion of Problems.* New York: Riverrun, 1985.

Shame. Center City, MN: Hazelden, 1981.

Siegel, Bernie S. *Love, Medicine and Miracles.* New York: Harper & Row, 1986.

Simon, S. B., L. W. Howe, and H. Kirschenbaum. *Values Clarification: A Handbook of Practical Strategies for Teachers and Students.* New York: Hart, 1972.

Simonton, Carl O., Stephanie Mathews-Simonton, and James L. Creighton. *Getting Well Again: A Step-by-Step, Self-Help Guide to Overcoming Cancer for Patients and Their Families.* New York: Bantam, 1978.

Simos, Bertha. *A Time to Grieve.* New York: Family Service, 1976.

Sinetar, Marsha. *Elegant Choices, Healing Choices: Finding Grace and Wholeness in Everything We Do.* New York: Paulist, 1988.

Smith, Ann W. *Grandchildren of Alcoholics: Another Generation of Co-Dependency.* Deerfield Beach, FL: Health Communications, 1988.

Smith, Manuel J. *When I Say No I Feel Guilty.* New York: Bantam, 1975.

Spiegelberg, H. (Ed.). *The Phenomenological Movement* (Vol. 2). The Hague: Martinus Nijhoff, 1965.

Steiner, Claude M. *Games Alcoholics Play: The Analysis of Life Scripts.* New York: Grove Press, 1971.

Steiner, Clark M. *What Do You Say after You Say Hello?* New York: Grove Press, 1972.

Steiner, Clark M. *Scripts People Live.* New York: Grove Press, 1974.

Steiner, Clark M. *Healing Alcoholism.* New York: Grove Press, 1979.

Stephanie, E. *Shame Faced.* Center City, MN: Hazelden, 1986.

Stevens, J. *Awareness.* Moab, UT: Bantam, 1971.

Stone, H., and S. Winkleman. *Embracing Ourselves*. San Rafael, CA: New World, 1989.

Strasser, S. *Phenomenology and the Human Sciences*. Atlantic Highlands, NJ: Humanistic Press, 1963.

Sturges, J. S. "Children's Reactions to Mental Illness in the Family." *Social Casework*, 59 (1978): 530–536.

Sutich, A. J., and M. A. Vich (Eds.). *Readings in Humanistic Psychology*. New York: Fress Press, 1969.

Thoele, Sue Patton. *The Courage to Be Yourself: A Woman's Guide to Growing beyond Emotional Dependence*. Nevada City: Pyramid, 1988.

Timmerman, Nancy G. *Step One for Family and Friends*. Center City, MN: Hazelden, 1985a.

Timmerman, Nancy G. *Step Two for Family and Friends*. Center City, MN: Hazelden, 1985b.

Vale Allen, Charlotte. *Daddy's Girl*. New York: Berkley, 1980.

VanKaam, K. *Existential Foundations of Psychology*. Garden City, NY: Doubleday, 1969.

VanKaam, K., and T. Wahl. *A Short History of Existentialism*. New York: Philosophic Library, 1949.

Viorst, Judith. *Necessary Losses*. New York: Fawcett, 1986.

Vitale, Barbara Meisten. *Free Flight: Celebrating Your Right Brain*. Rolling Hills, CA: Jalman, 1986.

Warch, William. *How to Use Your 12 Gifts from God*. Marina del Rey, CA: DeVorss, 1976.

Wegscheider-Cruse, Sharon. *Another Chance: Hope and Health for the Alcoholic Family*. Palo Alto, CA: Science & Behavior, 1981.

Wegscheider-Cruse, Sharon. *Choicemaking: For Co-Dependents, Adult Children and Spirituality Seekers*. Pompano Beach, FL: Health Communications, 1985.

Wegscheider-Cruse, Sharon. *Learning to Love Yourself*. Pompano Beach, FL: Health Communications, 1987.

White Eagle. *The Quiet Mind*. Hampshire, England: White Eagle Trust, 1972.

Whitfield, Charles. *Healing the Child Within*. Deerfield Beach, FL: Health Communications, 1987.

Whitfield, Charles. *Letting Go of Shame*. Deerfield Beach, FL: Health Communications, 1987.

Wholey, Dennis. *The Courage to Change*. Boston: Houghton Mifflin, 1984.

Wilde, Stuart. *Life Was Never Meant to Be a Struggle*. Taos, NM: White Dove, 1987.

Williams, Margery. *The Velveteen Rabbit*. New York: Doubleday, 1975.

Woititz, Janet. *Marriage on the Rocks*. Pompano Beach, FL: Health Communications, 1979.

Woititz, Janet. *Adult Children of Alcoholics*. Hollywood, FL: Health Communications, 1983.

Woititz, Janet. *Struggle for Intimacy*. Pompano Beach, FL: Health Communications, 1985.

Wood, Wendy, and Leslie Hutton. *Triumph over Darkness: Understanding and Healing the Trauma of Childhood Sexual Abuse*. Hillsboro, OR: Beyond Words, 1989.

Wright, Machaelle Small. *Behaving as If God in All Life Mattered: A New Age Ecology*. Jeffersonton, VA: Perelandra, 1987.

York, Phillis, David York, and Ted Wachtel. *Toughlove*. Garden City, NY: Doubleday, 1982.

Ziglar, Zig. *Raising Positive Kids in a Negative World*. New York: Ballantine, 1989.

Index